Revival Reader

Edited by

John Michael Greer

The Druid Revival Reader

Compiled and Edited by John Michael Greer

ISBN: 978-0-9837422-0-3

Greer, John Michael
The Druid Revival Reader/John Michael Greer

First Edition: July 2011

Printed in the United States of America

9 8 7 6 5 4 3 2 1 0

Starseed Publications
2204 E Grand Ave.
Everett, WA 98201

John Michael Greer

Starseed Publications

The Fires of Shalsa

a novel

The Druid Grove Handbook

A Guide to Ritual in the Ancient Order of Druids in America

Contents

Foreword:
The Imagination of a Nature Religion
John Michael Greer

Nearly three hundred years ago, in the midst of the eighteenth-century Enlightenment, a handful of British intellectuals turned their back on the social and cultural trends of their time and set out to reinvent the spirituality of the ancient Druids. That act of spiritual reimagination was unlikely enough; more improbably still, the movement they set in motion—the Druid Revival—found an enduring niche, not only in Celtic nations such as Wales and Brittany but also in more than a dozen other countries around the world, including the United States.

For the last century, at least, this remarkable movement has received less attention from scholars, as well as from the general public, than it deserves. It's true, of course, that alternative spiritual movements have had longer histories, more members, and greater cultural influence than the Druid Revival. Still, a movement that played a central role in struggles for cultural identity in most of the Celtic nations of Europe, and provided inspiration to such world-class creative talents as William Blake and Frank Lloyd Wright, has arguably earned a larger place in the history books than it has usually been given.

One source of this lack of attention is rooted in the cultural context of the twentieth century, and specifically in the emergence of archeology after the Second World War as a recognized source of authoritative knowledge about the past. From the 1950s on, Glyn Daniels and Stuart Piggott, leading figures in the first generation of British archeologists to benefit from this shift in attitudes, accordingly took public aim at those whose vision of the past strayed too far from the facts as archeology revealed them. The Druids of their time—"bodies of self-styled Druids which today represent the fag-end of the myth...at once misleading and rather pathetic," in Piggott's not exactly unbiased language[1]—were an easy target, because the Druidry of the Revival by that time did not have all that much to do with the ancient Druids.

It must also be said that the Revival traditions of the early and middle years of the twentieth century made life easy for critics of Piggott's

[1] Stuart Piggott, The Druids (Thames & Hudson, 1975), p.181.

stripe by claiming a direct lineal connection to the ancient Druids that they did not, in fact, possess. Generations had passed since the founding of most of the core Druid Revival movements, and the passage of time made it all too easy to lose track of the difference between a reinvention and a survival. This was especially true since at least one of the major figures of the Revival—the Welsh poet and literary forger Edward Williams (1747-1826), better known by his *nom de barde* Iolo Morganwg—had explicitly claimed ancient origins for his inventions.

The resulting squabbles between archeologists and archdruids spread in turn into the newly minted paganism of the twentieth century's latter half, and convinced far too many neopagans that they could bolster their own dubious claims to authenticity by assailing the Druid Revival in terms even more intemperate than Piggott's.

All of this disputation, however, missed the fact that at least two points were actually in question. The first was whether the Druid Revival descended from the ancient Druids. The second was whether the Druid Revival had anything to offer to the present. The obsessive concern with the first of these questions in the twentieth century debates too often failed to cast any light on the second.

A tradition can be gray with the dust of centuries, after all, and still be useless or actively harmful, while a newly minted tradition can have important lessons to teach, not least if this latter was created in response to changed conditions. Thus the question that should have been asked about the Druidry of the Druid Revival, and far too often was not, was whether it had anything to offer to people who lived in the modern world, rather than that of Celtic antiquity.

Starting from this latter question, a strong case can be made for the relevance ofthe Druid Revival. Born in the eighteenth century, as the industrial revolution radically redefined humanity's relationship to nature, the Revival embodied a principled response to industrialism that broke with many of the unthinking responses of its time—and ours. Where the scientific materialism of the period devalued nature in order to celebrate humanity's supposed conquest of it, and the dogmatic religion of the time devalued nature in order to celebrate God's supposed transcendence of it, the thinkers of the Revival, drawing inspiration from what was known about the ancient Druids, saw nature itself as a central source of value, meaning, and spiritual insight.

The idea that humanity somehow stands apart from nature, equally a commonplace of scientific materialism and religious orthodoxy, found no support in the Druid Revival tradition. To the Druids of the Revival, as many of the following texts show, human nature was a subset of nature as a whole, and the human mind was simply one expression of a capacity for consciousness and intelligence found throughout the natural world. Instead of turning to a scripture written by human hands, the Revival argued, human beings were capable of knowing spiritual truth by reflecting on nature itself, which fills the role in Druidry that scriptures hold in prophetic religions such as Christianity. None of these ideas have lost any of their validity in the light of the twenty-first century's looming environmental crises; quite the contrary, the Druid Revival is if anything more relevant now than it ever was.

It is in this light, ultimately, that the Druid Revival needs to be understood. Beginning in the eighteenth century, as the industrial revolution was just getting under way, a handful of visionaries saw the need for a nature religion in modern Western civilization, and set out to imagine one by using the ancient Druids as a template and a source of inspiration. Some of their efforts may seem strange in retrospect, and a great many more of them had little in common with the archaic Celtic priests on whose inkblot patterns they were projected. Still, the imagination of a nature religion in a newly industrializing society was an immense task, and the roundabout ways that process of imagining sometimes took do not detract from their ongoing achievement.

Most of the literature of the Druid Revival is long out of print, and even in today's Druid orders, few members have had the opportunity to read more than a few of the original texts from the eighteenth, nineteenth, and early twentieth century movements. *The Druid Revival Reader* is meant to help fill that gap by making some of the writers whose works influenced the Revival accessible to a new generation of Druids. Roughly half the authors whose essays appear in this volume considered themselves to be Druids, or heirs of the Druids; the others, while not themselves part of the Revival movement, helped to shape it by offering ideas and insights that were adopted into the Druidry of the Revival.

The texts included here cover almost exactly two centuries in the life of an evolving tradition. The first excerpt, drawn from William Stukeley's *Abury,* was published in 1743; the last, the complete text of

Ross Nichols' *An Examination of Poetic Myth*, saw print in 1946. During that period, like any living tradition, the Druid Revival changed and grew along a complex trajectory. The excerpts that follow track that trajectory in much of its richness; they appear in chronological order, so that the reader can trace the emergence and development of core themes in the Revival's thought.

In classic Celtic fashion, the selections in The Druid Revival Reader fall readily into three groups. The first group, from the eighteenth and early nineteenth century, includes William Stukeley's *Theology of the Druids*, James Thompson's *The Song of the Druid Bard*, Edward Davies' *The Mysteries of Ceridwen*, and Thomas Paine's *An Essay on the Origin of Free Masonry*. These show the tradition in its formative stages, making tentative ventures along lines that later Druids would explore more thoroughly. Stukeley's exploration of a theology of reason and nature, Thompson's first rough sketch of a scheme of spiritual evolution, Davies' enthusiastic reinterpretations of Welsh legend, and Paine's no less bold attempt to identify Freemasonry with Druid sun worship all staked claims to territory that would be central to the evolving Druid Revival tradition.

The second group, from the nineteenth century, begins with selections from Iolo Morganwg's massive *Barddas*, under the title of The *Bards of the Island of Britain*, and includes David James' *The Customs of the Druids*, W. Winwood Reade's *Mysteries of the Druids*, Robert Stephen Hawker's *The Quest of the Sangreal*, and Owen Morgan's *The Gods and Goddesses of the Druids*. With Iolo the Revival found its distinctive voice, and though each of the writers that follow him in this group draw on earlier sources, they build their own visions of Druidry on a foundation largely taken from *Barddas*. For all that, none of them portray anything like the same Druids in their works; James' Druids are wise proto-Christian sages, Reade's are a proto-scientific elite dominating an ignorant people, while Morgan's are the initiates of a dizzyingly complex cult that combines astronomy and sex. Hawker's poem would lack Druids altogether, except that the figure of Merlin sums up the Revival vision of the Druid and places him in a context of symbolism that would have many close equivalents in the years to come; though Hawker wrote before Morgan, and his poem therefore precedes Morgan's in the text, it offers a transition to the third group of texts.

That third group, from the twentieth century, includes Rudolf Steiner's *The Sun Initiation of the Druid Priests and their Moon Science*, Lewis Spence's *Druid Teachings and Initiations*, and Ross Nichols's *An Examination of Creative Myth*. In these selections, under the influence of the broader revival of Western esotericism that began in the late 19th century, the diverse threads of the Druid Revival begin to weave themselves into a coherent fabric. Steiner was not part of the Revival; a significant cultural force in his own right, he was influenced by the Theosophy of H.P. Blavatsky, as well as by older central European traditions and his own visionary experiences, and his essay on the Druids is among the best examples of the contributions made by esoteric thinkers outside Druidry to the Revival. Spence was both a Theosophist and a Druid, and drew extensively on the older Revival literature in writing his own influential studies of Druidry and Celtic lore; while Nichols, a poet and educator, went on to become perhaps the most influential figure in late twentieth century Druidry as author of *The Book of Druidry* and founder of the Order of Bards Ovates and Druids (OBOD), currently the world's largest Druid order.

This selection of writers and essays is not as complete as it probably should be. The most significant limitation was made necessary by the fact that neither I nor the Ancient Order of Druids in America, the Druid order I head, had the resources to attempt translations of Druid literature from languages other than English. The rich Druid Revival literatures in Welsh, Breton, and French, to name only the three most obvious examples, thus had to be left for another time. It is our hope that Druids or others with facility in these languages and an interest in the Druid Revival may be encouraged to fill the gap with anthologies of their own.

Another limitation comes from the tradition, common among Druid orders in the nineteenth and twentieth centuries, of retaining core elements of their teachings and traditions under obligations of secrecy. Several of those involved in compiling this anthology, myself included, have access to documents that might have enriched this collection substantially; in all cases, however, where the current custodians of those documents asked that they remain secret, that request has been honored.

Finally, of course, the provisions of copyright law have been honored as well, and for this reason the texts included here have almost entirely been drawn from the public domain. For the two exceptions, I would like to gratefully acknowledge the assistance of the Rudolf Steiner Press, which graciously permitted the reprinting of Rudolf Steiner's *The Sun Initiation of the Druid Priests and their Moon Science*, and of the Order of Bards Ovates and Druids and its Chosen Chief, Philip Carr-Gom, who no less graciously allowed the republication of Ross Nichols' *An Examination of Creative Myth*.

Thanks are also due to the officers and members of the Ancient Order of Druids in America (AODA), which enthusiastically supported this project, and AODA members Dana Driscoll and Dana Corby, who willingly volunteered for the by no means minor task of editing it and preparing it for publication.

William Stukeley
The Theology of the Druids
(from Abury, *A Temple of the British Druids*, 1743)

It's only a slight exaggeration to call William Stukeley the founder of the Druid Revival. One of the founding figures of British archeology, a Fellow of the Royal Society, a respected scholar and antiquary in his own time, and an Anglican vicar during the second half of his life, he was also the first person in modern times known to have organized a Druid grove and celebrated Druid rituals. Many of the core themes that would later be central to the Revival tradition first surfaced in his work.

While he was a prolific author, most of his fame rested on two books, *Stone-Henge: A Temple Restor'd to the British Druids* (1740) and *Abury, a Temple of the British Druids* (1743). These were the most complete studies published up to that time on Stonehenge and Avebury, and still the most detailed record of many landscape features that were obliterated after Stukeley's time. Stukeley was convinced that these and other megalithic sites had been built by the prehistoric inhabitants of Britain. From this conviction, he reached the conclusion, reasonable at the time though rejected by archeologists today, that these sites had been temples built by the ancient Druids and that encoded in their geometries were some of the lost secrets of Druid philosophy and theology. Both books thus devoted many pages to Druid teachings Stukeley believed he had recovered through careful study of the great stone circles and their surroundings.

As an Anglican clergyman, Stukeley brought a commitment to Christian faith and a solid background in Christian theology to his interpretation of the Druids. Still, his beliefs drew heavily on the Latitudinarian movement of the previous century, which argued for religious tolerance and an acceptance of diverse beliefs within a common religious communion, and also on the suggestion made by St. Augustine and other Church Fathers, many centuries earlier, that Christianity simply restated a body of religious truth that was as old as the world and had been known by sages and priests throughout all previous ages.

This latter belief, which was not uncommon during his time, nevertheless opened the door to a far more radical approach to spirituality than Stukeley himself was willing to embrace. By arguing that human thought could discover the basic truths of Christianity without help from divine revelation, and that reflection on nature could lead to the same insights as sacred scriptures, he provided a core justification for later Druid teachings that would step outside of Christian forms using the same arguments as their justification. Stukeley's cautious speculations about the process of "divine generation" by which God the Father produced God the Son would have an even more forceful impact, starting Druid thought down the road that led eventually to the robust sexual symbolism of Owen Morgan and Ross Nichols, outlined in later selections in this volume

The following selection, Chapter Fifteen of Stukeley's *Abury*, provides a good overview of the way he imagined Druidry as a religion of reason reflecting on nature.

Further Reading:

David Boyd Haycock, William Stukeley: *Science, Religion, and Archaeology in Eighteenth-century England* (Boydell Press, 2002).
Neil Mortimer, ed., *Stukeley Illustrated* (Green Magic, 2003).
Stuart Piggott, William Stukeley (Thames & Hudson, 1985).
William Stukeley, *Stonehenge: A Temple Restor'd to the British Druids* (repr. Garland, 1982). -----, *Abury, a Temple of the British Druids* (repr. Garland, 1982).

* * *

I have given the reader an account of three eminent builders of these *Dracontia*, or serpentine temples, in the earliest times after the flood, and in the more eastern parts of the world; as well as described one of those works in our island. There are many more such builders and buildings, which will be easily found out by those that are conversant in ancient learning. This figure of the circle and the snake, on which they are founded, had obtained a very venerable regard, in being expressive of the most eminent and illustrious act of the deity, the multiplication of his own nature, as the Zoroastrians and Platonists speak; and in being a symbol of that divine person who was the consequence of it.

We shall not wonder that the Druids had a perception of this great truth, when we consider that it was known, as far as necessary, to all the philosophic and religious sects of antiquity, as shown at large by several learned writers. My opinion is, that it was communicated to mankind, originally, by God himself. 'Tis the highest point of wisdom which the human mind can arrive at, to understand somewhat of the nature of the deity; and the studious, the pious, and thinking part of the world, would not fail to improve this knowledge by reflection and ratiocination.

Though my business is to speak more fully of the religion of the Druids in the next volume, yet I judge it very pertinent to the present subject to anticipate that intention, so as to show how far they might advance toward that knowledge, by the hint of reason; to further the works, wherein they have, in the largest characters that ever were made, consigned their notions of this sort, remaining to this day, such as we have been describing; and which may induce us to have the same sentiment concerning them as Pere Martin in his *Religion des Gaulois*, though he knew nothing of our antiquities; but this he writes, "that the Druids worshipped the true God, and that their ideas of religion were truly grand, sublime, magnificent."

We may therefore very justly affirm of them, that in their serious contemplations in this place, concerning the nature of the deity, which, as Caesar tells us, was one part of their inquiries, they would thus reason in their own minds.

A contemplative person, viewing and considering the world around him, is ravished with the harmony and beauty, the fitnesses of things in it, the uses and connections of all its parts, and the infinite agreement shining throughout the whole. He must bely all his senses to doubt, that it was composed by a being of infinite power, wisdom, and goodness, which we call God. But among all the most glorious attributes of divinity, goodness is preeminent. For this beautiful fabric of the world displays through every atom of it, such an amazing scene of the goodness and beneficence of its author; that it appears to such contemplative minds, that his infinite power and wisdom were but as the two hands, employed by the *goodness* of the sovereign architect.

Goodness was the beginning, the middle and the end of the creation. To explain, to prove, or illustrate this topic, would be an affront to the common understanding of mankind. The sum of what we can know of him is that he is good, essentially good. We are not more assured of the existence of the first being, than that he is good, *the* good, goodness itself, in eminence. He is God, because he is good; which is the meaning of the word in English, and in many other languages. This, in God almighty, is the attribute of attributes, the perfection of his all-perfect nature. He made and maintains those creatures which he multiplied to an infinite degree, the objects of his care and beneficence; those great characters of supreme love, that render him deservedly adorable.

All possible perfections, both moral and natural, must needs be inherent in this first and supreme being, because from him alone they can flow. This is in one comprehensive word, what we call good. But good unexercised, unemployed, incommunicate, is no good, and implies a contradiction, when affirmed of the all-good being. Therefore it undeniably follows, there never was a time, never can be, when God was useless, and did not communicate of his goodness.

But there was a time before creation, before this beautiful fabric of the world was made, before even chaos itself, or the production of the rude matter, of which the world was made. And this time must be affirmed, not only as to material creation, but to that of angels and spiritual beings. Reckon we never so many ages, or myriads of ages, for the commencement of creation, yet it certainly began, and there was a time before that beginning. For, by definition, creation is bringing that into being which was not there before. There must have been a time before it.

Here then occurs the difficulty, of filling up that infinite gap before creation. Consider the supreme, first being sitting in the center of a universal solitude, environed with the abyss of infinite nothing, a chasm of immense vacuity! What words can paint the greatness of the solecism? What mind does not start at the horror of such an absurdity? And especially supposing this state subsisted from infinite ages.

'Tis in vain to pretend, that a being of all perfections can be happy in himself, in the consciousness of those perfections, whilst he does no good to any thing; in the reflexive idea of his possessing all excellency, whilst he exerts no tittle of any one. This is the picture of a being quite different from the All-good. And as the Druids would, without difficulty, judge, that there must needs be one, only, self-originated first being, the origin of all things: so they would see the necessity of admitting one or more eternal beings, or emanations from that first being, in a manner quite distinct from creation.

That there ever was one eternal, self-existent, unoriginated being, is the very first and most necessary truth, which the human mind can possibly, by contemplation and ratiocination, obtain. Still by considering the matter intimately, they would find it impossible to conceive, that there should ever be a time, when there was but one being in the universe, which we call the first and self-originated being, possessing in himself all possible perfections, and remaining for endless myriads of ages, torpid, unactive, solitary, useless. This is a notion so abhorrent to reason, so contrary to the nature of goodness, so absolutely absurd, that we may as well imagine this great being altogether absent, and that there was no being at all.

This all the philosophers were sensible of, for good unexercised, that always lay dormant, never was put into act, is no goodness; it may as well be supposed to be absent, and even that there was no God. To imagine that God could be asleep all this while, shocks the mind, therefore it casts about, to remedy this great paradox.

Now it cannot be said of any part of creation, or of the whole, that God always did good to any created being or beings; for these are not, cannot be, commensurate in time with his own being. Count backward never so long to the beginning of things, still there was a time prior to this beginning of things; for eternal creation is an equal absurdity with an eternal absence of any being; where no part is necessary, to affirm that the whole is a necessarily and self-existing being, is a mere portent of reason.

So we see, in every light, an absolute necessity of admitting a being or beings coeval with the supreme and self-originating being, distinct from any creation, and which must needs flow from the first being, the cause of all existence. For two self-originating beings is as much an absurdity as any of the preceding.

But, as 'tis impossible that the act of creation should be coeval with the first being, what other act of goodness can be? For that being which is essentially good, must ever have been actively and actually so. To answer this great question, we must thus expostulate, as the prophet Isaiah does in the person of God, in his last chapter, when summing up the business of his prophetical office: "Shall I bring forth to birth and not beget, saith Jehovah; shall I cause to bring forth, and be myself barren, saith thy God?" He is there speaking of the birth of the son of God in human form; but we may apply it in a more eminent degree, to the son of God in his divine nature; and as the Druids may well be supposed to have done. The highest act of goodness which is possible, even to the supreme being, is the production of his like, the act of filiation, the begetting of his son. Proverbs 8:22, "The Lord begat me from eternity, before his works of old" (so it ought to be read); verse 30, "then I was by him, as one brought up with him" (*amoun* in the original), and I was daily his delight, rejoicing always before him."

This is the internal divine fecundity of the fruitful cause of all things. Creation is external fecundity. The Druids would naturally apply the term generation, to this act of producing this person, or divine emanation from the supreme, which we are obliged to admit of; and to affirm him coeval with the supreme. The difficulty of priority in time, between father and son, would easily be removed, by considering the difference between divine and human generation, the production of necessary and contingent beings.

If an artist produces an admirable and curious piece of mechanism, he is said to make it; if he produces a person or being altogether like himself, he is rightly said to generate that person; he begets a son, 'tis an act of filiation. So the like we must affirm of the supreme being generating another being, with whom only he could communicate of his goodness from all eternity, and without any beginning; or, in scripture language, *in whom he always had complacency*. This is what Plato means by "love being ancienter than all the gods; that the kingdom of love is prior to the kingdom of necessity." And this son must be a self-existent, all-perfect being, equally as the father, self-origination only excepted, which the necessary relation or economy between them forbids. If he is a son, he is like himself; if he is like himself, he is God; if he is God, an eternity of existence is one necessary part of his divine nature and perfection.

If the son be of the same substance and nature as the father, an eternity of being is one part of his nature; therefore no time can be assigned for this divine geniture, and it must be what we call eternal. Or perhaps we may express it as well by saying, it was before eternity, or that he is coeval with the almighty father. In this same sense Proclus in *De Patriarch.* uses the word *praeternus*. For though 'tis impossible that creation, whether of material or immaterial beings, should be coeval with God; yet, if the son be of the same nature with the father, which must be granted, then 'tis impossible to be otherwise, than that the son of God should be coeval with the father.

If goodness be, as it were, the essence of God, then he can have no happiness but in the exercise of that goodness. We must not say, as many are apt to do, that he was always and infinitely happy, in reflecting upon his own being and infinite perfections, in the idea of himself. This is no exercise of goodness, unless we allow this idea of himself which he produces, to be a being without him, or distinct from himself, and that is granting what we contend for. A true and exact idea of himself is the *logos* of the ancients, the first-born of the first cause. And this is the meaning of what the eastern and all other philosophers assert, "that it was necessary for good to communicate itself. There could be no time before then, for then he would be an imperfect unity, and may as well be termed a cipher, which of itself can never produce any thing." Agreeable to this doctrine, Philo in the second book of *On Monarchies* writes, "The *logos* is the express image of God, and by whom all the world was made." It would be senseless to think here, he meant only the wisdom of the supreme, the reason, the cunning of God, a quality, not a personality.

What difficulty here is in the thing, arises merely from the weakness of our conceptions, and in being conversant only with ordinary generation. A son of ours is of the same nature as his father. His father is begat in time, therefore the son the like. Not so in divine generation. But as the father is from eternity, so is the son. This only difference there is, or rather distinction; the father is self-existent, and unoriginate; the son is of the father.

Further, we must remove, in this kind of reasoning, all the imperfection of different sexes, as well as time, which is in human generations; and all such gross ideas incompatible with the most pure and perfect divine nature.

The whole of our reasoning further confirms, that the son is necessarily existing. It was necessary for God to be actively good always, and begetting his son was the greatest act of divine goodness, and the first, necessarily. But the word *first* is absurd, betraying our own imperfection of speech and ideas, when we treat of these matters; for there could be no *first*, where no beginning. And the very names of father and son are but relative and economical; so far useful, that we may be able to entertain some tolerable notion in these things, so far above our understanding.

But though it be infinitely above our understanding, yet we reach so far, as to see the necessity of it. And we can no otherwise cure that immense vacuum, that greatest of all absurdities, the indolence and uselessness of the supreme being, before creation. And all this the Druids might, and I venture to say, did arrive at, by ratiocination. And we can have no difficulty of admitting it, if we do but suppose, there were obscure notions of such being the nature of the deity, handed down from the beginning of the world. Whence in *Chronicon Alexandrinum, Malala,* and other authors, we read, for instance, "in those times (the most early) among the Egyptians reigned, of the family of Misraim, Sesosiris, that is, the branch or offspring of Osiris, a man highly venerable for wisdom, who taught, there were three greatest energies or persons in the deity, which were but one." This man was Lud, or Thoth, son of Misraim or Osiris, and for this reason, when idolatry began, he was consecrated by the name of Hermes, meaning one of those divine energies, which we call the Holy Spirit.

This is a short and easy account of that knowledge which the ancients had of the nature of the deity, deduced from reason in a contemplative mind, and which certainly was known to all the world from the beginning, and rightly called a mystery. For our reason is strong enough to see the necessity of admitting this doctrine, but not to see the manner. The how of an eternal generation is only to be understood by the deity itself.

The Druids would pursue this notion from like reasoning a little further, in this manner. Though from all that has been said, there is a necessity of admitting an eternal generation, yet the person so generated, all-perfect God, does not multiply the deity itself, though he is a person distinct from his father. For addition or subtraction is argument of imperfection, a thing not to be affirmed of the nature of the deity. They would therefore say, that though these two, the father and the son, are different divine personalities, yet they cannot be called two Gods, or two godheads; for this would be discerpting the deity or godhead, which is equally absurd and wicked.

That mankind did formerly reason in this wise, is too notorious to need my going about formally to prove it. 'Tis not to be controverted; very many authorities have done it substantially. And when there was such a notion in the world, our Druids, who had the highest fame for theological studies, would cultivate it in some such manner as I have delivered, by the mere strength of natural reason. Whether they would think in this manner *ex priori*, I cannot say; but that they did so think, we can need no weightier argument than the operose work of Abury before us; for nought else could induce men to make such a stamp, such a picture of their own notion, as this stupendous production of labour and art.

As our western philosophers made a huge picture of this their idea, in a work of three miles extent, and, as it were, shaded by the interposition of diverse hills; so the more eastern sages who were not so shy of writing, yet chose to express it in many obscure and enigmatic ways. Pythagoras, for instance, affirmed, the original of all things was from unity and an infinite duality: Plutarch, *On the Opinions of the Philosophers*. Plato makes three divine authors of all things, the first he calls king, the good. Beside him he names the cause, descended from the former; and between them he names dux, the leader, or at other times he called him the mind. Just in the same manner, the Egyptians called them father, mind, power. Therefore Plato, in his VIth epistle, writing to Hermias and his friends to enter into a most solemn oath, directs it to be made before "God the leader and prince of all things, both that are, and that shall be; and before the Lord, the father of that leader or prince; and of the cause; all whom," says he, "we shall know manifestly, if we philosophize rightly, as far as the powers of good men will carry us." And in *Timaeus* he makes Mind to be the son of Good, and to be the more immediate architect of the world. And in *Epinomis* he writes, "the most divine Logos or Word made the world," the like as Philo wrote, which is expressly a Christian verity.

'Tis not to be wondered at, that the ancients wrapped up this doctrine in an abstruse and symbolic way of speaking, of writing, and in hieroglyphic characters and works, as we have seen. It was communicated to them in the same manner; they did not, could not, comprehend it any more than we, but they held it as a precious depositum of sacred wisdom.

We may therefore make this deduction from what has been said, that the Christian doctrine of distinct personalities in the deity, is so far from being contrary to reason, as some would have it, or above human reason as others, that 'tis evidently deducible therefrom, at least highly agreeable thereto, when seriously proposed to our reason. And when most undoubtedly the ancients had such a notion, even from the creation, those minds that were of a contemplative turn, would embrace it and cultivate it, as being the most exalted knowledge we are capable of. Of such a turn were our Druids, as all accounts agree.

James Thompson
Song of the Druid Bard
(from *The Castle of Indolence*, 1748)

One of the leading British poets of his time, James Thompson was a contemporary of Stukeley's and, like him, had a wide range of interests and involvements. Today, he is best known as the author of *The Seasons*, though he also wrote the words to "Rule Britannia" for a musical drama about King Alfred, and a great deal of popular poetry on political and ethical themes.

The Castle of Indolence, his last work, was an allegorical poem in the style of Edmund Spenser—a literary genre much more popular in the eighteenth century than today—and accordingly neglected by recent critics and readers alike. This lack of attention is by no means entirely justified, for the poem is a lively and readable work, in which the evil wizard Indolence lures victims into his enchanted castle, until he is overthrown by the magic-dispelling wand of the Knight of Art and Industry. Accompanying the Knight on his quest to free the captives in the Castle of Indolence is the remarkable figure of a Druid Bard, whose song to the captives is given below.

Thompson's participation in the early stages of the Druid Revival is an open question. At his death, one of his friends wrote an elegy that begins, "In yonder grave a Druid lies..." This might simply have referred back to the Druid Bard of Thompson's last poem, or it might have had some further meaning; so far, scholars have not yet pursued the hint.

Still, Thompson and his Druid Bard had an unexpected impact on the later tradition of the Druid Revival. In the following lines, woven in among a great deal of more ordinary encouragement, appears a vision of human existence that would become central to Druidry in the work of Iolo Morganwg and his successors. To Thompson's Druid Bard, as to these later members of the species, the human soul rises

Up from unfeeling Mold,
To Seraphs burning round th'Almighty's Throne,
Life rising still on Life, in higher Tone,
Perfection forms, and with Perfection Bliss.

This is not the fallen humanity of the religious orthodoxy of Thompson's time, but a race of beings on a pilgrimage from matter to spirit that could be accomplished—had to be accomplished—by the combination of divine inspiration and individual effort.

Further Reading

Thompson, James, *The Castle of Indolence and Other Poems* (University of Kansas Press, 1961).

* * *

XLVI.
The Bard obey'd; and taking from his Side,
Where it in seemly Sort depending hung,
His British Harp, its speaking Strings he try'd,
The which with skilful Touch he deftly strung,
Till tinkling in clear Symphony they rung.
Then, as he felt the Muses come along,
Light o'er the Chords his raptur'd Hand he flung,
Anti play'd a Prelude to his rising Song:
The whilst, like Midnight mute, ten Thousands round
him throng.

XLVII.
Thus, ardent, burst his Strain. "Ye hapless Race;
"Dire-labouring here to smother Reason's Ray,
"That lights our Maker's Image in our Face,
"And gives us wide o'er Earth unquestion'd Sway;
"What is Th' Ador'd Supreme Perfection, say?
"What, but eternal never-resting Soul,
"Almighty Power, and all-directing Day;
"By whom each Atom stirs, the Planets roll;
"Who fills, surrounds, informs, and agitates the Whole?

XLVIIL
"Come, to the beaming God your Hearts unfold!
"Draw from its Fountain Life! 'Tis thence, alone,
"We can excel. Up from unfeeling Mold,
"To Seraphs burning round th'Almighty's Throne,
"Life rising still on Life, in higher Tone,
"Perfection forms, and with Perfection Bliss.
"In Universal Nature. This clear shewn,
"Not needeth Proof; To prove it were, I wis,
"To prove the beauteous World excels the brute Abyss.

XLIX.
"Is not the Field, with lively Culture green,
"A Sight more joyous than the dead Morass?
"Do not the Skies, with active Ether clean,
"And fan'd by sprightly Zephyrs, far surpass
"The foul November-Fogs, and slumbrous Mass,
"With which sad Nature veils her drooping Face?
"Does not the Mountain-Stream, as clear as Glass,
"Gay-dancing on, the putrid Pool disgrace?
"The same in all holds true, but chief in Human Race.

L.
"It was not by vile Loitering in Ease,
"That Greece obtain'd the brighter Palm of Art,
"That soft yet ardent Athens learn'd to please,
"To keen the Wit, and to sublime the Heart,
"In all supreme! complete in every Part!
"It was not thence majestic Rome arose,
"And o'er the Nations shook her conquering Dart;
"For Sluggard's Brow the Laurel never grows;
"Renown is not the Child of indolent Repose.

LI
"Had unambitious Mortals minded Nought,
"But in loose Joy their Time to wear away;
"Had they alone the Lap of Dalliance sought,

"Pleas'd on her Pillow their dull Heads to lay;
"Rude Nature's State had been our State To-day;
"No Cities e'er their towery Fronts had rais'd,
"No Arts had made us opulent and gay;
"With Brother-Brutes the Human Race had graz'd;
"None e'er had soar'd to Fame, None honour'd been,
None prais'd.

LII.
"Great Homer's Song had never fir'd the Breast
"To Thirst of Glory, and heroic Deeds;
"Sweet Maro's Muse, sunk in inglorious Rest,
"Had silent slept amid the Mincian Reeds;
"The Wits of modern Time had told their Beads,
"And monkish Legends been their only Strains;
"Our Milton's Eden had lain wrapt in weeds,
"Our Shakespeare stroll'd and laugh'd with Warwick swains,
"Ne had my Master Spenser charm'd his Mulla's Plains.

LIII.
"Dumb too had been the sage Historic Muse,
"And perish'd all the Sons of ancient Fame;
"Those starry Lights of Virtue, that diffuse
"Through the dark Depth of Time their vivid Flame,
"Had all been lost with Such as have no Name.
"Who then had scorn'd his Ease for other's Good?
"Who then had toil'd rapacious Men to tame?
"Who in the Public Breach devoted stood,
"And for his Country's Cause been prodigal of Blood?

LIV.
"But Should to Fame your Hearts impervious be,
"If right I read, you Pleasure All require:
"Then hear how best may be obtain'd this Fee,
"How best enjoy'd this Nature's wide Desire.
"Toil, and be glad! Let Industry inspire
"Into your quicken'd Limbs her buoyant Breath!

"Who does not act is dead; absorpt entire
"In miry Sloth, no Pride, no Joy he hath:
"O Leaden-hearted Men, to be in Love with Death!

LV.
"Better the toiling Swain, oh happier far!
"Perhaps the happiest of the Sons of Men!
"Who vigorous plies the Plough, the Team, or Car;
"Who hoes the Field, or ditches in the Glen,
"Delves in his Garden, or secures his Pen;
"The Tooth of Avarice poisons not his Peace;
"He tosses not in Sloth's abhorred Den;
"From Vanity he has a full Release;
"And, rich in Nature's Wealth, he thinks not of Increase.

LVI.
"Good Lord! how keen are his Sensations all!
"His Bread is sweeter than the Glutton's Cates;
"The Wines of France upon the Palate pall,
"Compar'd with What his Simple Soul elates,
"The native Cup whose Flavour Thirst creates;
"At one deep Draught of Sleep he takes the Night;
"And for that Heart-felt Joy which Nothing mates,
"Of the pure nuptial Bed the chaste Delight,
"The Losel is to him a miserable Wight.

LVII.
"But what avail the largest Gifts of Heaven,
"When sickening Health and Spirits go amiss?
"How tasteless then Whatever can be given?
"Health is the vital Principle of Bliss,
"And Exercise of Health. In Proof of This,
"Behold the Wretch, who slugs his Life away,
"Soon swallow'd in Disease's sad Abyss;
"While he whom Toil has brac'd, or manly Play,
"Has light as Air each Limb, each Thought as clear as Day.

LVIII.
"O who can speak the vigorous Joys of Health!
"Unclogg'd the Body, unobscur'd the Mind:
"The Morning rises gay; with pleasing Stealth,
"The temperate Evening falls serene and kind..
"In Health the wiser Brutes true Gladness find.
"See I how the Younglings frisk along the Meads,
"As May comes on, and wakes the balmy Wind;
"Rampant with Life, their Joy all Joy exceeds
"Yet what save high-strung Health this dancing
Pleasaunce breeds?

LIX
"But here, instead, is foster'd every Ill,
"Which or distemper'd Minds or Bodies know.
"Come then, my kindred Spirits! do not spill
"Your talents here. This Place is but a Shew,
"Whose Charms delude you to the Den of Woe;
"Come, follow me, I will direct you right,
"Where Pleasure's Roles, void of Serpents, grow,
"Sincere as sweet; come, follow this good Knight,
"And you will bless the Day that brought him to your sight.

LX.
"Some he will lead to Courts, and Some to Camps;
"To Senates Some, and public sage Debates,
"Where, by the solemn Gleam of Midnight-Lamps,
"The World is pois'd, and manag'd mighty States;
"To high Discovery Some, that new-creates
"The Face of Earth; Some to the thriving Mart;
"Some to the Rural Reign, and softer Fates;
"To the sweet Muses Some, who raise the Heart:
"All Glory shall be yours, all Nature, and all Art!

LXI.
"There are, I see, who listen to my Lay,
"Who wretched sigh for Virtue, but despair.
"All may be done, (methinks I hear them say)
"Even Death despis'd by generous Actions fair;
"All, but for Those who to these Bowers repair,
"Their every Power dissolv'd in Luxury,
"To quit of torpid Sluggishness the Lair,
"And from the powerful Arms of Sloth get free.
"Tis rising from the Dead—Alas!—It cannot be!

LXII.
"Would you then learn to dissipate the Band
"Of these huge threat'ning Difficulties dire,
"That in the weak Man's Way like Lions stand,
"His Soul appall, and damp his rising Fire?
"Resolve! resolve! and to be Men aspire!
"Exert that noblest Privilege, alone,
"Here to Mankind indulg'd: control Desire;
"Let Godlike Reason, from her sovereign Throne,
"Speak the commanding Word—I will!—and it is done.

LXIII.
"Heavens! can you then thus waste, in shameful wise,
"Your few important Days of Trial here?
"Heirs of Eternity! born to rise
"Through endless States of Being, still more near
"To Bliss approaching, and Perfection clear,
"Can you renounce a Fortune so sublime,
"Such glorious Hopes, your backward Steps to steer,
"And roll, with vilest Brutes, through Mud and Slime?
"No! No!—Your Heaven-touch'd Hearts disdain the
piteous Crime!"

Edward Davies
The Mysteries of Ceridwen
(from *The Mythology and Rites of the British Druids*, 1809)

Rev. Edward Davies was one of countless Anglican clergymen whose leisure time was spent in scholarly pursuits and who enriched the intellectual life of their time to a degree that is hard to imagine today. The rector of Bishopston in the county of Glamorgan, in southern Wales, he produced two works widely read in his time, *Celtic Researches* (1804) and *The Mythology and Rites of the British Druids* (1809), which interpreted Welsh traditions and legendry through the lens of the Helio-Arkite theory of the origins of religion.

Baffling though it seems nowadays, the Helio-Arkite theory was a reasonable hypothesis at a time when the infant science of geology seemed to support the traditional belief in the historical reality of Noah's flood. (Until Louis Agassiz proposed the radical theory of an ice age in 1837, the traces of the last great glaciation were considered by geologists as evidence for a titanic flood.) Accepting the biblical account, though, meant that every human culture was descended from the survivors of the Flood, Noah and his family, who had all been devout monotheists. How, then, had classical Paganism, Hinduism, and other robustly polytheist faiths emerged?

The Helio-Arkite theory offered an answer. Jacob Bryant's *New System, or an Analysis of Ancient Mythology* (1774-1776), Davies' primary source for the theory, argued that as the descendants of Noah scattered around the world, they took with them traditions about the Flood, and these gave rise to a cult in which the sun and the ark were the primary symbols—thus, "helio-arkite." Given time and humanity's penchant for idolatry, the sun and Noah fused into the father god of Pagan religion, and the ark became first a feminine symbol, and then the mother goddess of Pagan religion. Misunderstood incidents from the Flood gave rise to other deities and filled out the emerging pantheons. Meanwhile commemorations of the Flood and the ark evolved into the first of the ancient mystery initiations.

Davies applied all this theory to the traditions of his native Wales with more energy than critical thought. It is easy to criticize the results, though it bears remembering that the fashionable scholarship of the present will likely seem equally foolish fifty or a hundred years from now. More to the point is Davies' impact on later Druid writers, including those at the core of the Revival tradition; most Druid writers of the late 19th and early 20th centuries used Davies' colorful vision of Druid initiations and teachings as a central source.

Davies' writing style is among the most rambling and discursive in the Druid tradition, including long quotations from other authors and equally long divagations on subjects that often strayed far from his theme. The following selection, from Chapter 3 of *The Mythology and Rites of the Ancient British Druids*, has undergone substantial editing for the sake of clarity.

Further Reading:

Edward Davies, *The Mythology and Rites of the British Druids* (J. Booth, 1809).

* * *

The detection of those divine honours, which the British sage awarded to the patriarch Noah, under whatever title; the magnificent mention of the ship of Nevydd; and the commemorations of the deluge upon the borders of the lakes of Cambria, encourage me to search for some farther vestiges of that kind of superstition, and of those mystic rites. I shall now proceed to the Druidical precinct, in search of the British Ceres: and I think I distinguish her character and history in the celebrated goddess Kêd, or Ceridwen, whom I have already remarked in close connexion with the Arkite god.

In the introductory section of this Essay, I quoted several passages from those Bards who lived under the Welsh princes, in which Ceridwen is mentioned. They uniformly represent this character, as having pertained to the superstition of the primitive Bards, or Druids. They describe her, as having presided over the most hidden mysteries of that ancient superstition; and as a personage, from whom alone the secrets of their fanatical priesthood were to be obtained in purity and perfection. They also intimate, that it was requisite for those who aspired to the chain of presidency, to have tasted the waters of inspiration front her sacred cauldron; or, in other words, to have been initiated into her mysteries.

All this clearly points towards some solemn rites of our remote progenitors: and, for such rites, we can find no parallel amongst the heathen priesthood of other nations, if we except the celebrated mysteries of Ceres, Isis, or Cybele. But it may be asked, if Ceridwen has the attributes of Venus, why should I labour to connect her more particularly with the character of Ceres? I must observe, in reply, that this station seems to be pointed out for her, by the most obvious mythological analogy. The most familiar idea which was entertained of Ceres, presented her as the goddess of corn; as having introduced the art of tillage, and taught mankind to sow the land, and cultivate the various species of grain.

The reader may recollect a passage of Cuhelyn, a Bard of the sixth or eighth century, which I have already quoted, and which delineates the character of Ceridwen by one impressive epithet—she is styled Ogyrven Amisad, *the goddess of various seeds*. Thus Ceres and Ceridwen unite by a single touch.

The history and character of Ceridwen are exhibited in a very curious mythological tale, called *Hanes Taliesin,* the *History of Taliesin*. It is prefixed to the works of that Bard, and has been supposed to contain some romantic account of his birth; but, in reality, it has nothing to do with the history of a private individual, or with romance, in the common acceptation of that term. It is a mythological allegory, upon the subject of initiation into the mystical rites of Ceridwen. And though the reader of cultivated taste may be offended at its seeming extravagance, I cannot but esteem it one of the most precious morsels of British antiquity, which is now extant.

Before I exhibit the tale itself, it may be proper to obviate an objection to the era of the incidents which it recites. Ceridwen is represented as living in the time of Arthur. Hence it may be argued, that she could neither have been the great mother, nor have belonged at all to the ancient superstition of the Druids.

But the Arthur here introduced, is a traditional character, totally distinct from the prince who assumed that name in the beginning of the sixth century.

He is placed high in the mythological ages, and far beyond the reach of authentic, profane history. The great bear is his representative in the heavens, and the constellation, Lyra, is his harp. He is the son of

Uthyr Pendragon, the *wonderful supreme leader*, and Eigyr, the *generative power*. His adventures, as related in the mythological tales, had evidently a common origin with those of Hercules, the Argonauts, & I think that *Arthur* was one of the titles of the deified patriarch Noah. And with this idea, the account which we have of him in the Bards and the Triads, perfectly accord.

He is represented as having had three wives, the daughter of mythological personages: each of these wives had the name of Gwenhwyvar, that is, the *lady of the summit of the water*. These three wives of Arthur are only so many copies of the same mystical character, the import of which may be perceived in the construction of the name.

And as for Arthur himself, Taliesin's *Spoils of the Deep*, a poem which treats wholly of Diluvian mythology, represents this prince as presiding in the ship which brought himself, and seven friends, safe to land, when that deep swallowed up the rest of the human race. This has no connection with the history of the sixth century. It relates entirely to the deluge; and the personage here commemorated, was the same as his mystical parent, Uthyr Pendragon, or the deified patriarch Noah.

It appears from Taliesin, that Ceridwen also was esteemed a character of the most remote antiquity: for the Bard places the origin of her mysteries very remote in the primitive ages.

"I implore my sovereign, to consider the inspiring muse (a title of this goddess)—what did necessity produce, more early than Ceridwen! The primary order in the world was that of her priests."

These mystical characters, it must be acknowledged, were still regarded as existing in the sixth century; and so they would have been to this day, had they been still personified in their priests, and had the superstition which upheld them continued to prevail.

To this short defence of the antiquity of the British mysteries, or rather of the characters to which they were consecrated, I must add, that I have thought it convenient to divide the story of Hanes Taliesin into chapters, in order to place the long annotations which it may require, as near as possible to the subject from which they arise. I have also translated the names of men and places: for this I need but little apology. Though many of these names occur in history, yet in the present, and in similar cases, they are evidently selected for the purpose of carrying on the allegory, without wholly removing the mystic veil: their import, therefore, ought to be known to the reader.

Hanes Taliesin: Chapter I

"In former times, there was a man of noble descent in Penllyn, the end of the lake. His name was Tegid Voel, bald serenity, and his paternal estate was in the middle of the lake of Tegid, or Pemble mere.

"His espoused wife was named Ceridwen, By his wife he had a son, named Morvran ap Tegid, *raven of the sea, the son of serenity,* and a daughter called Creirvyw[1], *the sacred token of life.* She was the most beautiful damsel in the world. But these children had a brother, named Avagddu, *utter darkness,* or *black accumulation,* the most hideous of beings. Ceridwen, the mother of this deformed son, concluded in her mind, that he would have but little chance of being admitted into respectable company, unless he were endowed with some honourable accomplishments, or sciences; for this was in the first period of Arthur, and the round table."

This opening of the tale carries us at once into mythological ground. In the situation of Tegid's paternal estate, in the figure presented by that personage, and in the names and characters of his children, we have the history of the deluge presented to our view; and that history is sketched upon British canvas.

The Britons, as we have seen in the preceding section, represented the deluge as having been occasioned by the bursting forth of the waters of a lake. Hence they consecrated certain lakes, as symbols of the deluge; whilst the little islands which rose to the surface, and were fabled to have floated, or else artificial rafts, representing such floating islands, were viewed as emblems of the ark, and as mystical sanctuaries. They also regarded certain rocks, or mounts, attached to such lakes, as typifying the place of the patriarch's debarkation; and in the midst of these hallowed scenes, they celebrated the memorials of the deluge by some periodical rites. We are therefore told, that the paternal estate of Tegid Voel, the husband of Ceridwen, was in the centre of Pemble mere, the largest of the Welsh lakes. This estate must have been limited to the space of a raft, ship, or boat, which could have floated in such a situation; or else it must be supposed to have suffered that kind of submersion, by which our ancestors commemorated the destruction of the ancient world.

[1] In other passages, this name is written Creirwy, the token of the egg.

We may infer from these coincident circumstances, that this lake and its neighbourhood were deeply impressed with the characters of arkite superstition; and that our mythological narrator was fully aware of this fact, when he placed the paternal estate of Tegid, the husband of Ceridwen, in the bosom of Pemble Mere.

Let us, therefore, take a brief view of the proprietor of this estate.

Tegid Vohel, bald serenity, presents himself at once to our fancy. The painter would find no embarrassment in sketching the portrait of this sedate, venerable personage, whose crown is partly stripped of its hoary honours. But of all the gods of antiquity, none could with propriety, sit for this picture, excepting Saturn, the acknowledged representative of Noah, and the husband of Rhea; which was but another name for Ceres, the genius of the ark.

As consort of the arkite goddess, Tegid was evidently the deified patriarch. Is has, however, been observed, that this deity was a Pantheos, comprehending in his own person, most of the superior gods of the heathens; here then, we contemplate him—in the character of Saturn. The particulars of Tegid's appropriate history have disappeared; but by a little mythological deduction, we shall discover him under another name.

Tegid, as we have already seen, was the father of Creirwy, the token of the egg, or the British Proserpine; and Creirwy was the same personage as Llywy, the putting forth of the egg, mentioned by .Aneurin and Taliesin, in conjunction with Hu or Aeddon.

This identity appears from the poems of Hywel, son of Owen, prince of North Wales, who styles Llywy his sister and that, in consequence of his matriculation into the mysteries of Ceridwen. She could not have become the mystical sister of Hywell by this means, had she not been the daughter of that goddess.

The same princely Bard says, that Llywy had stolen his soul, as she had stolen that of Garwy; but the mistress of Garwy was Creirwy, the daughter of Ceridwen:

"Am I not deprived of spirit! I am enchanted like Garwy, by her who equals Creirwy, sprightly and fair."

Creirwy and Llywy being thus the same personage, it follows, that the father of Creirwy was also the father of Llywy; but the parent of the latter is mentioned in the Triads, by the name of Seithwedd Saidi. And here it must be remarked of the lady, that, notwithstanding her exquisite beauty and delicacy, she is classed with two other mythological personages, under the character of Gwrvorwyn, a man-maid, which must imply a virago at least, it not something still less attractive.

From these premises it is clear, that Seithwedd Saidi was a name of Tegid, the father of this mystical lady; and this name, as well as Tegid, must be referred to the character of Saturn.

We shall now have an opportunity of investigating his mythology. Seithwedd is an epithet, implying either septiform, or else, having seven courses. This may allude to the multitude of his names and functions, or to the annual feasts of Saturn, which were continued for the space of seven days. If Saidi be a British term, it must be derived from Sâd, firm or just. From this word, and Wrn, a covered vessel, Mr. Owen deduces the Welsh name of Saturn; so that Sad-wrn is the just man of the vessel. This description is not inapplicable to the patriarch Noah, and to his history, the character of Saturn is referred by mythologists in general.

As our British Saturn was named Saidi, so his mystical spouse seems to have had a title of nearly the same sound; for her chair or sanctuary was called Caer Sidi, the sanctuary of Sidi. The consideration of this subject I must defer for the present, and go on to examine, whether the children of Tegid and Ceridwen have any similar relation to the history of the deluge.

Their first born was named Morvran, raven of the sea. Of this personage, a few particulars are recorded. He was dark and hideous in his person; he was addicted to contention; and he escaped from the army of the mythological Arthur, or the deified patriarch.

From these hints I conjecture, that the character of Morvran represents the raven which Noah sent forth. This was the first animal that proceeded from the ark: hence, mythology might regard him as her first-born son. It is remarked, that Noah sent the raven out of the ark, by way of experiment; but that it disappointed him and never returned—hence a tradition is mentioned, that the raven was once sent out upon a message by Apollo, but deserted him, and did not return when he was expected. But this faithless messenger was for the most part, esteemed a bird of ill omen. His very croaking would put a stop to the process of matrimony.

Morvran may then be regarded as the representative of Noah's raven; but what are we to understand by the forlorn condition of Avagddu, utter darkness, or black accumulation, whose misfortune was the grief of his mother; and who could not be relieved, as we learn from the sequel of the tale, till the renovating cauldron of the deluge had boiled for a year and a day. And what are we to think of his subsequent illuminated state, when he became the pride of Ceridwen, and if I mistake not, married the rainbow?

Avagddu is made a son of Tegid; but as mythological genealogy is mere allegory, and the father and son are frequently the same person under different points of view; this character, in his abject state, may be referred to the patriarch himself, during his confinement in the internal gloom of the ark, where he was surrounded with utter darkness, a circumstance which was commemorated in all the mysteries of the gentile world. If this be granted, then the son of Ceridwen, or the ark in his renovated state, is the same patriarch, born anew to light and life, at the close of the deluge.

And as our complex mythology identified the character of the patriarch, with that of the sun; so Avagddu may also have been viewed as a type of that luminary, in his veil of darkness, and gloom, during the melancholy period of the deluge. This gloom was afterwards changed into light and cheerfulness; and thus the son of Ceridwen may be recognized, in his illuminated state, under the titles of Elphin and Rhuvawn Bevyr, which implies bursting forth with radiancy, and seems to be an epithet of the Helio-arkite god.

The chair of Ceridwen, represents Gwydion, or Hermes, in the act of forming the Iris, as a consort for the renovated sun; and the allegory is as just as it is beautiful: for what was the secondary cause of this sacred token, but the rays of the sun just bursting forth from the gloom, and mixing with the humid air?

Avagddu, thus considered as a type of the Helio-arkite god in his afflicted and renovated state, has a striking coincidence of character with Eros, the blind god of the Greeks, who was a distinguished agent in the Arkite mysteries, whose name, in the course of those mysteries, was changed into Phanes, a title of the sun, not dissimilar to our El-phin; and whose symbol was the bow, which, as well as the bow of Apollo, alluded to the Iris.

I am not sure, however, that the character of Avagddu had not a secondary allusion, in his forlorn state, to the uninitiated, and in his renovation, to the adept in the mysteries of Druidism: as the former was regarded as living in darkness, whereas the latter was illuminated and endowed with all knowledge.

Creirwy, the token, or sacred symbol of the egg, otherwise called Llywy, the manifestation, or putting forth of the egg, is not the least remarkable of Ceridwen's children.

As it will appear presently, that the mother is described as a hen, or female bird of some species, there seemed to be an analogous propriety in the names of the daughter, who though a Gwrvorvyn, or virago, was esteemed a paragon of beauty: and, as such, she is classed with Arianrod merch Don, the lady of the silver wheel, the daughter of Jove whom Ceridwen represents as conducting the rainbow, which she was, therefore, the appropriate genius; and with Gwen, Venus, the daughter of Cy-wryd, Crydon, the manhood of Crodon, or Saturn.

Creirwy, as daughter of Ceridwen, or Ceres, was the Proserpine of the British Druids. The attributes of the mother and daughter, in the Bardic mythology, as well in that of other heathens, are so much confounded together as not to be easily distinguished.

All the difference which I can perceive in their character is this. Ceridwen was the genus of the ark throughout its whole history; hence she was viewed as a severe matron supposed to preside in those public sanctuaries, where the Arkite rites were celebrated: whilst Creirwy, on the other hand, was regarded as the genius of the same sacred vessel, only during its perilous conflict with the waters of the deluge; and therefore represented as a helpless virgin, exposed to dreadful calamities, from which she was at length delivered. She did not preside in the Arkite temples, though she was occasionally associated with her mother; but the private and portable tokens delivered to the initiated, and the wand or branch, which was a badge of the Bardic office, were regarded as her gift.

This mystical lady is also called Creirddylad, the token of the flowing or floating, and described as the daughter of Lludd Llaw Eraint, the chief who governed the vessel, or of Llyr, the margin of the sea: and here she is an old acquaintance of the English nation, being no less a personage than Cordelia, the daughter of King Lear.

In an old poem, in which Gwyn ab Nudd, King of Annwn, is introduced as a speaker, this potentate describes himself. as Gordderch

Creirddylad merch Lludd, "The paramour of Creirddylad, the daughter of Lludd."

Here we have a hint of a British tradition upon the subject of the rape of Proserpine. Gwyn ab Nudd was the Pluto of the Britons. Annwn, the kingdom of that god, in its popular acceptation, is hell, or the infernal regions; but in the mystical poems and tales, Annwn seems to be no other than that deep or abyss, the waters of which burst forth at the deluge. Gwyn, the King of Annwn, was therefore the genius of the deluge; and the fable means nothing more, than that the ark was forcibly carried away by the flood.

In the short chapter which gave rise to these remarks, our mythological narrator appears, with a master's hand, to have directed our attention to the history of the deluge, and to the local notions of the Britons relative to that event. We shall now observe his dexterity in delineating the character and operations of Ceridwen herself.

Hanes Taliesin: Chapter II

"Then she (Ceridwen) determined, agreeably to the mystery of the books of Pheryllt, to prepare for her son a cauldron of Awen a Gwybodeu, *water of inspiration and sciences,* that he might be more readily admitted into houourable society, upon account of his knowledge, and his skill in regard to futurity.

"The cauldron began to boll, and it was requisite that the boiling should be continued, without interruption, for the period of a year and a day; and till three blessed drops of the endowment of the spirit could be obtained.

"She had stationed Gwion the Little, the son of Gwreang the Herald, of Llanvair, *the fane of the Lady,* in Caer Einiawn, *the city of the just,* in Powys, *the land of rest,* to superintend the preparation of the cauldron: and she had appointed a blind man, named Morda, *ruler of the sea,* to kindle the fire under the cauldron, with a strict injunction that he should not suffer the boiling to be interrupted, before the completion of the year and the day.

"In the mean time Ceridwen, with due attention to the books of astronomy, and to the hours of the planets, employed herself daily in botanizing, and in collecting plants of every species, which possessed any rare virtues.

"On a certain day, about the completion of the year, whilst she was thus botanizing and muttering to herself, three drops of the efficacious water happened to fly out of the cauldron, and alight upon the finger of Gwion the Little. The heat of the water occasioned him putting his finger into his mouth.

"As soon as these precious drops had touched his lips, every event of futurity was opened to his view: and he clearly perceived, that his greatest concern was to beware of the strategems of Ceridwen, whose knowledge was very great. With extreme terror he fled toward his native country.

"As for the cauldron, it divided into two halves; for the whole of the water which it contained, excepting the three efficacious drops, was poisonous; so that it poisoned the horses of Gwyddno Garanhir, which drank out of the channel into which the cauldron had emptied itself. Hence that channel was afterwards called, The poison of Gwyddno's horses."

The most. remarkable subject brought forward in this chapter, is the preparation of the cauldron of inspiration and science. Ceridwen, like Ceres and Isis, appears to have been a great botanist, and well skilled in the virtues of plants. The Pheryllt, according to whose ritual she proceeds in her selection, are often mentioned by the Bards, as well as by the prose writers of Wales. The poet Virgil, whose sixth Aeneid treats so largely of the mysteries of heathenism, has been dignified with that title; and an old chronicle, quoted by Dr. Thomas Williams, asserts that the Pheryllt had an establishment at Oxford, prior to the founding of the university by Alfred.

These Pheryllt are deemed to have been the first teachers of all curious arts and sciences; and, more particularly, are thought to have been skilled in every thing that required the operation of fire. Hence some have supposed, that the term implies chemists or metallurgists. But chemistry and metallurgy seem rather to have taken their British name from these ancient priests; being called Celvyddydau Pheryllt, 'the arts of the Pherylit, or some of those mysteries in which they were eminently conversant.

As primary instructors in the rites of Ceridwen, or Ceres, I regard the Pheryllt as priests of the Pharaon, or higher powers, who had a city or temple amongst the mountains of Snowdon, called also Dinas Emrys, or the ambrosial city.

The tale before us also mentions books of astronomy. Whether the Druids actually had such books or not, it is certain that Caesar enumerates astronomy amongst the sciences which they professed; and that they not only remarked the periodical return of their festivals, but also mixed with their arkite superstition, an idolatrous veneration of the heavenly bodies, and paid a religious regard to their influence.

I come now to the cauldron of Ceridwen, which makes a very conspicuous figure in the works of the mystical bards, from the beginning of the sixth, to the close of the twelfth century. In these authors, we find the term pair, or cauldron, used metaphorically to imply the whole mass of doctrine and discipline, together with the confined circle of arts and sciences, which pertained to the ancient priesthood of Britain. The preparation of this vase being a necessary preliminary, to the celebration of their most sacred mysteries, it stands as a symbol of the mysteries themselves, and of all the benefits supposed to result from them.

Hence it becomes a subject of some importance in British antique ties, to inquire into the meaning of this mystical vessel, and to determine the question, whether the ancient superstition of other heathens present us with any thing analogous to it.

From the best information which I can collect upon the subject, it does not appear that this cauldron implies one identical vessel, or at least, that its contents were designed for one simple purpose. In the tale before us it is described as used in the preparation of a decoction of various select plants, which was to constitute the water of inspiration and science. A few drops of this water fall upon the finger of the attendant, he puts it into his month, and immediately all futurity is open to his view. Such knowledge, however, must not be regarded as the result of merely tasting the water, or of any single ceremony whatever; but of a complete course of initiation, of which the tasting of this water was an essential rite.

The poem called Taliesin's Chair, enumerates a multitude of ingredients, which entered into the mystical decoction, and seems to describe it as designed, for purification by sprinkling, then, for the preparation of a bath, and again, as used in the rite of libation, and lastly, as constituting a particular kind of drink for the aspirants. The sacred vessel is there called Pair Pumwydd, the cauldron of the five trees or plants, alluding, I suppose, to five particular species of plants, which were deemed essentially requisite in the preparation.

Some of the mythological tales represent this Pair, as constituting a bath, which conferred immortality or restored dead persons to life, but deprived them of utterance: alluding to the oath of secrecy, which was administered previous to initiation.

In the poem called Preiddeu Annwn, Taliesin styles it the cauldron of the ruler of the deep (the arkite god), which first began to be warmed by the breath of nine damsels (the Gwyllion, or Gallicenae). He describes it as having a ridge of pearls round its border, and says, that it will not boil the food of a coward, who is not bound by his oath.

Yet the author of Hanes Taliesin, speaks of the residue of the water, after the efficacious drops had been separated, as a deadly poison.

From these various accounts, it may be inferred, that the Pair, was a vessel employed by the Druids, in preparing a decoction of potent herbs and other ingredients, to which superstition attributed some extraordinary virtues; that this preparation was a preliminary to the mysteries of the arkite goddess; that in those mysteries, part of the decoction was used for the purpose of purification by sprinkling; that another part was applied to the consecration of the mystic bath: that a small portion of the same decoction, was infused into the vessels which contained the liquor, exhibited in the great festival, for the purpose of libation, or for the use of the priests and aspirants, which liquor, is described, as consisting of Gwin a Bragawd, that is, wine with mead, and wort, fermented together: that all the sacred vessels employed in the mysteries of Ceridwen, being thus purified and consecrated by the Pair, passed under its name; and that, in these appropriations, the water of the cauldron was deemed the water of inspiration, science, and immortality, as conducing to the due celebration of mysteries, which were supposed to confer these benefits upon the votaries.

But it seems that the residue of the water, being now supposed to have washed away the mental impurities of the initiated, with which impurities, of course it became impregnated, was now deemed deleterious, and accursed. It was therefore emptied into a deep pit or channel in the earth, which swallowed it up, together with the sins of the regenerate.

But the mystical cauldron of Ceridwen was also employed in preparing the liquor of those magnanimous aspirants, who took and kept the oath. It was one of its functions to boil that beverage, or else a certain portion of its contents was added, by way of consecration to the Gwin a Bragawd, or composition of wine, honey, waters and the extract of malt, or barley.

But we are told, the residue of the water in Ceridwen's vessel, was of a poisonous quality. It now contained the sins and pollutions of the noviciates: the cauldron was therefore divided into two equal parts, and the water ran out of it into a certain terrestrial channel.

But whence came the original idea of the purifying water, prepared in this celebrated cauldron?

In the tradition of our ancestors, we find that the mystical vase was peculiarly sacred to the god and goddess of the ark. It must then be referred to something in the history of the deluge; for the discovery of which, it may be proper to take a brief view of the ideas which the Britons entertained respecting that awful event.

The following circumstances may be verified by passages in the Bards and the Triads:

The profligacy of mankind had provoked the great Supreme to send a pestilential wind upon the earth. A pure poison descended—every blast was death. At this time the patriarch, distinguished for his integrity, was shut up together with his select company, in the inclosure with the strong door. Here the just ones were safe from injury. Presently, a tempest of fire arose. It split the earth asunder, to the great deep. The lake Llion burst its bounds; the waves of the sea lift themselves on high, round the borders of Britain; the rain poured down from heaven, and the water covered the earth. But that water was intended as a lustration, to purify the polluted globe, to render it meet for the renewal of life, and to wash away the contagion of its former inhabitants into the chasma of the abyss. The flood, which swept from the surface of the earth the expiring remains of the patriarch's contemporaries, raised his vessel, or inclosure, on high, from the ground, bore it safe upon the summit of the waves, and proved to him and his associates the water of life and renovation.

Agreeably to these ideas, the cauldron which was kept boiling for a year and a day; which purified the sacred utensils, and the company assembled at the mystic festival; and with its dregs washed away the sins of the regenerate into the terrestrial channel, may have been regarded as an emblem of the deluge itself.

Hanes Taliesin: Chapter III

"Ceridwen entering just at this moment, and perceiving that her whole year's labour was entirely lost, seized an oar, and struck the blind Morda upon his head, so that one of his eyes dropped upon his cheek.

"'Thou hast disfigured me wrongfully,' exclaimed Morda, 'seeing I am innocent: thy loss has not been occasioned by any fault of mine.'

"'True,' replied Ceridwen, 'it was Gwion the Little who robbed me.' Having pronounced these words, she began to run in pursuit of him. Gwion perceiving her at a distance, transformed himself into a hare, and doubled his speed: but Ceridwen instantly becoming a greyhound bitch, turned him, and chased him towards a river.

"Leaping into the stream, he assumed the form of a fish: but his resentful enemy, who was now become a otter bitch, traced him through the stream; so that he was obliged to take the form of a bird, and mount into the air.

"That element afforded him no refuge; for the lady, in the form of a sparrow hawk was gaining upon him—she was just in the act of pouncing him.

"Shuddering with the dread of death, he perceived a heap of clean wheat upon a floor, dropped into the midst of it, and assumed the form of a single grain.

"Ceridwen took the form of a black, high-crested hen, descended into the wheat, scratched him out, distinguished and swallowed him. And, as the history relates, she was pregnant of him nine months, and when delivered of him, she found him so lovely a babe, that she had no resolution to put him to death.

"She placed him, however, in a coracle, covered with skin, and, by the instigation of her husband, cast him into the sea on the twenty-ninth of April."

Through the fabulous wildness of this chapter, we may discover constant allusions to the history of Ceres, and her mystical rites. Ceridwen here assumes the character of a fury. Under that idea, she is elsewhere represented. Taliesin says of himself, that he had been nine months in the womb of Ceridwen Wrach, the hag, or fury. This fury was the goddess of death. The death of Arthur is implied by his contending with the fury in the hall of Glastonbury. And, as Ceridwen was the genius of a sacred ship; so death, of which she was the goddess, is represented under the character of the ship of the earth.

But let us proceed to consider the incidents of the story—Ceridwen seizes an oar, and strikes the Daemon of the sea upon his head.

This instrument was a proper symbol to be employed by the genius of a floating vessel, and the action an emblem of her triumph over the watery element.

The goddess then transforms herself into a bitch; whilst the aspirant was converted into a hare. This animal, as we learn from Caesar, was deemed sacred by the Britons; at the same time it was an emblem of timidity, intimating the great terror to which the noviciate was exposed, during the mystical process.

This hare is turned, and driven towards a river. Bit he is still in the road to initiation. Here our noviciate takes the form of a fish, whilst the goddess herself, or rather her priest, assumes the character of an otter. The next change of the aspirant was into a bird. The species is not named. It was probably the Dryw, which implies both a wren and a Druid; and Taliesin tells us that he had been in that form. His adversary became a hawk.

At last, the novitiate becomes a grain of pure wheat, and mixes with an assemblage of the same species and character. He was now cleansed from all his impurities, and he had assumed a form, which was eminently sacred to Ceres. In this form, therefore, the goddess receives him into her bosom. In order to accomplish this design, she transforms herself into a hen, which was deemed a sacred animal by the Britons, in the days of Caesar.

The singular representation of Ceridwen, as swallowing the aspirant; and of the latter, as continuing for a considerable time imprisoned in her womb, must imply something more than his mere introduction into the sanctuary. This aspirant was intended for the priesthood: and we have here the history of his inclosure, in some ship, cell, or cave, which more immediately symbolized the person of the mystical goddess. In this inclosure, he was subjected to a rigid course of discipline. Here he studied the fanatical rites, and imbibed the sacred doctrines of Ceridwen.

As the completion of the initiatory rites was deemed by the Gentiles a regeneration, or new birth, and distinguished by that name; so our aspirant is represented as having been born again, of the mystical

Ceridwen. As yet, however, we seem to have been only contemplating the lesser mysteries—the greater are still to succeed.

After the aspirant had completed his course of discipline in the cell, had gone through the ceremonies of the lesser mysteries, and had been born again of Ceridwen; we are told, that this goddess inclosed him in a small boat, covered with skin, and cast him into the sea. Let us observe the progress of the British ceremony.

Hanes Taliesin: Chapter IV

"In those times, Gwyddno's weir stood out in the beach, between Dyvi and Aberystwyth, near his own castle. And in that weir, it was usual to take fish, to the value of a hundred pounds, every year, upon the eve of the first of May.

"Gwyddno had an only son, named Elphin, who had been a most unfortunate and necessitous young man. This was a great affliction to his father, who began to think that he had been born in an evil hour.

"His counsellors, however, persuaded the father to let this son have the drawing of the weir on that year, by way of experiment; in order to prove whether any good fortune would ever attend his, and that he might have something to begin the world.

"The next day, being May-eve, Elphin examined the weir, and found nothing: but as he was going away, he perceived, the coracle, covered with a skin, resting upon the pole of the dam.

"Then one of the weirmen said to him, 'Thou hast never been completely unfortunate before this night; for now thou hast destroyed the virtue of the weir, in which the value of a hundred pounds was always taken upon the eve of May-day.

"'How so?' replied Elphin—'that coracle may possibly contain the value of a hundred pounds.'

"The skin was opened, and the opener perceiving the forehead of an infant, said to Elphin—'Behold Taliesin, radiant front!' 'Radiant front be his name,' replied the prince, who now lifted the infant in his arms, commiserating his own misfortune, and placed him behind him upon his own horse, as if it had been in the most easy chair.

"Immediately after this, the babe composed for Elphin a song of consolation and praise; at the same time, he prophesied of his future renown. The consolation was the first hymn which Taliesin sung, in order to comfort Elphin, who was grieved for his disappointment in the draught of the wear; and. still more so, at the thought that the world would impute the fault and misfortune wholly to himself."

Elphin carries the new-born babe to the castle, and presents him to his father, who demands whether he was a human being or a spirit; and is answered in a mystical song, in which he professes himself a general primary Bard, who had existed in all ages, and identifies his own character with that of the sun.

Gwyddno, astonished at his proficiency, demands another song, and is answered as follows:

"Water has the property of conferring a blessing. It is meet to think rightly of God. It is meet to pray earnestly to God; because the benefits which proceed from him cannot be impeded.

"Thrice have I been born. I know how to meditate. It is woeful that men will not come to seek all the sciences of the world, which are treasured in my bosom; for I know all that has been, and all that will be hereafter."

I have already taken notice that Taliesin, radiant front, was properly a title of the sun, and thence transferred to his priest. This priest had now, for a complete year, attended the preparation of the mystical cauldron: he had received the water of inspiration, and with it the sacred lessons of Ceridwen: he bad been received and swallowed up by that goddess, and had remained for some time in her womb, or had been subjected to a course of discipline in the mystical cell, and at length he had been born again.

But after this, we find him inclosed in a coracle, or small boat, cast into the sea, and consigned into the hands of Gwyddno Garanhir, and his son Elphin.

According to this tale, therefore, the Britons celebrated the commemoration of the deliverance out of the ark upon the eve of May day. And if they supposed the deluge to have continued for a year and a day, the period which was employed in preparing the mystical cauldron, the anniversary or commencement would fall, of course, upon the twenty-ninth of April.

As Ceridwen threw the coracle into the sea upon that day, so opportune for the drawing of Gwddno's weir on the morrow, it may be inferred, that Gwyddno and his son were intimately connected with the family of Ceridwen. Taking all circumstances into account, we may even premise, that they were the same as her husband Tegid, and her unfortunate son Avagddu.

Tegid, indeed, is said to have had two sons, whereas Gwyddno is described as having but one at this time: but it may be replied, that Morvran, the raven of the sea, had deserted his family, previous to the debarkation from the ark.

The idea here suggested respecting Gwyddno, differs from the received opinion of the Welsh, which Mr. Owen thus details in his Cambrian Biography.

"Gwyddno Garanhir, or Dewrarth Wledig, was a Prince of Cantrey y Gwaelod, and also a poet, some of whose composition is in the Welsh Archaiology. He flourished from about A.D. 460, to 520. The whole of his territory was inundated by the sea in his life-time, and it forms the present Cardigan Bay."

The whole of this account, though literally understood in the country, appears to me nothing more than a piece of local mythology, of the same kind as those tales which assert the submersion of cities in the lakes of Wales. But let us hear the record of the catastrophe, as preserved in the Triads.

"Seithinin the Drunkard, the son of Seithin Saidi, King of Dyved, in his liquor let in the sea, over Cantre'r Gwaelod, so as to destroy all the houses and lands of the place, where, prior to that event, there had been sixteen cities, the best of all the towns and cities of Wales excepting Caerleon upon Usk. This district was the dominion of Gwyddnaw Garanhir, King of Caredigion. The event happened in the time of Emrys, the sovereign. The men who escaped the inundation, came to land in Ardudwy, in the regions of Avon, and in the mountains of Snowdon, and other places which had hitherto been uninhabited."

This is, undoubtedly, the substance of an old Mabinogi, or mythological tale, and ought not to be received as authentic history. For, in the first place, Cardigan Bay did exist in the time of Ptolemy, who marks the promontories by which it is circumscribed, and the months of the rivers which it receives, in nearly the same relative situations which they retain at present. But neither Ptolemy, nor any other ancient geographer, takes notice of one of those sixteen cities, which are said to have been lost there in the sixth century.

In the next place, we know enough of the geography of Wales, both ancient and modern, to form a decisive conclusion, that a single Cantrev, or hundred, never did contain sixteen towns, which would bear the slightest comparison with Caerleon, such as it was in the supposed age of Gwyddno.

Again: the incident is generally represented as having happened, in consequence of having neglected to close a sluice; a cause inadequate, surely, to the alleged effect. And the omission is imputed to a son of Seithin Saidi, King of Dyved, a character who we have already traced into the regions of mythology. We have marked his intimate connexion with the history of the deluge, and the mystic rites by which it was commemorated, and have ascertained his identity with Tegid, the husband of Ceridwen.

The landing of those who escaped from this drowned country, upon the mountains of Snowdon, is like the landing of Deucalion upon Mount Parnassus. It is not history, but mythology. The district of Snowdon, from the remotest period of British mythology, was famous for its Arkite memorials. Here was the city of Enrys, or the ambrosial city—this was also called the city of Pharäon, or the higher powers; that is, the Baalim, or Arkite patriarchs. Here the dragons were concealed in the time of Beli (the solar deity), and in the time of Prydain, the son of Aedd the Great, a mystical personage of the same family. As dragons were harnessed in the car of the British Ked, as well as in that of Ceres, the concealing of these animals, in a city of the higher powers, must imply an establishment of her mysteries.

The land of Gwyddno is said to have been inundated in the time of Emrys, the sovereign. This is the personage from whom the temple of Stonehenge, as well as the sacred city in Snowden, derived its name. If the Britons of the fifth century had a monarch who bore this title, we can only say, that like his successors Uthyr and Arthur, he was complimented with a name out of the vocabulary of the Druids; and that the age of Emrys was any age, which acknowledged the Helio-arkite superstition.

Thomas Paine
An Essay on the Origin of Freemasonry
(unpublished pamphlet, c. 1810)

Thomas Paine needs no introduction to those who still recall the history they learned in school. A firebrand on the far end of Enlightenment radicalism, Paine denounced monarchy and Christianity with equal heat, and his most famous book—*Common Sense*, an incendiary tract that helped spark the American Revolution—was simply the most politically successful product of a lifetime of literary rabble-rousing. The essay included here, unpublished during his lifetime, was probably written for the third volume of his sprawling *The Age of Reason*, but was edited out at some stage; it saw print after his death in a collection of his philosophical and theological works.

Its theme was the proposal that Freemasonry was descended from the mysteries of the ancient Druids. In Toland's time Freemasonry was among the most influential social organizations in the English-speaking world; its colorful initiation rituals, its advocacy of religious and political tolerance, and the traditional secrecy of its meetings and ceremonies made it a magnet for exotic theories. The idea that the ancient Druids might have gone underground with the coming of Christianity, and preserved their teachings under the guise of stonemasons, was by no means the strangest of these speculations. This theory was not original to Paine, though his essay played a significant role in popularizing it. John Cleland, better known as the author of the pornographic classic *Fanny Hill*, published a book of eccentric etymology in 1766, *The Way to Things through Words*. Among Cleland's arguments was the claim that the word "Masons" had nothing to do with building things from stone, but came from "May's sons," a reference to the Druids, whose most important holy day he believed to have been May Day.

Finding new origins for Freemasonry was a popular sport in the eighteenth century. The intense class-consciousness of the time clashed awkwardly with the actual origins of the Masonic fraternity in the resolutely working-class stonemason's guilds of the late Middle Ages. The market for more romantic origin stories was thus a sizeable one, and the writers of the time did their best to fill it. Nearly every ancient or medieval organization with a reputation for secret knowledge ended up being drafted into service in this quest, the Druids among them; if the Knights Templar had not become the most popular choice by the mid-nineteenth century, a recent runaway bestseller might have been titled *The Merlin Code*.

The idea of a connection between the ancient Druids and the Freemasons, though, had significant impacts on the course of the Revival. It inspired the creation of Druid orders based on either Freemasonry itself, or the wider world of fraternal lodges and friendly societies that came into being during the eighteenth century. Much of what came to be standard practice in the later Druid Revival found its way into the tradition by this means, and proved to be a source of ideas and inspirations nearly as rich as Celtic tradition itself.

Further Reading:

Margaret Jacobs, *The Radical Enlightenment* (George Allen and Unwin, 1981).

Thomas Paine, *The Writings of Thomas Paine*, ed. Moncure Daniel Conway (G.P. Putnam's Sons, 1908).

* * *

It is always understood that Free Masons have a secret which they carefully conceal; but from every thing that can be collected from their own accounts of Masonry, their real secret is no other than their origin, which but few of them understand; and those who do, envelope it in mystery.

The Society of Masons is distinguished into three classes or degrees. 1st. the Entered Apprentice. 2nd. the Fellow-craft. 3rd. the Master Mason.

The entered apprentice knows but little more of Masonry, than the use of signs and tokens, and certain steps and words by which Masons can recognise each other, without being discovered by a person who is not a Mason. The fellow craft is not much better instructed in masonry, than the entered apprentice, It is only in the Master Mason's lodge, that whatever knowledge remains of the origin of masonry is preserved and concealed.

In 1730, Samuel Pritchard, member of a constituted lodge in England, published a treatise entitled *Masonry Dissected*; and made oath before the Lord Mayor of London that it was a true copy.

"Samuel Pritchard maketh oath that the copy hereunto annexed, is a true and genuine copy in every particular."

In his work he has given the catechism, or examination, in question and answer, of the apprentice, the fellow craft and the Master Mason. There was no difficulty in doing this, as it is mere form.

In his introduction, he says, "the original institution of masonry consisted in the foundation of the liberal arts and sciences, but more especially on Geometry, for, at the building of the Tower of Babel, the art and mystery of Masonry was first introduced, and from thence handed down by Euclid, a worthy and excellent Mathematician of the Egyptians; and he communicated it to Hiram, the Master Mason concerned in building Solomon's Temple in Jerusalem."

Besides the absurdity of deriving masonry from the building of Babel, where, according to the story, the confusion of languages prevented builders understanding each other and consequently of communicating any knowledge they had, there is a glaring contradiction in point of chronology in the account he gives.

Solomon's Temple was built and dedicated 1004 years before the christian era; and Euclid, as may be seen in the tables of chronology, lived 277 years before the same era. It was therefore impossible that Euclid could communicate any thing to Hiram, since Euclid did not live till 700 years after the time of Hiram.

In 1783 Captain George Smith, inspector of the Royal Artillery Academy at Woolwich, in England, and Provincial Grand master of Masonry for the county of Kent, published a treatise entitled *The Use and Abuse of Free-Masonry*.

In his chapter of the antiquity of masonry, be makes it to be coeval with creation. "When," says he, "the sovereign architect raised on masonic principles, the beauteous globe, and commanded that master science, Geometry, to lay the planetary world, and to regulate by its laws the whole stupendous system in just, unerring proportion, rolling around the central sun."

"But," continues he, "I am not at liberty publicly to undraw the curtain, and thereby to descant on this head, it is sacred, and ever will remain so; those who are honoured with the trust will not reveal it, and those who are ignorant of it cannot betray it." By this last part of the phrase, Smith means the two inferior classes, the fellow craft and the entered apprentice, for he says, in the next page of his work: —"It is not every one that is barely initiated into Free Masonry that is entrusted with all the mysteries thereto belonging; they are not attainable as things of course, nor by every capacity."

The learned, but unfortunate Doctor Dodd, Grand Chaplain of Masonry, in his oration at the dedication of Free-Masons Hall, London, traces Masonry through a variety of stages. Masons, says he, are well informed from their own private and interior records that the building of Solomon's Temple is an important era, from whence they derive many mysteries of their art. "Now," says he, "be it remembered that this great event took place about 1000 years before the Christian era, and consequently more than a century before Homer, the first of the Grecian Poets, wrote; and above five centuries before Pythagoras brought from the east his sublime system of truly masonic instruction to illuminate our western world.

"But remote as this period is, we date not from thence the commencement of our art. For though it might owe to the wise and glorious king of Israel some of its many mystic forms and hieroglyphic ceremonies, yet certainly the art itself is coeval with man, the great subject of it.

"We trace," continues he, "its footsteps in the most distant, the most remote ages and nations of the world. We find it amongst the first and most celebrated civilizers of the East. We deduce it regularly from the first astronomers on the plains of Chaldea, to the wise and mystic kings and priests of Egypt, the sages of Greece, and the philosophers of Rome."

From these reports and declarations of Masons of the highest order in the institution, we see that masonry, without publicly declaring so, lays claim to some divine communication from the Creator in a manner different from and unconnected with the book which the Christians call the Bible; and the natural result from this is, that masonry is derived from some very ancient religion wholly independent of and unconnected with that book.

To come then at once to the point, masonry (as I shall shew from the custom, ceremonies, hieroglyphics, and chronology of masonry) is derived, and is the remains of the religion of the ancient Druids; who like the magi of Persia, and the priests of Heliopolis in Egypt, were priests of the Sun. They paid worship to this great luminary, as the great visible agent of a great invisible first cause, whom they styled, Time without limits.

The Christian religion and masonry have one and the same common origin, both are derived from the worship of the sun, the difference between their origins is, that the Christian religion is a parody on the worship of the sun, in which they put a man whom they call Christ, in the place of the sun, and pay him the same adoration which was originally paid to the sun, as I have shewn in the chapter on the origin of the Christian religion.

In masonry, many of the ceremonies of the Druids are preserved in their original state, at least without any parody. With them the sun is still the sun; and his image in the form of the sun, is the great emblematical ornament of Masonic Lodges and Masonic dresses. It is the central figure on their aprons, and they wear it also pendant on the breast in their lodges, and in their processions. It has the figure of a man, as at the head of the sun, as Christ is always represented.

At what period of antiquity, or in what nation, this religion was first established, is lost in the lahyrinth of unrecorded times. It is generally ascribed to the ancient Egyptians, the Babylonians and Chaldeans, and reduced afterwards to a system regulated by the apparent progress of the sun through the twelve signs of the zodiac, by Zoroaster the lawgiver of Persia, from whence Pythagoras brought it into Greece. It is to these matters Dr. Dodd refers in the passage already quoted from his oration.

The worship of the sun as the great visible agent of a great invisible first cause, time without limits, spread itself over a considerable part of Asia and Africa, from thence to Greece and Rome, through all ancient Gaul, and into Britain and Ireland.

Smith, in his chapter on the antiquity of masonry in Britain, says, that "notwithstanding the obscurity which envelopes masonic history in that country, various circumstances contribute to prove that Free Masonry was introduced into Britain about 1030 years before Christ."

It. cannot be masonry in its present state that Smith here alludes to. The Druids flourished in Britain at the period he speaks of, and it is from them that masonry is descended. Smith has put the child in the place of the parent.

It sometimes happens is well in writing as in conversation, that a person lets slip an expression that serves to unravel what he intends to conceal, and this is the case with Smith, for in the same chapter he says, "The Druids, when they committed any thing to writing, used the Greek alphabet, and I am bold to assert that the most perfect remains of the Druids' rites and ceremonies are preserved in the customs and ceremonies of the masons that are to be found existing among mankind. My brethren," says he, "may be able to trace them with greater exactness than I am at liberty to explain to the public."

This is a confession from a Master Mason, without intending it to be so understood by the public, that masonry is the remains of the religion of the Druids. The reason for the Masons keeping this a secret I shall explain in the course of this work.

As the study and contemplation of the Creator in the works of the creation, of which the sun, as the great visible agent of that Being, was the visible object of the adoration of Druids, all their religious rites and ceremonies had reference to the apparent progress of the sun through the twelve signs of the Zodiac, and his influence upon the earth. The Masons adopt the same practices. The roof of their temples or lodges is ornamented with a sun, and the floor is a representation of the variegated face of the earth, either by carpeting or Mosaic work.

Free Mason's Hall, in Great Queen Street, Lincoln's Inn Fields, London, is a magnificent building, and cost upwards of 12,000 pounds sterling. Smith, in speaking of this building, says (page 152) The roof of this magnificent hall, is in all probability the highest piece of finished architecture in Europe. In the centre of this roof, a most resplendent sun is represented in burnished gold, surrounded with the 12 signs of the Zodiac with their respective characters:

♈ Aries	♎ Libra
♉ Taurus	♏ Scorpio
♊ Gemini	♐ Sagittarius
♋ Cancer	♑ Capricorn
♌ Leo	♒ Aquarius
♍ Virgo	♓ Pisces

After giving this description he says, "The emblematical meaning of the sun is well known to the enlightened and inquisitive Free Mason; and as the real sun is situated in the centre of the universe, so the emblematical sun is the centre of real masonry. We all know", continues he, "that the sun is the fountain of light, the source of the seasons, the cause of the vicissitudes of day and night, the parent of vegetation, the friend of man; hence the scientific Free Mason only knows the reason why the sun is placed in the centre of this beautiful hall."

The Masons, in order to protect themselves from the persecution of the Christian church, have always spoken in a mystical manner of the figure of the sun in their lodges or, like the astronomer Lalande, who is a Mason, been silent upon the subject. It is their secret, especially in Catholic countries, because the figure of the sun is the expressive criterion that denotes they are descended from the Druids, and was that wise, elegant, philosophical religion, the faith opposite to the faith of the gloomy Christian church.

The lodges of the Masons, if built for the purpose, are constructed is a manner to correspond with the apparent motion of the sun. They are situated East and West. The master's place is always in the East. In the examination of an entered apprentice, the master, among many other questions asks him,

Q. How is the lodge situated?

A. East and West.

Q. Why so?

A. Because all churches and chapels are or ought to be so.

This answer, which is mere catechismal form, is not an answer to the question. It does no more than remove the question a point further, which is, why ought all churches and chapels to be so? But as the entered apprentice is not initiated into the Druidical mysteries of Masonry, he is not asked any question to which a direct answer would lead thereto.

Q. Where stands your master?

A. In the East.

Q. Why so?

A. As the sunrises lit the East, and opens the day, so the master stands in the East (with his right hand upon his left breast, being a sign, and the square about his neck) to open the lodge and set his men to work.

Q. Where stands your wardens?
A. In the West.
Q. What is their business?
A. As the sun sets in the West to close the day; so the wardens stand in the West with their right hands upon their left breasts, being a sign, and the level and plumb rule about their necks to close the lodge, and dismiss the men from labour, paying them their wages.

Here the name of the sun is mentioned, but it is proper to observe, that lit this place it has reference only to labour or to the time of labour, and not to any religious Druidical rite or ceremony, as it would have with respect to the situation of Lodges East and West. I have already observed in the chapter on the origin of the Christian religion, that the situation of churches East and West is taken from the worship of the sun which rises in the East, and has not the least reference to the person called Jesus Christ. The Christians never bury their dead on the North side of a church; and a Masonic Lodge always has, or is supposed to have, three windows which are called fixed lights, to distinguish them from the movable lights of the sun and the moon. The master asks the entered apprentice,

Q. How are they (the fixed lights) situated?
A. East, west, and south.
Q. What are their uses?
A. To light the men to and from their work.
Q. Why are there no lights in the North?
A. Because the sun casts no rays from thence.

This among numerous other instances shews that the Christian religion, and Masonry, have one and the same common origin, the ancient worship of the sun.

The high festival of the Masons is on the day they call St. John's day; but every enlightened Mason must know that holding their festival on this day has no reference to the person called St. John; and that it is only to disguise the true cause of holding it on this day, that they call the day by that name. As there were Masons, or at least Druids, many centuries before the time of St. John, if such person ever existed, their holding their festival on this day must refer to some cause totally unconnected with John.

The case is, that the day called St. John's day is the 24th of June, and is what is called Midsummer day. The sun is then arrived at the summer solstice; and with respect to his meridional altitude, or height at high noon, appears for some days to be of the same height. The Astronomical longest day, like the shortest day, is not every year, on account of leap year, on the same numerical day, and therefore the 24th of June, is always taken for Midsummer day; and it is in honour of the sun, which has then arrived at his greatest height in our hemisphere, and not anything with respect to St. John, that this annual festival of the Masons, taken from the Druids, is celebrated on Midsummer day.

Customs will often outlive the remembrance of their origin, and this is the case with respect to a custom still practised in Ireland, where the Druids flourished at the time they flourished in Britain. On the eve of St. John's day, that is on the eve of Midsummer day, the Irish light fires on the tops of the hills. This can have no reference to St. John—it has emblematical reference to the sun which on that day is at his highest summer elevation, and might in common language be said to have arrived at the top of the hill.

As to what Masons, and books of Masonry tell us of Solomon's Temple in Jerusalem, it is in no wise improbable that some masonic ceremonies may have been derived from the building of the Temple, for the worship of the sun was in practice many centuries before that temple existed, or before the Israelites came out of Egypt. And we learn from the history of the Jewish Kings, 2 Kings, chap. xxii. xxiii. that the worship of the sun was performed by the Jews in that temple. It is, however, much to be doubted, if it was done with the same scientific purity and religious morality, with which it was performed by the Druids, who by all accounts that historically remain of them, were a wise, learned, and moral class of men. The Jews, on the contrary, were ignorant of astronomy, and of science in general, and if a religion founded on astronomy, fell into their hands, it is almost certain it would be corrupted. We do not read in the history of the Jews, whether in the Bible or elsewhere, that they were the inventors or the improvers of any sort of science. Even in the building of this temple, the Jews did not know how to square and frame the timber for beginning and carrying out the work, and Solomon was obliged to send to Hiram, King of Tyre, (Zidon) to procure workmen; "for thou knowest, (says Solomon to Hiram, 1 Kings, chap. v. ver. 6.) that there is not among us any that can skill to hew timber like unto the Zidonians." This temple was more properly Hiram's temple than Solomon's, and if the Masons derive any thing from the building of it, they owe it to the Zidonians and not to the Jews—But to return to the worship of the sun in this temple.

It is said, 2 Kings chap. xxiii. ver. 8. "And King Josiah put down all the idolatrous priests that burned incense unto the sun, the moon, the planets and to all the host of heaven." And it is said at the 11th verse "and he took away the horses that the kings of Judah had given to the sun, at the entering of the house of the Lord and burned the chariots of the sun with fire, ver. 13 and the high places that were before Jerusalem, which were on the right hand of the mount of corruption, which Solomon the King of Israel had builded for Ashtoreth, the abomination of the Zidonians (the very people that built the temple) did the king defile."

Besides these things, the description that Josephus gives of the decorations of this Temple, resembles on a large scale those of a Masons Lodge. He says that the distribution of the several parts of the Temple of the Jews represented all nature, particularly the parts most apparent of it, as the sun, the moon, the planets, the zodiac, the earth, the elements, and that the system of the world was retraced there by numerous ingenious emblems. These, in all probability, are what Josiah, in his ignorance, calls the abominations of the Zidonians.[2] Every thing, however, drawn from this temple,[3] and applied to Masonry, still refers to the worship of the sun, however corrupted or misunderstood by the Jews, and, consequently, to the religion of the Druids.

Another circumstance which shews that Masonry is derived from some ancient system, prior to and unconnected with, the Christian:

[2] Smith, in speaking of a Lodge, says, when the Lodge is revealed to an entering Mason, it discovers to him a representation of the world; in which from the wonders of nature, we are led to contemplate her great original, and to worship him from his mighty works; and we are thereby also moved to exercise those moral and social virtues which become mankind as the servants of the great architect of the world.

[3] It may not be improper here to observe, that the law called the law of Moses could not have been in existence at the time of building this temple. Here is the likeness of things in heaven above, and in the earth beneath. And we read in I Kings, chap 6, 7, that Solomon made cherubs and cherubims, that he carved all the walls of the house round about with cherubims and palm trees, and open flowers, and that be made a molten sea, placed on twelve oxen, and the ledges of it were ornamented with lions, oxen, and cherubims; all this is contrary to the law called the law of Moses.

religion, is the chronology, or method of counting time, used by the Masons in the records of their lodges. They make no use of what is called the Christian era; and they reckon their months numerically, as the ancient Egyptians did, and as the Quakers do now. I have by me, a record of a French Lodge, at the time the late Duke of Orleans, then Duke de Chartres, was Grand Master of Masonry in France. It begins as follows: "*te trentième jour du sixième mois de l'an de la V. L. cinq mil sept cent soixante et treize,*" that is, the thirtieth day of the sixth month of the year of the venerable Lodge, five thousand seven hundred and seventy three. By what I observe in English books of Masonry, the English Masons use the initials A. L and not V. L. By A. L. they mean in the year of the lodge, as the Christians by A.D. mean by the year of the Lord. But. A. L like V. L refers to the same chronological era, that is, to the supposed time of the Creation. In the chapter on the origin of the Christian religion, I have shewn that the cosmogony, that is the account of the creation, with which the book of Genesis opens, has been taken and mutilated from the Zend-Avesta of Zoroaster, and is fixed as a preface to the Bible, after the Jews returned from captivity in Babylon, and that the rabbis of the Jews do not hold their account in Genesis to be a fact, but mere allegory. The six thousand years in the Zend Avesta, is changed or interpolated into six days in the account of Genesis. The masons appear to have chosen the same period, and perhaps to avoid the suspicion and persecution of the church, have adopted the era of the world, as the era of Masonry. The V. L of the French, and A. L. of the English Mason, answer to the A.M. Anno Mundi or year of the world.

Though the Masons have taken many of their ceremonies and hieroglyphics from the ancient Egyptians, it is certain that they have not taken their chronology from thence. If they had, the church would soon have sent them to the stake; as the chronology of the Egyptians, like that of the Chinese, goes many thousand years beyond the Bible chronology.

The religion of the Druids, as before said, was the same as the religion of the ancient Egyptians. The priests of Egypt were the professors and teachers of Science, and were styled priests of Heliopolis, that is, of the city of the sun. The Druids in Europe, who were the same order of men, have their name from the Teutonic or ancient German language; the Germans being anciently called Teutones. The word Druid signifies a wise man. In Persia they were called magi, which signifies the same thing.

"Egypt," says Smith, "from whence we derive many of our mysteries, hath always borne a distinguished rank in history, and was once celebrated above all others for its antiquities, learning, opulence, and fertility. In their system, their principal hero-gods, Osiris and Isis, theologically represented the supreme Being and universal nature; and physically, the two great celestial luminaries, the sun and the moon, by whose influence all nature was actuated. The experienced brethren of the Society" (says Smith in a note to this passage) "are well informed what affinity these symbols bear in masonry, and why they are used in all Masonic Lodges."

In speaking of the apparel of the Masons in their Lodges, part of which as we see in their public processions, is a white leather apron, he says, "the Druids were apparelled in white at the time of their sacrifices and solemn offices. The Egyptian Priests of Osiris wore snow white garments. The Grecian and most other priests, wore white garments. As Mason, we regard the principles of those *who were the worshippers of the true God*, imitate their apparel, and assume the badge of innocence.

"The Egyptians," continues Smith, "in the earliest ages, constituted a great number of Lodges, but with assiduous care kept their secrets of Masonry from all strangers. These secrets have been imperfectly handed down to us by tradition only, and ought to be kept undiscovered to the labourers, crafts men, and apprentices, till by good behaviour, and long study, they become better acquainted in Geometry and the liberal arts, and thereby qualified for Masters and Wardens, which is seldom or never the case with English Masons."

Under the head of Free Masonry, written by the astronomer Lalande, in the French Encyclopedia, I expected from his great knowledge in astronomy, to have found much information on the origin of Masonry; for what connection can there be between any institution and the sun and twelve signs of the Zodiac, if there be not something in that institution, or in its origin, that has reference to astronomy. Every thing used as an hieroglyphic, has reference to the subject and purpose for which it is used; and we are not to suppose the Free Masons, among whom are many very learned and scientific men, to be such idiots as to make use of astronomical signs without some astronomical purpose.

But I was much disappointed in my expectation from Lalande. In speaking of the origin of Masonry, he says *"L origine de la maçonnerie se perd, comme tant d'autres, dans la obscurité des temps;"* that is, the origin of Masonry, like many others, loses itself in the obscurity of time. When I came to this expression, I supposed Lalande a Mason, and on enquiry found he was. This passing over saved him from the embarrassment which Masons are under respecting the disclosure of their origin, and which they are sworn to conceal. There is a society of Masons in Dublin who take the name of Druids; these Masons must be supposed to have a reason for taking that name.

I come now to speak of the cause of secrecy used by the Masons.

The natural source of secrecy is fear. When any new religion over-runs a former religion, the professors of the new become the persecutors of the old. We see this in all the instances that history brings before us. When Hulkiah the Priest and Shaphan the scribe, in the reign of King Josiah, found or pretended to find the law, called the law of Moses, a thousand years after the time of Moses, and it does not appear from the 2nd Book of Kings; chapters 22, 23, that such law was ever practised or known before the time of Josiah; he established that law as a national religion, and put all the priests of the sun to death. When the Christian religion over-ran the Jewish religion, the Jews were the continual subjects of persecution in all Christian countries. When the Protestant religion in England over-ran the Roman Catholic religion, it was made death for a Catholic priest to be found in England. As this has been the case in all the instances we. have any knowledge of, we are obliged to admit it with respect to the case in question, and that when the Christian religion over-ran the religion of the Druids in Italy, ancient Gaul, Britain, and Ireland, the Druids became the subjects of persecution. This would naturally and necessarily oblige such of them as remained attached to their original religion to meet in secret and under the strongest injunctions of secrecy. Their safety depended upon it. A false brother might expose the lives of many of them to destruction; and from the remains of the religion of the Druids thus preserved, arose the institution which, to avoid the name of Druid, took that of Mason; and practised, under this new name, the rites and ceremonies of Druids.

Iolo Morganwg

The Bards of the Island of Britain

(from *Barddas*, edited by J. Williams ab Ithel, 1862)

Poet, visionary, scholar, trickster, forger, and opium addict, Iolo Morganwg had a more potent influence on the Druid Revival than any other single person. His birth name was Edward Williams; Iolo Morganwg, "Ned from Glamorgan," was the bardic title he gave himself, as part of his claim to be the heir of the Welsh bardic tradition and the lore of the ancient Druids.

Born in 1747, he lived during the years when Welsh national identity was reinventing itself, inspired by the romantic nationalism that a generation or two later would sweep Europe in the wake of the Napoleonic wars. Iolo himself played no small role in that process, giving traditional Welsh poetry a new momentum and social role that placed it near the center of a renewed national culture. That a good deal of that momentum came through allegedly medieval poems and lore that he actually wrote himself is simply part of the complex character of the man.

He was far from the only romantic nationalist to manufacture some of the national identity he celebrated, and far from the only figure in the Druid Revival to project onto the Druids of the past his ideas of what the Druids of present and future should be. Among the gifts he brought to his work was a mastery of medieval Welsh literature and verse so far beyond that of his contemporaries, and indeed most later scholars, that some of his inventions were not identified as such until the 1950s. Welsh scholar Ceri Lewis was not exaggerating when she said that, "he was, beyond doubt, the most accomplished and successful forger in literary history."

The core of his project, especially toward the end of his life, was the reconstruction of the traditions of the old Welsh bards. There is some reason to think that he may have received some scraps of tradition from several elderly Welsh poets in his youth, and more reason to believe that he had access to a few documents of poetry and bardic lore that have not survived elsewhere, but the great majority of his bardism was his own brilliant creation. In his vision, the Bards of the Island of Britain were the custodians of the lore of the ancient Druids, an intact tradition of wisdom dating from pre-Christian times and enriched by a Christianity that proved to be remarkably close to Iolo's own Unitarian beliefs.

His system proved as popular in its time as Gerald Gardner's equally unhistorical tradition of Wicca became in the second half of the twentieth century, and had a similarly broad influence. Unlike Wicca, which drew most of its adherents from the avant-garde of its time, Iolo's bardic inventions found an audience in the Welsh cultural mainstream. His Gorsedd rituals were adopted by the Welsh *eisteddfodau* or bardic assemblies, beginning with the Caermarthen eisteddfod of 1819, and remain in use today by Gorseddau in Wales, Cornwall and Brittany.

Outside the Welsh community, his major impact came with the publication of his collected papers and fragments of Bardic lore. Iolo himself spent much of his old age trying to piece these together, and his son, Taliesin Williams, put years into the same task; the work was finally completed by John Williams ab Ithel, another enthusiastic Anglican clergyman, and published as *Barddas (Bardism)* in 1862. The following extracts from *Barddas* give some sense of the flavor and quality of Iolo Morganwg's work, but only a close study of *Barddas* and later Druid literature can communicate the measure of his impact on the tradition.

Further Reading:

Geraint H. Jenkins, *Fact, Fantasy, and Fiction: The Historical Vision of Iolo Morganwg* (Canolfan Uwchefrydiau Cymreig a Cheltiadd Prifysgol Cymru, 1997). -----, ed., *A Rattleskull Genius: The Many Faces of Iolo Morganwg* (University of Wales Press, 2005).

J.Williams ab Ithel, ed., *The Barddas of Iolo Morganwg* (Weiser, 2003)

* * *

The Origin and Progress of Letters—The Name of God—The Bardic Secret

Pray, my skilful and discreet teacher, if it be fair to ask, how was the knowledge of letters first obtained!

I will exhibit the information of men of wisdom and profound knowledge, thus;—When God pronounced His name, with the word sprang the light and the life; for previously there was no life except God

Himself. And the mode in which it was spoken was of God's direction. His name was pronounced, and with the utterance was the springing of light and vitality, and man, and every other living thing; that is to say, each and all sprang together. And Menw the Aged, son of Menwyd, beheld the springing of the light, and its form and appearance, not otherwise than thus, /I\ in three columns; and in the rays of light the vocalization—for one were the hearing and seeing, one unitedly the form and sound; and one unitedly with the form and sound was life, and one unitedly with these three was power, which power was God the Father. And since each of these was one unitedly, he understood that every voice, and hearing, and living, and being, and sight, and seeing, were one unitedly with God; nor is the least thing other than God. And by seeing the form, and in it hearing the voice—not otherwise —he knew what form and appearance voice should have. And having obtained earth under him co-instantaneousty with the light, he drew the form of the voice and light on the earth. And it was on hearing the sound of the voice, which had in it the kind and utterance of three notes, that he obtained the three letters, and knew the sign that was suitable to one and other of them. Thus he made in form and sign the Name of God, after the semblance of rays of light, and perceived that they were the figure and form and sign of life; one also with them was life, and in life was God, that is to say, God is one with life, and there is no life but God, and there is no God but life.

It was from the understanding thus obtained in respect of this voice, that he was able to assimilate mutually every other voice as to kind, quality, and reason, and could make a letter suitable to the utterance of every sound and voice. Thus were obtained the Cymraeg, and every other language. And it was from the three primary letters that were constructed every other letter,—which is the principal secret of the Bards of the Isle of Britain; and from this secret comes every knowledge of letters that is possible.

Thus was the voice, that was heard, placed on record in the symbol, and meaning attached to each of the three notes:—the sense of O was given to the first column, the sense of I to the second or middle column, and the sense of V to the third; whence the word OIV. That is to say, it was by means of this word that God declared His existence, life, knowledge, power, eternity, and universality. And in the declaration was His love, that is, coinstantaneously with it sprang like lightening all the universe into life and existence, co-vocally and co-jubilantly with the uttered Name of God, in one united song of exultation and joy—then all the worlds to the extremities of Annwn. It was thus, then, that God made the worlds, namely, He declared His Name and existence OIV.

Why is it not right that a man should commit the Name of God to vocalization, and the sound of language and tongue?

Because it cannot be done without misnaming God, for no man ever heard the vocalization of His Name, and no one knows how to pronounce it; but it is represented by letters, that it may be known what is meant, and for Whom it stands. Formerly signs were employed, namely, the three elements of vocal letters. However, to prevent disrespect and dishonour to God, a Bard is forbidden to name Him, except inwardly and in thought.

Pray, my beloved and discreet teacher, show me the signs that stand for the Name of God, and the manner in which they are made.

Thus are they made;—the first of the signs is a small cutting or line inclining with the sun at eventide, thus, / ; the second is another cutting, in the form of a perpendicular, upright post, thus, | ; and the third is a cutting of the same amount of inclination as the first, but in an opposite direction, that is, against the sun, thus \ ; and the three placed together, thus, /|\. But instead of, and as substitutes for these, are placed the three letters O I V. And it was in this manner that the Bard inserted this name in his stanza, thus,

> The Eternal, Origin, Self-existent, Distributor—holy be the lips
> That canonically pronounce them;
> Another name, in full word,
> Is O. I. and W—OIW the word.—Ieuan Rudd sang it.

This name God gave to Himself, to show that He is in existence, and that there is no one but Himself, except by gift and permission; for truly all of us men, and other living beings, are and exist only by the gift and permission of God. It is considered presumptuous to utter this name in the hearing of any man in the world. Nevertheless, every thing calls Him inwardly by this name—the sea and land, earth and air, and all the visibles and invisibles of the world, whether on the earth or in the sky—all the worlds of all the celestials and terrestrials—every intellectual being and existence—every thing animate and inanimate; wherefore none that honours God, will call Him by this name, except inwardly.

The three mystic letters signify the three attributes of God, namely, love, knowledge, and truth; and it is out of these three that justice springs, and without one of the three there can be no justice. Which one so ever of the three stands up, the other two will incline towards it; and every two of them whatsoever will yield precedency and pre-eminence to the third, whichever of the three it may be. It was according to this order and principle that three degrees were conferred upon the Bards of the Isle of Britain, and each of the three was invested with privilege, precedency, and pre-eminence, in respect of the particularity of necessity, over the other two, whichsoever they might be. Out of the three attributes of God spring every power and will and law.

It was out of the knowledge and understanding of the vocalization of language and speech, by reason of the three principal letters, that sixteen letters were formed, constructed from the primary columns, namely, the three principal letters in the form of rays of light. And it was thus that form and appearance could be imparted to every vocalization of language and speech, and to every primary sound, and symbolic forms of memory be made visible on wood and stone. Accordingly the memory of seeing could thus take place simultaneously with the memory of hearing; and, by means of signs, every sound of voice could be rendered visible to the eye, as far as the ear could hear what the tongue spoke, and what awen from God was capable of. Then when sixteen letters were constructed out of the principal columns, namely these /|\ —since no letter can be found on the Coelbren, or in the Secret of the Bards of the Isle of Britain, that has not its elements and modifications derived from one or other of the three principal columns—and because these signs were cut on wood, they were called llythyrau. And when every one of the letters was cut on wood, each of them received a name and meaning in respect of sound and voice, warranted and systematized; that is to say, each had its own peculiar vocalization, confirmed by art. Thus were obtained the signs and rudiments of warranted speech, which is called Abic, but others call it Abcedilros. Thus was ocular and manual art applied to speech and thought, whence arose ocular memorials and the materials of knowledge. Then wise men and aspirants engaged themselves in improving sciences and language and speech, and in discriminating vocalization and the variety of sound with greater skill and minuteness; and they elaborated them, until they were able to make two more letters, so that the Alphabet consisted of eighteen letters. After that the need of two more was observed, until they became twenty; then twenty-two; and to complete the work, twenty-four principal letters; nor are there more in the Alphabet of the Coelbren that are simple, that is to say, of primary sound. Nevertheless, there are others that are compound letters, significative of the mutation of voice, and of the accentuation of letters, of which, according to highly skilful teachers, there are sixteen in number, whilst others will have them to be eighteen. Some of them cannot have authority or warrant, at least they cannot have necessity, in virtue of indispensable reason; nevertheless it is not allowable to forbid the improvement of sciences, whilst every awen and art are free, provided they do not injure, obscure, or confound laudable sciences.

It is by means of letters that sciences and history are committed to rational memory. The three foundations of sciences are memory, understanding, and reason, and without the memory little is the utility of memory, understanding, and reason. After the discovery of the knowledge of letters it was that every understanding, and consideration, and every meditation of awen were committed to the memorial of letters; and from long acquaintance therewith room was seen for improving, amplifying, and varying the order and system of language and speech, and the art of letters, that letters might be warranted, which should be suitable to every circumstance of language and speech, and for the purpose of showing visibly every sound and utterance of word, voice, and speech, that they might harmonize with the ratiocination of the art of language and letters, and that speech might agree with speech between man and man, in respect of the sound and meaning of a sentence, the effort of language, and the encounter of the art and sciences of language and letters. Hence easy and warranted became the understanding, and understanding arose from understanding, and all men became of one judgment in respect of the meaning of word and sentence, and in respect of the sense, accent, and signification of letters. And hence fixed confirmation was bestowed upon the sciences of letters, and upon all sciences that were committed to the memory and under the auspices of letters; and it became easy, also, to learn and understand what was thus arranged systematically and with a fixed meaning; and it was easy for all men to be of one judgment, and of one sense in respect of such. That is to say, from the long co-reasoning of wise men and aspirants, and men of art, improvement and fixedness of meaning and system, are obtained, in respect of all sciences, and in respect of every one of them. After letters had been improved and amplified, as occasion required, in respect of meaning and number, there were exhibited twenty-four primaries—in the opinion of others, the three nines, tint is to say, twenty-seven; nor is there any need or occasion for more primaries, for, say they, there cannot be symbols of every sound of word and speech in the Cymraeg under twenty-seven letters—but they formed secondaries and two primary letters.

Pray, my far knowing teacher, why is it said that only a Bard of thorough secrecy knows how the Name of God is to be spoken audibly, that is to say, by means of the three principal columns of letters?

Because only a Bard of secrecy knows properly the old system of letters, and their meaning, accent, and powers, in respect of their stability in the system of the eighteen letters; for when the system of the eighteen was established, new letters were employed for the Name of God, namely O I U, but previously, during the era of the sixteen, no letters stood for the Name of God, other than the three columns of primary letters, that is / | \ , which was called the system of God and light, and only a Bard of thorough secrecy now knows properly either the one or the other of the two old systems, which I have mentioned.

Why is not that secret committed to letter and audible speech, that it may be known of all?

Because it is misjudged by him who would have credence from another for more than he knows, and it is the wicked man, with the view of pillaging belief from the ignorant, that does so, and that bestows unjust imaginations upon a letter, and its meaning, accent, pronunciation, and sound, rather than the true and just. It is by such men that divine sciences are and have been corrupted, therefore the secret ought not to be divulged to other than to him who, in the judgment and sight of man, is warranted as having awen from God. Nor is there any other who knows the vocalization of the Name of God, without telling a falsehood, and the greatest falsehood is to falsify God and His Name.

Why is it not free from falsehood to commit the Name of God to speech and the hearing of the ear?

Because that cannot be done without its being falsely spoken, by any man or living being and existence possessed of soul and intellect, but by God Himself;—to exhibit and pronounce it in speech otherwise is falsehood, and the devastation and spoliation of God, for there is no being but God and in God, and whoso says otherwise speaks falsehood, which is falsehood against God, and depredatory usitrpation over Him. But he who possesses awen from God will perceive the secret, and will know it, and wherever a man may have awen from God, warranted in respect of reason and conduct, it is not unjust to divulge to him the secret, but it is not just to do so to any other, lest the Name of God be spoken erroneously, falsely, and through unjust and vain imagination, and thereby be mocked, disparaged, and dishonoured. There is also another cause, namely, to induce a man to excercise his understanding and reason upon just and firm meditation; for he who does so, will understand the character and meaning of the primitive system of sixteen letters, and the subsequent system of eighteen, and hence will perceive and understand the Name of God, and the just reverence due to Him; for he who does truth will do justice.

The three principal signs of sciences, namely,—the three rays of light, for from them were obtained appearance and colour and form—the three voices of light, and from them were obtained hearing and speech and vocal song—and the three symbolic letters, and from them were obtained the memory of sight, and the form of voice, visibly, and mental understanding in regard to what can have no colour, or form, or voice. And it was from these three that fixedness and authority were obtained for sciences and art.

The Invention of Letters by Einigan and Menw—The Secret of Bardism

Einigan the Giant beheld three pillars of light, having in them all demonstrable sciences that ever were, or ever will be. And he took three rods of the quicken tree, and placed on them the forms and signs of all sciences, so as to be remembered and exhibited them. But those who saw them misunderstood, and falsely apprehended them, and taught illusive sciences, regarding the rods as a God, whereas they only bore His Name. When Einigan saw this, he was greatly annoyed, and in the intensity of his grief he broke the three rods, nor were others found that contained accurate sciences. He was so distressed on that account that from the intensity he burst asunder, and with his [parting] breath he prayed God that there should be accurate sciences among men in the flesh, and there should he a correct understanding for the proper discernment thereof. And at the end of a year and a day, after the decease of Einigan, Menw, son of the Three Shouts, beheld three rods growing out of the mouth of Einigan, which exhibited the sciences of the Ten Letters, and the mode in which all the sciences of language and speech were arranged by them, and in language and speech all distinguishable sciences. He then took the rods, and taught from them the sciences—all, except the Name of God, which he made a secret, lest the Name should be falsely discerned; and hence arose the Secret of the Bardism of the Bards of the Isle of Britain. And God imparted His protection to this secret, and gave Menw a very discreet understanding of sciences under this His protection, which understanding is called Awen from God; and blessed for ever is he who shall obtain it. Amen, so be it.

Druidism

Disciple and Teacher.

This is the Druidism of the Bards of the Isle of Britain, with their opinion respecting God and all living beings, of whatsoever grade or kind they may be. It is rudimentally taught as follows:

1. Question. What is God?

Answer. What cannot be otherwise.

Q. Why cannot it be otherwise?

A. Could it be otherwise, we should have no knowledge of any animation, being, existence, or futurity, in respect of any thing now known to us.

Q. What is God?

A. Complete and perfect life, and the total annihilation of every thing inanimate and death, nor can any species of mortality concur with Him. And God is life, full, entire, imperishable, and without end.

2. God is perfect life, which cannot be limited or confined, and, in virtue of His proper essence, is possessed of perfect knowledge, in respect of sight, sufferance, and intention, having His origin in Himself, without communion with any thing else whatsoever, and wholly free from all participation in evil.

3. God is absolute good, in that lie totally annihilates all evil, and

there cannot be in Him the least particle of the nature of evil.

4. God is absolute power, in that He totally annihilates inability, nor can power and will in Him be restrained, since He is almighty, and all good.

5. God is absolute wisdom and knowledge, in that He totally annihilates ignorance, and folly; and therefore no event can by any chance happen, which He knows not of. And in view of these qualities and properties no being or animation can be conceived or contemplated other than coming from God, except natural evil, which annihilates all life and goodness.

6. What would utterly annihilate and reject God and life, and therein all goodness, is absolute and natural evil; which is thus in complete opposition, and of a contrary nature, and essence, to God, life, and goodness.

7. And by means of this direction, may be seen two things existing of necessity, namely: the living and dead; good and evil; God and Cythraul, and darkness in darkness, and powerless inability.

8. Cythraul is destitute of life and intention—a thing of necessity, not of will, without being or life, in respect of existence and personality; but vacant in reference to what is vacant, dead in reference to what is dead, and nothing in reference to what is nothing. Whereas God is good with reference to what is good, is fulness in reference to fulness, life in life, all in all, and light in light.

9. And from what has been said, it may be seen that there can be no existence of original nature but God and Cythraul, the dead and living, nothing and occurrence, issue from what is issueless, and existence from mutual union.

10. God mercifully, out of love and pity, uniting Himself with the lifeless, that is, the evil, with the intention of subduing it unto life, imparted the existence of vitality to animated and living beings, and thus did life lay hold of the dead, whence intellectual animations and vitality first sprang. And intellectual existences and animations began in the depth of Annwn, for there is the lowest and least grade, and it cannot but be that there and in that state intellectual life first began, for it cannot be otherwise than that the least and lowest grade of every thing should be the original and primordial one. The greatest cannot exist in an intellectual existence before the least; there can be no intellectual existence without

gradation, and in respect of gradation there cannot but be a beginning, a middle, and an end or extremity,—first, augmentation, and ultimate or conclusion. Thus may be seen that there is to every intellectual existence a necessary gradation, which necessarily begins at the lowest grade, progressing from thence incessantly along every addition, intervention, increase, growth in age, and completion, unto conclusion and extremity, where it rests, for ever from pure necessity, for there can not be any thing further or higher or better in respect of gradation and Abred.

11. All intellectual existences partake of good and evil, and that, more or less, according to their degree in Abred, from the dead in the depth of Annwn, to the living in the extremity of goodness and power, even so far as would not be at all possible for God to conduct them further.

12. Animations in Annwn are partakers of life and goodness in the lowest possible degree, and of death and evil in the highest degree that is possibly compatible with life and personal identity. Therefore, they are necessarily evil, because of the preponderance of evil over the good; and scarcely do they live and exist; and their duration and life are necessarily short, whilst by means of dissolution and death they are removed gradually to a higher degree, where they receive an accumulation of life and goodness, and thus they progress from grade to grade, nearer and nearer to the extremity of life and goodness, God, of His merciful affection for animated beings, preparing the ways along Abred, out of pure love to them, until they arrive at the state and point of human existence, where goodness and evil equiponderate, neither weighing down the other. From this spring liberty and choice and elective power in man, so that he can perform which ever he likes of any two things, as of good and evil; and thus is it seen that the state of humanity is a state of probation and instruction, where the good and evil equiponderate, and animated beings are left to their own will and pleasure.

13. In every state and point of Abred that is below humanity, all living beings are necessarily evil, and necessarily bound to evil, from utter want of will and power, notwithstanding all the exertion and power put forth, which vary according as they are situate in Abred, whether the point be high or low. On this account God does not hate or punish them, but loves and cherishes them, because they cannot be otherwise, and because they are under obligation, and have no will and choice, and whatever the

amount of evil may be, they cannot help it, because it is from obligation, and not willingly, that they are in this condition.

14. After having arrived at the point of humanity in Abred, where evil and good equiponderate, man is free from all obligation, because goodness and wickedness do not press one upon the other, nor does either of them preponderate over the other. Therefore, the state of man is a state of will and freedom and ability, where every act is one of project and selection, consent and choice, and not of obligation and dislike, necessity and inability. On this account man is a living being capable of judgment, and judgment will be given upon him and his acts, for he will be good or bad according to his works, since whatever he does he could do differently; therefore it is right that he should receive punishment or reward, as his works require.

God in the Sun

Question. Why is the face turned toward the sun in every asseveration and Prayer?

Answer. Because God is in every light, and the chief of every light is the sun. It is through fire that God brings back to Himself all things that have emanated from Him; therefore it is not right to ally one's self to God, but in the light. There are three kinds of light, namely: that if the sun, and hence fire; that which is obtained in the sciences of teachers; and that which is possessed in the understanding of the head and heart, that is, in the soul. On that account, every vow is made in the face of the three lights, that is, in the light of the sun is seen the light of a teacher, or demonstration; and from both of these is the light of the intellect, or that of the soul.

The Book of Bardism

Here is the Book of Bardism, that is to say, the Druidism of the Bards of the Isle of Britain, which I, Llywelyn Sion of Llangewydd, extracted from old Books, namely, the books of Einion the Priest, Taliesin, the Chief of Bards, Davydd Ddu of Hiraddug, Cwtta Cyvarwydd, Jonas of Menevia, Edeyrn the Golden-tongued, Sion Cent, Rhys Goch, and others, in the Library of Rhaglan, by permission of the lord William Herbert, earl of Pembroke, to whom God grant that I may prove thankful as long as I live. The first is a Treatise in the form of Question and Answer, by a

Bard and his Disciple—the work of Sion Cent, which contains many of the principal subjects of the primitive wisdom, as it existed among the Bards of the Isle of Britain from the age of ages. In this Dialogue, the Disciple first puts the question, and the Bard, his Teacher, answers, and imparts to him information and knowledge. In the second place the Bard examines, and the Disciple answers.

The second examination.

Q. Prithee, who art thou? and tell me thy history.

A. I am a man in virtue of God's will, and the necessary consequence that follows, for "what God wills must be."

Q. Whence didst thou proceed? and what is thy beginning?

A. I came from the Great World,' having my beginning in Annwn.

Q. Where art thou now? and how camest thou to where thou art?

A. I am in the Little World, whither I came, having traversed the circle of Abred,[4] and now I am a man at its termination and extreme limits.

Q. What wert thou before thou didst become a man in the circle of Abred?

A. I was in Annwn the least possible that was capable of life, and the nearest possible to absolute death, and I came in every form, and through every form capable of a body and life, to the state of man along the circle of Abred, where my condition was severe and grievous during the age of ages, ever since I was parted in Annwn from the dead, by the gift of God, and His great generosity, and His unlimited and endless love.

Q. Through how many forms didst thou come? and what happened unto thee?

A. Through every form capable of life, in water, in earth, and in air. And there happened unto me every severity, every hardship, every evil, and every suffering, and but little was the goodness and gwynfyd before I became a man.

Q. Thou hast said, that it was in virtue of God's love thou camest through all these, and didst see and experience all these; tell me how can

[4] Abred, Gwynvyd, and Ceugant are the Three Circles of Existence in Iolo's cosmology. They are respectively incarnate life, spiritual life, and the divine life that only God can experience.

this take place through the love of God? And how many were the signs of the want of love during thy migration in Abred?

A. Gwynvyd cannot be obtained without seeing and knowing every thing, but it is not possible to see and to know every thing without suffering every thing. And there can be no full and perfect love that does not produce those things which are necessary to lead to the knowledge that causes Gwynvyd, for there can be no Gwynvyd without the complete knowledge of every form of existence, and of every evil and good, and of every operation and power and condition of evil and good. And this knowledge cannot be obtained without experience in every form of life, in every incident, in every suffering, in every evil and in every good, so that they may be respectively known one from the other. All this is necessary before there can be Gwynvyd, and there is need of them all before there can be perfect love of God, and there must be perfect love of God before there can be Gwynvyd.

Q. Why are the things, which thou hast mentioned, necessary before there can be Gwynvyd?

A. Because there can be no Gwynvyd without prevailing over evil and death, and every opposition and Cythraul, and they cannot be prevailed over without knowing their species, nature, power, operations, place, and time, and every form and kind of existence which they have, so that all about them may be known, and that they may be avoided, and that wherever they are they may be opposed, counteracted, and overcome, and that we may be cured of them, and be restored from under their effect. And where there is this perfect knowledge, there is perfect liberty, and evil and death cannot be renounced and overcome but where there is perfect liberty; and there can be no Gwynvyd but with God in perfect liberty, and it is in perfect liberty that the circle of Gwynvyd exists.

Q. Why may not perfect knowledge be obtained, without passing through every form of life in Abred?

A. On this account, because there are no two forms alike, and every form has a use, a suffering, a knowledge, an intelligence, a gwynvyd, a quality, an operation, and an impulse, the like and complete uniformity of which can not be had in any other form of existence. And as there is a special knowledge in each form of existence, which cannot be had in another, it is necessary that we should go through every form of existence, before we can acquire every form and species of knowledge and understanding, and consequently renounce all evil, and attach ourselves to every gwynvyd.

Q. How many forms of existence are there? and what is the use of them?

A. As many as God saw necessary towards the investigation and knowledge of every species and quality in good and evil, that there might be nothing, capable of being known and conceived by God, without being experienced, and consequently known. And in whatsoever thing there may be a knowledge of good and evil, and of the nature of life and death, there is a form of existence which corresponds with the attainment of the knowledge required. Therefore, the number of the kinds and modes of forms of existence is the sum that could conceive and understand with a view to perfect goodness, knowledge, and gwynvyd. And God caused that every living and animate being should pass through every form and species of existence endued with life, so that in the end every living and animate being might have perfect knowledge, life, and gwynvyd; and all this from the perfect love of God, which in virtue of His Divine nature He could not but exhibit towards man and every living being.

Q. Art thou of opinion that every living being shall attain to the circle of Gwynvyd at last?

A. That is my opinion, for less could not have happened from the infinite love of God, God being able to cause, knowing the manner how to cause, and continually willing every thing to exist that can be conceived and sought in His own love, and in the desire of every animation whilst opposed to evil and death.

Q. When will this condition happen to every living being, and in what manner will occur the end of the life of Abred?

A. Every living and animate being shall traverse the circle of Abred from the depth of Annwn, that is, the extreme limits of what is low in every existence endued with life; and they shall ascend higher and higher in the order and gradation of life, until they become man, and then there can be an end to the life of Abred by union with goodness. And in death they shall pass to the circle of Gwynvyd, and the Abred of necessity will end for ever. And there will be no migrating through every fqrm of existence after that, except in right of liberty and choice united with Gwynvyd, with a view to re-experience, and re-seek knowledge. And this will remain for ever, as a variation and novation of Gwynvyd, so that no one can fall into Ceugant, and thence into Abred; for God alone can endure and traverse the circle of Ceugant. By this it is seen that there is no Gwynvyd without mutual communication, and the renewal of proof, experience, and knowledge, for it is in knowledge that life and Gwynvyd consist.

Q. Shall every man, when he dies, go to the circle of Gwynvyd?

A. No one shall at death go to Gwynvyd, except he who shall attach himself in life, whilst a man, to goodness and godliness, and to every act of wisdom, justice, and love. And when these qualities prepon4erate over their opposites, namely, folly, injustice, and uncharitableness, and all evil and ungodliness, the man, when he dies, shall go to Gwynvyd, that is heaven, from whence he will no more fall, because good is stronger than evil of every kind, and life subdues death, prevailing over it for ever. And he shall ascend nearer and nearer to perfect Gwynvyd, until he is at its extreme limits, where he will abide for ever and eternally. But the man who does not thus attach himself to godliness, shall fall in Abred to a corresponding form and species of existence of the same nature as himself, whence he shall return to the state of man as before. And then, according as his attachment may be to either godliness or ungodliness, shall he ascend to Gwynfyd, or fall in Abred, when he dies. And thus shall he fall for ever until he seeks godliness, and attaches himself to it, when there will be an end to the Abred of necessity, and to every necessary suffering of evil and death.

Abred—Gwynvydd—Awen

Q. How often may one fall in Abred?

A. No one will fall once of necessity, after it has been once traversed, but through negligence, from cleaving to ungodliness, until it preponderates over godliness, a man will fall in Abred. He will then return to the state of man, through every form of existence that will be necessary for the removal of the evil, which was the cause of his fall in Abred. And he will fall only once in Abred on account of the same ungodliness, since it will be overcome by that fall; nevertheless, because of many other impieties he may fall in Abred, even numberless times, until every opposition and Cythraul, that is, all ungodliness, shall have been vanquished, when there will be an end to the Abred of necessity.

Q. How many have fallen in Abred? and for what cause have they fallen?

A. All living beings below the circle of Gwynvyd have fallen in Abred, and are now on their return to Gwynvyd. The migration of most of them will be long, owing to the frequent times they have fallen, from having attached themselves to evil and ungodliness; and the reason why they fell was, that they desired to traverse the circle of Ceugant, which God alone could endure and traverse. Hence, they fell even unto Annwn, and it was from pride, which would ally itself with. God, that they fell, and there is no necessary fall as far as Annwn, except from pride.

Q. Did all, who reached the circle of Gwynvyd after the primary progression of necessity from Annwn, fall in Abred from pride?

A. No; some sought after wisdom, and hence saw what pride would do, and they resolved to conduct themselves according to what was taught them by God, and thereby became divinities, or holy angels, and they acquired learning from what they beheld in others, and it was thus that they saw the nature of Ceugant and eternity, and that God alone could endure and traverse it.

Q. Does not the danger of falling in Abred, from the circle of Gwynvyd, exist still as it did formerly?

A. No; because all pride and every other sin, will be overcome before one can a second time reach the circle of Gwynvyd, and then by recollecting and knowing the former evil, every one will necessarily abhor what caused him to fall before, and the necessity of hatred and love will last and continue for ever in the circle of Gwynvyd, where the three stabilities, namely, hatred, love, and knowledge, will never end.

Q. Will those, who shall return to the circle of Gwynvyd after the fall in Abred, be of the same kind as those who fell not?

A. Yes; and of the same privilege, because the love of God cannot be less towards one than towards another, nor towards one form of existence than another, since He is God and Father to them all, and exercises the same amount of love and patronage towards them all, and they will all be equal and co-privileged in the circle of Gwynvyd, that is, they will be divinities and holy angels for ever.

Q. Will every form and species of living existence continue for ever as they are now? If so, tell me why?

A. Yes, in virtue of liberty and choice, and the blessed will go from one to another as they please, in order to repose from the fatigue and tediousness of Ceugant, which God only can endure, and in order to experience every knowledge and every gwynvyd that are capable of species and form; and each one of them will hate evil of necessary obligation, and know it thoroughly, and consequently of necessity renounce it, since he will perfectly know its nature and mischievousness—God being a help, and God being chief, supporting and preserving them for ever.

Q. How are these things to be known?

A. The Gwyddoniaid, from the age of ages, from the time of Seth, son of Adam, son of God, obtained Awen from God, and thence knew the mystery of godliness; and the Gwyddoniaid were of the nation of the Cymry from the age of ages. After that, the Gwyddoniaid were regulated according to privilege and usage, in order that unfailing memory might be kept of this knowledge. After that, the Gwyddoniaid were called Bards according to the privilege and usage of the Bards of the Isle of Britain, because it was after the arrival of the Cymry in the island of Britain, that this regulation was made; and it is through the memorials of Bardism and Awen from God that this knowledge has been acquired, and no falsehood can accrue from Awen from God. In the nation of Israel were found the holy prophets, who through Awen from God knew all these things as described in the Holy Scriptures. And after Christ, the Son of God, had come in the flesh from Gwynvyd, further knowledge of God, and His will, was obtained, as is seen in St. Paul's Sermon. And when we, the Cymry, were converted to the faith in Christ, our Bards obtained a more clear Awen from God, and knowledge about all things divine beyond what had been seen before, and they prophesied, improving Awen and knowledge. Hence is all knowledge concerning things divine and what appertains to God.

Q. How is Awen to be obtained, where it is not, so that a Bard may be made of him, who would be a Bard?

A. By habituating one's self to a holy life, and all love towards God and man, and all justice, and all mercy, and all generosity, and all endurance, and all peace, and practising good sciences, and avoiding pride and cruelty and adultery, and murder and ambuscade, and theft, and covetousness, and all injustice, that is, the things that will corrupt and destroy Awen, where it exists, and will prevent the obtaining it, where it does not exist.

Q. Is it in the way it was first obtained, that Awen from God is still obtainable?

A. It is in this way that Awen is obtained, that the truth may be known and believed. Some, however, are of opinion that the way in which the truth was first known, was, that the divinities, or holy angels, and the saints or godly men, who went to heaven, and especially Jesus Christ, the Son of God, came down from Gwynvyd to the Little World in the condition of man, in order to teach, warn, direct, and inform those who seek to be divine. That is, they came in the capacity of messengers sent by God in His infinite love, and in virtue of their own great love co-operating with the love of God, and as His obedient messengers. And we shall have what of Awen from God is necessary for us, by attaching ourselves to the good and godly with sincerity, and out of pure love for all goodness.

The Creation—The First Man—The Primary Letters

Disciple and his Teacher.

Disciple. Tell me, my kind and discreet Master, whence originated the world, and all visible, all audible, all sensible, and all intelligible things, and whence did they come, and were made?

Teacher. God the Father made them by pronouncing His Name, and manifesting existence. In the same instant, co-simultaneously, lo! The world, and all that appertains to it, sprang together into being, and together celebrated their existence with a very loud and melodious shout of joy; even as we see them to be now, and as they shall exist whilst God the Father lives, Who is not subject to dissolution and death.

D. Of what, in respect of materials, were formed living and dead beings, which are eognizable to the human sight, hearing, feeling, understanding, perception, and the creation of the imagination?

T. They were made of the manred, that is, of the elements in the extremities of their particles and smallest atoms, every particle being alive, because God was in every particle, a complete Unity, so as not to be exceeded, even in all the multiform space of Ceugant, or the infinite expanse. God was in each of the particles of the manred, and in the same manner in them collectively in their conjoined aggregation; wherefore, the voice of God is the voice of every particle of the manred, as far as their numbers or qualities may be counted or comprehended, and the voice of every particle is the voice of God—God being in the particle as its life, and every particle or atom being in God and His life. On account of this view of the subject, God is figuratively represented as being born of the manred, without beginning, without end.

D. Was existence good or bad before God pronounced His Name?

T. All things were thoroughly good, without beginning, without end, as they are now, and ever shall be; though in Abred neither the mode, nor the thing that exists, is seen, except from learning by means of demonstrative hearing and seeing, or by means of reason making it comprehensible, namely, God and His peace in every thing, and nothing existing without God and His peace. Therefore, there was good in every thing,—a blissful world, and a blissful deliverance from every evil, as an unconquerable predominance. And where God exists in every atom of manred, evil is impossible; because there neither is, nor can be room for it, since God and all goodness fill the infinitude, which is without beginning and without end, in respect of place and duration of time. Therefore, evil or its like cannot exist, nor the least approximation to it.

D. What judgment is formed concerning the act of God in giving existence to the world, that is, heaven and earth, and all that are in and from them?

T. God, with a view to every goodness of which He is capable, branched Himself out of His majesty, incomprehensible to man further it was so. And from this there was an increase of all finite goodness, and all goodness cannot be had, without finite goodness in infinite space.

D. Who was the first man?

T. Menyw the Aged, son of the Three Shouts, who was so called because God gave and placed the word in his mouth, namely, the vocalization of the three letters, which make the unutterable Name of God, that is, by means of the good sense of the Name and Word. And, co-instantaneously with the pronunciation of God's Name, Menyw saw three rays of light, and inscribed on them figure and form, and it was from those forms and their different collocations that Menyw made ten letters, and it was from them, variously placed, that he invested the Cymraeg with figure and form, and it is from understanding the combination of the ten letters that one is able to read.

D. My beloved Teacher, show me the power and mysteries of the three primitive letters, and the forms of the ten letters, which Menyw made from the varied combination of the three.

T. This is not allowed and permitted to me, for the ten letters are a secret, being one of the three pillars of the mystery of the Bards of the Isle of Britain. And before the disciple is brought under the obligation and power of a vow, the mystery may not be revealed to him. And even then it can only be displayed to the eye, without utterance, without voice. It can only take place, when the disciple shall have gone through all the cycle and course of his pupillage. Nevertheless, the sixteen letters are formed very differently, and I am at liberty to show and declare their names and their powers, before the cycle of the vow of pupillage shall have been traversed; and thus are the sixteen symbols, and the way in which they are enforced by usage.

Privilege and Usage

This is the Voice of Gorsedd of the Bards of the Isle of Britain, in which may be seen the Privileges and Usages of the Bards of the Isle of Britain, as originally exercised and confirmed. With them also are the Triads of the Bards of the Chair of Glamorgan, and other matters intended for Bardic instruction.

The Cymry first came into the Isle of Britain with Prydain, son of Aeddan the Great. And when they wore safely settled in the country, there arose among them three men, whose names were Plennydd, Alawn, and Gwron, each of them having Awen from God, and who consequently were Bards. These were the first who devised the Privileges and Usages of the Bards of the Isle of Britain, which they appointed for instruction, custom, and law in the Isle of Britain; nor were there any Bards previous to these men. The Bards maintained these usages, and improved them by means of Awen from God, so that the Bardism of the Bards of the Isle of Britain became the supreme learning and wisdom; and many of the wise men of distant countries desired to learn it, but they impaired and corrupted it by means of Awen which was not from God, until at last there was no pure Bardism in any country or place in the world, but among the Bards of the Isle of Britain, who were of the nation of the Cymry. The following treats of the Privileges and Usages, which the Bards of the Isle of Britain ought to preserve by means of the memorial of vocal song, and to recite with the Voice of Gorsedd: that is to say—

1. The principal usages of the Bards of the Isle of Britain are to maintain the memory and teaching of peace, truth, and justice in a country, and to bestow praise upon the good, and dispraise upon the bad; and all this by means of Awen from God.

2. They are not to bear a naked weapon in the presence of, or against any one; and it is not lawful for any one to bear a naked weapon where there is a Bard.

3. There are three kinds of Primitive Bards. The Bard positive, of original appointment, or a Poet, in virtue of discipleship, whose duty it is to preserve order and rule, in respect of the Privilege, Usage, and Voice of Gorsedd, so that Bardism be not lost, but be maintained and preserved, in right of original usage, incorrupt and unchanged. And it is incumbent upon a Poet to sing praise and dispraise, according to what is just and requisite, and, by means of song and oration, to preserve the memory of the Privileges and Usages of the Bards of the Isle of Britain, and their appurtenances. A Poet is adjudged to be one of presidency after three Chairs, that is, when ho shall have gained the privilege of three Chairs; and every office and employment, in respect of song and Bardism, are free to him in virtue of his Chair; and he may exercise the func-tion of Poet, Ovate, and Druid, as he pleases, in virtue of occasion, without a degree, without a grant. In this particular he is the chief of the Bards, and no one can be made master of song who is not a presiding Bard. His dress is to be of serene sky blue, and unicoloured, for unicolour is of the same hue as truth, and the serene sky blue is of the same hue as peace, a Poet, or a privileged Bard, being a man of peace and truth; he is also called a Licensed Bard, a privileged Licentiate, and Primitive Bard positive. Nor is it lawful for him to bear arms, nor for any one to bear a weapon, where he may be in his unicoloured vestment, by which he is to be distinguished. The second of the primitive Bards is the Ovate, and it is incumbent upon him to be acquainted with literature, that is, to read and write, and to know the kinds of arts which may be beneficial to Bards and to the world, and to exhibit them in their authenticity before a Gorsedd or Chair, or a Bard of presidency. It is incumbent upon him, also, to collect and to search for knowledge, and to impart instruction in it, after it shall have obtained the judgment and privilege of Gorsedd; he is not bound to do more, except in virtue of a degree and grant. The dress of an Ovate is to be green, being of the same colour as knowledge

and learning, which grow like the green vegetation of spring; and in the attainment of knowledge the Ovate is the chief of the Bards. The third of the primitive Bards is the Druid, and it is incumbent upon him to teach, according to reason, nature, obligation, and choice, what he sees to be true, of the original learning, usages, and judgment of the Poets, as preserved in the memory and by the voice of Gorsedd, and of the learning, art, and attainment of the Ovate-bard. And his principal function is to teach divine knowledge, and justice, truth, and peace; and in respect of learning and knowledge, according to reason, nature, and obligation, the chief of the Bards is the Druid. From knowing how to sing and exhibit a song of his own composition before a Gorsedd, which shall confer upon it the privilege of a Chair, he will be entitled to the privilege of a Poet, that is, a Bard of privilege, without either a degree or a grant. The dress of a Druid is to be of unicoloured white, being thus of the same colour positively as the sun and light, and consequently of the same colour as holiness of life, purity of godliness, and sanctity. If he cannot compose a song, a Druid has nothing to do with the function of a Bard of Privilege, except by grant and courtesy; but he is privileged, without either a degree or a grant, to perform what may be necessary, and what may seem good to him, in the employment and office of an Ovate. Should a Druid be an original Bard of Privilege, he has no need of either a degree or a grant, but will act according to privilege.

4. Discipleship is the instruction of a master, who is a presiding Bard; that is, he who desires to receive instruction and privilege in respect of song and Bardism, must apply to a presiding master, and put himself under his charge, and must attend every Gorsedd of song with his master. Those who seek instruction and privilege in respect of song are called Aspirants, Disciples, privileged Licentiates, and Protected, because protection will be afforded to them, that they should bear no arms, and that none should bear arms where they are. Aspirants have no more privileges, until they obtain a degree in right of a Gorsedd; and no degree can be conferred upon an Aspirant until the end of three years of discipleship, though in right of an Ovate he may have a degree sooner, where there is a presiding Bard, who will aver on his word and conscience that the candidate is competent to be a Bard. No man can be admitted into discipleship, who knows not his right hand, how to count a hundred, the names of the months of the year, and the four parts of

the world, namely, south, east, north, and west, and who knows not his mother's tongue in such a way as it may be easy to understand him. When he shall have been a disciple for three years, he is privileged to become a candidate for the degree of a Primitive Bard Positive, if he has a beard; if he has no beard, let him wait until he has, or let him seek the degree of an Ovate. And when he obtains a beard, he is privileged to become a candidate for the degree of a Primitive Bard, if he has been a disciple for three years, or is an Ovate; and if he cannot at that time answer poetically and judiciously, according to the instruction of Privilege and Usage, a degree must be forbidden to him, unless he is better acquainted with his necessity, his feat, and his employment, in which case ho is privileged to obtain a degree.

An Ovate is to be graduated, as before mentioned, in virtue of a presiding Bard, who shall aver on his word and conscience, that the candidate is competent to become a Bard, or according to the judgment of a Gorsedd, to which application has been made, or from having been a disciple for less than three years, if he can answer the questions put to him by an Ovate. An Ovate of privilege is a Bard of privilege, or a Druid, who exercises the vocation of an Ovate, or verifies the claim of an Ovate candidate, or an original Ovate; and there is no need to a Bard of privilege, or a Druid, of a degree or grant, since they are entitled by privilege to assume the office of an Ovate.

The privilege of grant, or privilege by the courtesy of Gorsedd, is that, when a Bard must needs exercise a function, which is not his by privilege and degree, as when an Ovate, or original Druid, in ease of necessity, exercises the vocation of a Primitive Bard Positive, where that person is wanting; or when an Ovate, in case of need, exercises the vocation of a Druid. Some say, that an Aspirant of three years, can, in right of courtesy, and of the grant of usage, engage in the office of a Primitive Bard Positive, where there is none, or a sufficient number of such already; and in the same manner, engage also in the offices of an Ovate and a Druid. It is not lawful for any one to assume the office of degree and Gorsedd, in right of the gift of courtesy, except where there is a deficiency of presiding Bards, or of Bards of institutional degree and privilege.

A person may share in the privilege of grant and courtesy, by giving notice of a year and a day; and unless an institutional Bard enters his protest against it before the expiration of that time, then all, who have enjoyed grant and courtesy, are entitled to the privilege of usage; this is the privilege of necessity, lest Bardism should be lost.

Where there are three presiding Bards, there is the privilege of an institutional Gorsedd. Where there are not three, there can be no institutional privilege, but the privilege of grant, or the privilege of courtesy, in virtue of a year and a day, when it becomes institutional, in case the claim has not been negatived.

Positive privilege takes place where there is only one presiding Bard, such being ordained lest Bardism should become lost. That is to say, the presiding Bard is empowered to confer the privilege of degree and Gorsedd upon three persons, if he pleases, for the sake of holding a Gorsedd, which takes place at the end of an institutional year and a day; after that, they become presiding in right of three Chairs, or three Gorsedds.

Where there is not one presiding Bard, or chief of song, and hence there is a prospect of Bardism being lost, let those, who know the usages and privileges of the Bards of the Isle of Britain from the lips and voice of country, or from Book and Coelbren, or from a very old song, give public notice of a year and a day throughout the country, in the name of the Bards of the Isle of Britain, who are adjudged to be always living. And when the year and a day are expired, it is lawful for them to hold a Gorsedd, according to what is institutional, as indicated by the memory and voice of country, and the memorial of Book and Coelbren. And at the end of a year and a day after that they will be Bards of privilege and usage, according to claim and acknowledgment, and unless they are protested against before the end of a year and a day after that by an institutional Bard of Gorsedd, under the privilege of the primitive Bards of the Isle of Britain, then they will be privileged and institutional, as well as their Gorsedd, since they will now be Bards according to privilege and usage in virtue of the same notice, grant, and courtesy, which first of all conferred privilege and usage upon the Bards of the Isle of Britain, that is, the privilege of necessity.

The Bardic Secret

'O I W are the three letters, and in very old books O I U, because U was used instead of W, in the olden times. It is the secret word of the primitive Bards, which it is not lawful to speak or utter audibly to any man in the world, except to a Bard who is under the vow of an oath. The letters may be shown to any one in the world we like, without uttering the vocalization, which, under the protection of secrecy, is due to them, though he be not under an oath; but should he utter them in speech audibly, he violates his protection, and he cannot be a Bard, nor will it be lawful to shew him any more of the secret, either in this world that perishes, or in the other world that will not perish for ever and ever.' Sion Bradford.

The Sacred Symbol

/|\ . That is to say, they are called the three columns, and the three columns of truth, because there can be no knowledge of the truth, but from the light thrown upon it; and the three columns of sciences, because there can be no sciences, but from the light and truth.

The Dasgubell Rodd

Question. What is the Dasgubell Rodd?

Answer. The keys of the primitive Coelbren.

Q. What is it that explains the primitive Coelbren?

A. The Dasgubell Rodd.

Q. What else?

A. The secret of the Dasgubell Rodd.

Q. What secret?

A. The secret of the Bards of the Isle of Britain.

Q. What will divulge the secret of the Bards of the Isle of Britain?

A. Instruction by a master in virtue of a vow.

Q. What kind of vow?

A. A vow made with God.

David James
The Customs of the Druids
(from *The Patriarchal Religion of Britain, or a complete manual of ancient British Druidism*, 1836)

Another of the Anglican clergymen whose leisure pursuits contributed so much to the Druid Revival, David James was the rector of Almondbury, Yorkshire during the years when he wrote the selection excerpted here. He was also an enthusiastic member of the Ancient Order of Druids, the first fraternal order to adopt the traditions of the Druid Revival for its own, and dedicated his book *The Patriarchal Religion of Britain* to the members of that order in the West Riding of Yorkshire. Welsh by birth and culture, he was an enthusiastic participant in Welsh bardic competitions, and took the bardic name Dewi o Ddyfed (David of Dyfed).

The Druidry of which James wrote was a reflection of his own values, as a clergyman, a Welshman, and a member of the Gorsedd of Bards and the Ancient Order of Druids—the two leading organizations in the Druid Revival at that time. The Gorsedd of Bards, the institution organized by Iolo Morganwg, had by James' time become an important force in the Welsh cultural revival, and had won support from a range of Welsh churches; the Ancient Order of Druids was pioneering the fraternal and social dimension of the Revival, with lodges and initiations largely modeled on those of Freemasonry and a similar role in public life.

For James, as a result, the Druids were simply the Anglican clergy of an earlier day, educated in a slightly more primitive version of Oxford or Cambridge, and their role in society was an idealized version of the one that the Anglican Church wished to fill in James' own time. At the same time, they offered an equally idealized image of wisdom and learning to which members of the Ancient Order of Druids might choose to aspire.

In assembling his "complete manual," James drew on much of the existing Druid Revival literature, especially Edward Davies and the then-published work of Iolo Morganwg. His work can be used as a tolerably complete summary of the way that Druids were imagined by the more Christian wing of the Revival movement in the first half of the nineteenth century. The radical wing of the Revival represented by Thomas Paine is conspicuous by its absence. In the years to come, however, a great many Druids would take James' detailed accounts of Druid customs and ceremonial garb, and fuse it with a far more radical vision of what Druidry had been—or, in a broader sense, could be.

Further Reading:

David James, *The Patriarchal Religion of Britain, or a complete manual of ancient British Druidism* (Whittaker and Co., 1836).

* * *

The Religion of Noah Preserved in Britain under the Name of Druidism

The descendants of Japheth that first took possession of Britain, though composed of several distinct tribes yet formed but one nation as we have already seen, having sprung from the same stock, and all speaking the same language. Agriculture and Pasturage were their primary pursuits: Their great chieftain Hu had taught them the former, "When they were in the Summer Country, [probably Bithynia in Asia Minor,] before they came to the Isle of Britain:"—Triad 55. And as the latter had universally prevailed in the East, and required less art, no instruction was necessary, and the Triads mention none.

Their form of government at this time was pure Patriarchism: that is, they were all subject to the heads of their respective families, who, according to the simple dictate of nature, and by invariable custom, inherited the right and privilege of governing those that had sprung from themselves, or that were employed by them in the capacity of men and women servants. Such had been the form of government among all pious people down to the time of the dispersion. And it continued in the East after that event among the descendants of Shem for many generations; and in the West among the progeny of Japheth, until it either degenerated into absolute clanship, or was changed into a monarchy for the better protection of the country.

These heads of families were also in Britain as well as in the East the ministers of religion to their respective tribes. With them rested the responsibility of instructing all that composed the clan under their immediate jurisdiction, in the principles of morality and divine worship;

and of performing the sacred rites of religion, more especially those of sacrificing. So that every patriarch or head of family was not only the Governor but also the Priest of his tribe.

These Priests or religious Instructers of the Kymry were at first simply called Gwyddon, the plural of Gwydd which implies wisdom or knowledge. The term therefore in its application to them as Teachers of religion, implied in its singular form the man of knowledge;—in its plural form, Wise men or Teachers of wisdom; illustrating in a most striking manner that maxim of the Mosaic law and priesthood, which says, "The Priest's lips shall keep knowledge, and the people shall seek the law at his mouth: for he is the messenger of the Lord of hosts." (Mal. ii. 7.) Wisdom and knowledge were emphatically the terms used in primitive ages for religion, as appears from the book of Job, the most ancient of all the inspired Records, and from the Psalms of David, and the Proverbs of Solomon: not forgetting that the same terms also obtained in Chaldea, Persia, and Greece.

But as these patriarchal Priests in Britain, chose to instruct the people, and perform their solemn rites in groves, and especially under the oak, their official name Gwyddon acquired in course of time another syllable by way of prefix, taken from Derw, their own Kimbric appellation of the oak or oak-groves. The name compounded of Derw and Gwyddon stood thus, Der-wyddon, which implied the Oak-wise-men, or Priests of the oak. And this is the term we render Druids in English. But it is more probable that the English term Druids was originally taken from the Gaelic word Druidh, which is an abbreviation of Derwydh the singular of Derwyddon, or from the Greek word Drus or Druades, an oak, or inhabitants of oak-groves. However, we have given the etymology of the Kimbric word from the language of the Druids themselves, in which language alone the genuine roots of all their technical and official terms must be sought.

But here we must stay for a moment to justify the conduct of the British Druids, in worshipping God under the oak, and sacrificing to him in groves. This practice was no innovation of the Druids, the Lord had been invariably worshipped in the open air, either on a mountain, in a plain, under a hill, or in a grove, from the creation down to the time of the general dispersion: and the same custom prevailed after the dispersion in the East among the descendants of Shem, for five or six hundred years; that is until the departure of the Israelites out of Egypt, and the erection of the tabernacle in the wilderness, "which probably was the first building ever formed as an habitation for the Deity." (Scott.) And the Israelites were then forbidden to worship in groves as incompatible with the worship of the Tabernacle; and because groves had been desecrated by the idolatrous Canaanites, the descendants of Ham, and made the scenes of the vilest abominations. Under other circumstances the Almighty had no objection to be worshipped in groves, or in high places.

We read in Genesis, that "Abraham passed through the land (of Canaan) unto the place of Sichem, unto the plain of Moreh:" according to the Hebrew, "unto the oak, or oak-grove of Moreh." The Hebrew word is Aluq, which the LXX have generally rendered by the Greek word for oak. The English translation seems to have been made from the Vulgate Latin. Parkhurst and other eminent Critics agree that the original implies a species of oak, and should have been rendered in this and several other places by that word instead of plain. We shall now read the passage according to this amended translation : "And Abraham passed through the land unto the place of Sichem, unto the Oak of Moreh: "And the Lord appeared unto Abraham and said, Unto thee seed will I give this land: and there builded he an altar, unto the Lord who appeared unto him," (Gen. xii.)

Again it is said, "Then Abram removed his tent, and came and dwelt in the plain of Mamre;" according to the Hebrew—the same noun occurring again in its plural form, "dwelt in or among the oaks of Mamre, which is in Hebron, and built there an altar unto the Lord," (Gen. xiii.) Once more, "And Abraham planted a grove in Beersheba, and called there on the name of the Lord, the everlasting God." (Gen. xxi.) On this last passage Mr. Scott remarks, "Perhaps Abraham planted this grove to shelter his tent; and to form a shade for the performance of sacred worship, which was at that time usually performed in the open air."

Other instances occur, but these are amply sufficient to shew that the custom of worshipping the Divine Being in groves, and particularly beside or under an oak, was not an invention of the Druids, but a faithful perpetuation on their part of a custom that had prevailed among the patriarchs in the East from the most remote times. Abraham and the Druids of Britain derived the usage from a common source; there was therefore nothing remarkable in the coincidence. The custom was first debased and perverted to idolatrous purposes by the wicked Canaanites, long after the time of Abraham and the arrival of the elder branch of Japheth in Britain.

But we cannot conceal the satisfaction we feel in being able to adduce the example of the most eminent Patriarch of antiquity, "the father of the faithful," in defence of the custom of the Druids in our native country. While Abraham, a descendant of Shem, was planting groves, building altars, and sacrificing thereon under oak trees to the God of heaven in the East, the Druids, the descendants of Japheth, were doing the same thing in the West, especially in Britain. And as the worship of Abraham was accepted, so was that of the Druids. Hence how true the declaration of our Saviour, "That many shall come from the East and West, and shall sit down with Abraham, and Isaac, and Jacob, in the kingdom of heaven." (Matt. chap, viii.)

Orders of the Bardo-Druidic Institution

No sooner had the original colony increased into a great and prosperous nation, expanding over the whole extent of the country, than it became necessary to divide the Bardo-Druidic Order into three distinct classes, and assign to each distinct and specific duties. These orders and their duties are thus described in the Institutes of Bardism:—

"The three orders of primitive Bards: the Presiding Bard, or Primitive Bard positive, according to the rights, voice, and usage of the Bardic Convention; whose office it is to superintend and regulate;—the Ovate according to poetical genius, exertion, and contingency; whose function it is to act from the impulse of poetical inspiration—and the Druid according to the reason, nature, and necessity of things; whose office it is to instruct,"—(Institutional Triads.)

This is merely an epitome of what is explained at full length in the Triads of the Social State; one of which we here subjoin with some few omissions which we shall have occasion to introduce in another place.

"There are three orders of the profession of Bardism:

1. "The Chief Bard, or the Bard of full privilege who has acquired his degree and privilege through discipline under a master duly authorised, being a Conventional Bard. His office is to preserve the memory of the Arts and Sciences, whilst he shall continue in his office of Bard regularly instituted; and also to preserve every record and memorial of the country

and tribe respecting marriages, pedigrees, arms, inheritances, and rights of the country and nation of the Kymry.

2. "The Ovate, whose degree is acquired in right of his possessing natural poetic genius, or praiseworthy knowledge, which he shall prove by the correctness of his answers when examined before a customary and honourable Congress of the Bards: or where there is no such Congress, by a lawful Session granted by the tribe of the lord of the district; or by twelve of the judges of his Court; or by twelve jurors of the Court in the customary manner. The Ovate is not to be interrogated respecting any regular discipline through which he may have passed, nor respecting any thing else, except that his view of the sciences be strictly accurate. This is so regulated for the maintenance of science, lest there should be a deficiency of regular teachers, and the arts and sciences depending upon memory and regular instruction should be lost: and also for the further improvement of arts and sciences by the addition of every new discovery approved by the judgment of masters and wise men; and confirmed as such by them: and also lest the advantage arising from the powers of natural genius and invention should be repressed.

3. "The Druid-Bard; who must be a Bard regularly initiated and graduated, of approved wisdom and knowledge, and of elocution sufficient to express what his judgment and intelligence dictate. His duty is to give moral and religious instruction in the convention of the Bards in the palace, in the place of worship, and in every family, in which he has full privilege. He is raised to this office according to the privilege granted by reason and the regular court of the tribe, and is elected by lot, which election is guaranteed by the vote of the convention."—Triad 71.

The Druid-Bard, though mentioned last in this Triad, was by no means inferior to the other two orders; but the circumstance of his being elected to his office from amongst the privileged Bards, called in this triad Chief Bards, seems to imply that he stood higher than the rest: And his office being more exclusively sacred naturally gave him that distinction. "In him," remarks Mr. Owen, "sanctity of life and celebrity for wisdom were always looked for as necessary qualifications. He was most immediately the instructer of youth, and was from the necessary obligations of his office the residentiary Bard of his district—an obligation which the others did not lie under. But though the Druid was more peculiarly, yet he was not exclusively the minister of religion, for the

Privileged Bard, and even the Ovate might officiate as such after being confirmed by reception into the Order at a Congress, But as a matter of convenience, the religious establishment was allotted to an appropriate set of Bards called Druids to give notoriety and discriminate visibility to their function. The Druid-order was exempted from some offices that were incumbent on each of the others.

"The Ovate" observes the same writer, "was the third order, being an honorary degree, to which the candidate could immediately be admitted without being obliged to pass through the regular discipline. This degree appears to have been intended to create a power that was capable of acting on emergencies, on a plan different from the regular mode of proceeding, and for the purpose of bringing within the system such kind of knowledge as was unknown, or foreign to the original Institution.

"Each of the orders had a peculiarity of estimation. Thus the Privileged Bard was peculiarly the ruling order,—the Druid the religious functionary,—and the Ovate, the literary or scientific order."—Owen's Llywarch Hen.

The Bardo-Druidic Institution appears from the preceding account to hare gradually assumed in many respects the character of an University, in which not only Religion, hut also all the Arts, Sciences, and Faculties then known and practised, were taught and studied.

Originally Music formed a part of the profession of the Bardic Druids. But from having advanced and become more consolidated in the course of ages, Minstrelsy became a distinct order under its own rules. Yet the connexion was not quite dissolved, for the latter was always considered in some degree as a subordinate branch of the original system.

That this Bardo-Druidic College or University was not merely an assemblage of nominal functionaries, but of men deeply learned and highly accomplished in every branch of useful knowledge, appears beyond a doubt from the high state of cultivation into which they had brought their own language before the arrival of the Romans under Julius Caesar. Ever since the Roman invasion the ancient British language has had to contend with the most untoward circumstances. Attempts have been repeatedly made at its entire extinction, but it still lives, and invites a comparison at the present moment with any language in the world for antiquity, purity, copiousness, force, melodiousness, and adaptability to every kind of poetry. Its vocabulary contains not fewer than one hundred thousand words, and its system of versification is superior to anything of the kind in the whole world: It is reduced to twenty-four elementary classes, from which every kind of verse is deducible. And it has been strictly ascertained that there is not in any language, ancient or modern, any kind of verse that is not used in the ancient British. Many kinds are in common use in the Principality at this day, so singularly different from what has ever yet been known in Europe, that no conception of them can be conveyed except by acquaintance with the language itself. And will it be believed that this language, which has so often been objected to on account of its supposed overplus of consonants, contains some stanzas of poetry, composed according to the strictest rules of alliteration entirely of vowels.

Costume of the Bardo-Druidic Orders

1. Of the Druid-Bard—His dress was pure white, the emblem of holiness. Taliesin calls the dress of this order, "The proud white garment which separated the elders from the youth." But several French authors assert that the white garment of the Continental Druids had a purple border.

A Druid in full Costume—On his head a garland or crown of oak leaves; in his right hand the crescent, or the first quarter of the moon, to signify that the time of the festival had arrived; around his neck a string of white glass beads called Glain; short hair, long beard, and a linen robe of pure white flowing down from the shoulders to the ankles, differing in shape from the surplices which are now worn by the ministers of religion, in that one side folded over the other in front and was fastened by a loop and button at the shoulder like a cassock: The sleeves were also open on the upper side along the arm as far as the shoulder, disclosing at once the tunic or white jacket worn underneath, which had tight sleeves with cuffs turned up at the wrists, and cut in points. The crescent was of pure gold.

2. The Chief or Privileged Bard—The distinguishing dress of this order was the unicoloured robe of skye-blue, an emblem of peace. Thus Cynddelw in his ode on the death of Cadwallon, calls these Bards "Wearers of long blue robes." And since the sky without a cloud appears

serene, and exhibits to an advantage its vivid blue, this colour was the best that could have been chosen as an emblem of peace, of which the Bards were professedly the advocates and heralds.

A Bard in full Costume—In addition to the robe we have just described, the Privileged Bard on all occasions that he officiated, wore a cowl or hood of the same colour, as a graduated badge or literary ornament. This custom was borrowed from the British Bards by the Druids of Gaul, and from them by the Romans. Whence this cowl on its being made use of at Rome obtained the name of "Bardo-cucullus" or the Bard's hood, which was adopted by the monks, and is still worn by the Capuchin Friars, and something like it by the graduates of the English Universities.

But the dress of the Bards differed a little in shape as well as colour from that of the Druid- order. It seems to have been more open in front and with narrower sleeves, lest they should be in the way when the Bard had occasion to perform on the harp. Around his neck was a string of blue glass beads called, as before, the Glain. His hair was short and his beard long, similar to the Druid or Priest.

The Original British harps were strung with hair, and consisted probably of the same number of strings as the ribs of the human body, viz. twelve. And such harps were used at first by scholars so late as the tenth century, as appears by the laws of Howel the Good, who directed a fee to be paid to the master of the art, when the minstrels left off playing on them.

3. The Ovate—The dress of this order was green, the symbol of nature, the mysteries of which the Ovate was considered more particularly to study as the Physician of the tribe. He studied astronomy, the revolution of the seasons, and the use of letters; but above all, the productions of nature with a view to ascertain their medicinal qualities. Taliesin in one of his poems makes an Ovate to say, "With my robe of light green, possessing a place in the assembly." He also had a cucullus or hood attached to his robe, and a string of green glass beads around his neck, and a staff with a golden top in his hand which measured about five feet six inches—a badge of his being an honorary member of the Bardo-Druidic Institution. His hair was also short, and his beard long. With the people it was otherwise. Their hair was allowed to grow like that of Absalom; and their beard was kept close, except on the upper lip.

It will have been observed that each of the three orders wore an Unicoloured robe, whether white, blue, or green. This was considered essential as an emblem of truth which is always one. Truth was that to which all the orders adhered with the most unbending spirit, and truth admits of no mixture. It was, it is, and ever will be, one and the same.

4. The Judicial Druid—or the Druid in his Judicial habit.

He was clothed in a stole of virgin white, over a closer robe of the same that was fastened by a girdle on which appeared the crystal stone, which was worn as an emblem of the transparency of every case that was brought before him as Judge, and of the clear or impartial judgment which he should give accordingly. This was incased in gold. Hence Taliesin says, "O thou with pure gold upon thy clasp."

Hound his neck was the breastplate of judgment in the form of a crescent with a full moon or circle fixed to each point, so as to present an even superficies to the spectators. Below the breastplate appeared the string of white glass beads set in gold. Encircling his temples was a wreath of oak leaves, and a tiara of pure gold in the form of a crescent placed behind it, the narrow points of which were concealed behind the ears, whilst the broad or middle part presented a bold front over the crown of the head. On the middle finger of the left hand was a ring, and a chain ring on the next to it, while the hand itself rested on the Peithynin or Elucidator, supported by an altar of stone. This Elucidator consisted of several staves called omen-sticks or lots, on which the judicial maxims were cut, and which being put into a frame were turned at pleasure, so that each staff or bar when formed with three flat sides represented a triplet; when squared or made with four flat sides, a stanza. The frame itself was an oblong with right angles.

The appearance of the National Priest in his judicial robes was splendid and imposing; inferior certainly to the Jewish High Priest, but not altogether dissimilar in the distant view of him.

5. The Bardic Disciple—As none could become Druids that were not previously admitted into the order of privileged Bards or Bards of Presidency, the disciples were all aspirants for the latter order, and the candidates retained their original habit or dress until they were actually admitted as disciples. After admission they wore a variegated dress of the three Bardo-Druidic colours—white, blue, and green.

The Bardic disciple in full Costume—He appeared in a loose robe of blue, green, and white, intermingled in stripes or otherwise. The sleeves wide, and little shorter than those of the Orders already described. In his right hand a cup full of wine and bragget (Gwin a Bragod)—a kind of delicious mead, still made in the Principality, which the Druids and the Ancient Britons used on their great festivals as drink offering, and otherwise, much after the manner of the Israelites. In his left hand was a bird, the symbol of an aspirant, which is generally believed to have been the wren, for the British word Dryw implies both a wren and a Druid; probably because the former was fixed upon in that age of emblems, as the symbol of an aspirant to the office of the latter.

A custom prevails in the Principality at this day of carrying about for a fortnight or three weeks after Christmas a small chest in imitation of Noah's Ark inhabited by a live wren, one or more. This is done by the young men of the village who go from door to door in the dusk of the evening and sing a song relative to the history of the Ancient Britons, reminding the present generation that they are descended from Noah who was saved by an Ark, and exhibiting the Dryw (or wren) as the ancient symbol of the Druid, the primitive Priest or minister of Noah's religion in Britain.

The Influence of the Druids

The Druids have been grossly calumniated by Toland and others on this head. They have been represented as tyrants, fond of power, and guilty of deposing kings, and working on the passions of the people through the medium of superstition to keep them in the most humiliating state of bondage and degradation. Toland, though professing to give the history of the Druids, evidently describes the Roman Catholic priesthood. That was the standard before his eyes. And others who knew less of the subject have followed in his train softening down his expressions a little, but adding to the heap of falsehood and confusion.

There never was a class of religions men mere favourable to the prosperity of the nation and liberties of the people, than the primitive Druids of Britain. Liberty animated their every thought and breathed in every sentence that fell from their lips. Let the laws of Dyvnwal Moelmud which were framed and drawn up by them be read, and it will be perceived that they breathe a spirit of freedom which would not disgrace the polish of the nineteenth century. Nevertheless, it is quite true that the Druids possessed great influence in Britain at all times, but they never used it except in subordination to that of the Prince or Chief of the tribe. In confirmation of this assertion we beg again to cite from the laws of the ancient Britons.

"There are three privileged Conventions (Courts or Assemblies) that have a right to the homage of all who apply for protection, employment, honour, or emolument arising from the arts or sciences, according to the privilege and equality of these conventions respectively.

"First, the convention of the Bards of the Isle of Britain, which requires the respectful homage of every person that seeks for the emoluments of song, and of the scientific branches of Bardism.

"Second, the convention of the King or the Lord of the district, with his jurors, judges, and barons; that is every Briton who is a landed proprietor, thus assembled for the purpose of forming a court and deciding on legal causes.

"And third, a convention assembled for independence, which is a collective assembly of the country and its dependencies; and to this the two others owe homage, and the preservation of their privileges. For though the convention of the Bards is the most ancient in dignity, and the source of all the sciences, yet the convention of the collective power of the country and its dependencies takes precedence by right of power and necessity, for the regulation and establishment of justice, privilege, and protection in the country and the neighbouring country, and the annexed and separated territories in alliance. Without this general constitutional assembly, the other two could possess neither privilege nor power: for this general court of legislation possesses three glorious qualifications, that is to say, it consists of the wisdom, the power, and the will, of country and dependency, clan and clan united, to make, amend, and confirm law and union. This genial convention controls all other right of determination, power, law, or authority so that none other is equal to it." —Triad 60.

"There are three things which must not be done but by the consent of the country, the neighbouring country, and particularly the tribe: abrogating the king's law;—dethroning the sovereign;—and teaching new Doctrines, and new regulations in the convention of the Bards, For these things (as to the Bards) must not be done until the country and the tribe understand their nature, tendency, and regular order, according to the judgment and legal illustration of learned and wise men who are regularly inducted teachers in the efficient convention of the Bards of the Isle of Britain. For neither law, regulation, art, nor any kind of knowledge of the sciences, can acquire any privilege unless they are shown to be true by illustration and instruction; and this is to be done by the decision of masters and wise men who are duly authorized by instruction, sciences, and authority according to the privileged regulations of the country and the tribe." —Triad 63.

Whilst the Druids made no attempt to usurp undue authority, or oppose the civil power, the people were always ready to listen td their calm advice, and yield to their remonstrance. Their remarkable wisdom, piety, and disinterestedness of conduct, obtained for them the highest place in the estimation of all. Hence they were always employed in embassies and negotiations. And they observed the most inviolable secrecy on all such occasions between the parties that engaged them in confidential offices.

Universal peace and good will to man being one of the fundamental doctrines of the religion they taught, they appeared often as heralds of peace, and were never at rest until they could bring about a reconciliation between the contending tribes. And so sacred was the person of the Druid held that if he presented himself in his unicoloured robe of sky-blue between two contending armies on the point of engaging in battle, they instantly laid down their arms in accordance with the custom or motto that "a naked weapon was never to be held in the presence of a Bard;" thus affording an opportunity which was often successful of reconciling the contending parties and establishing a covenant of peace. On such occasions a pillar of unhewn stone was erected to be a monument to each party of the solemn compact into which it had entered with the neighbouring tribe to avoid future encroachment and be at peace. How like the custom that prevailed among the Eastern patriarchs!

When Jacob left Padan-arain to return to Caanan, Laban pursued after him, with the view of revenging, but God withheld him. "And Laban said unto Jacob, now, therefore, come thou, let us make a covenant, I and thou; and let it be for a witness between me and thee. And Jacob took a stone and set it up for a pillar. And Jacob said unto his brethren. Gather stones: And they took stones, and made an heap: and Laban said this heap is a witness between me and thee this day, therefore was the name of it called the Heap of witness. And Laban said to Jacob, This heap be witness, and this pillar be witness that I will not pass over this heap to thee, and that thou shall not pass over this heap and this pillar unto me, for harm," (Gen. chap. xxxi.) Such a custom among the Druids in Britain accounts for the numerous pillars, and cairns or heaps of loose stones, with which Scotland, some parts of England, and the principality of Wales abound, they were erected in the earliest ages as monuments of peace, of victory, or of national thanksgiving for a rich harvest. But some of them were set up for other purposes as appears by the following extracts from the Law Triads:—

1. For boundary stones or landmarks. "It is ordered and established for the purpose of preventing the uncertainty of a claim, that the Bards shall keep an orderly record of pedigrees, nobility, and inheritances. For the same purpose also is the memorial of the back-fire stones, the boundary stone, and the horse block. And he that removes them offers an insult to the court and the judges."—Triad 91.

2. As guides to travellers over mountains and desolate tracts of land in the absence of well formed roads. Such were called "The posts of the country and the King." "There are three stones which if any man remove he shall be indicted as a thief, the boundary stone, the white stone of the convention, and the guide stone: And he that destroys them shall forfeit his life, (or be guilty of capital offence.")— Triad 100.

Will the reader consider this punishment too severe? Let him remember the penalty annexed to a similar offence in the law of Moses: " Cursed be he that removeth his neighbour's landmark. And all the people shall say Amen."— (Deut. chap. xxxii.)

Druidical Forms of Oath

"There are three conclusive testimonies: an oath upon the entrails; a mutual confession; and a chain of circumstantial evidence that cannot be doubted."—Law Triad 184.

Mr. Probert, the elegant translator of the Triads, observes in a note under this, that "swearing upon the entrails of any animal was used on certain occasions by the patriarchal Jews, and also by the Greeks, and that the form therefore must be very ancient." There can be little doubt that it prevailed long anterior to the dispersion from Babel. Again, "There are three sacred objects (or relics) to swear by: the rod of office (or truncheon) of the minister of religion, the name of God, and hand joined in hand; and these are called hand relics. There are three other modes of swearing; a declaration upon conscience, a declaration in the face of the sun, and a strong declaration by the protection of God and his truth." —Triad 219.

An oath was considered of so sacred a character that whosoever was found guilty of perjury, was never again to be credited.

"There are three persons whose testimony is never to be credited: A minister of religion who has broken his covenant;—a witness who has been found to swear falsely by his pledge of truth, in court or any other place;—and a notorious habitual thief." —Triad 111.

We need not add any remarks on these extracts: They speak explicitly for themselves, and afford additional testimony in support of the great position which pervades the whole of this Treatise, that the Druids taught the worship of the true God. They understood the nature and obligation of an oath.

The Druidical Use of the Mistletoe

It has been observed by naturalists that the blossom of the mistletoe falls off within a few days of the summer solstice, and the berry within a few days of the winter solstice. These incidents therefore marked the return of two of the usual seasons for holding the Bardic conventions and festivals. Hence, it is not improbable that thence arose one of the reasons for which the mistletoe was held in so high a veneration among the Druids.

Again it is stated that the Ancient Britons commenced their year on the sixth day of the new moon, on which occasion a sacred festival was held throughout the country, and sacrifices were offered to the God of heaven under the oak in acknowledgment of his manifold blessings on the past, and to supplicate the same on the coming year. The oak had become peculiarly sacred as the house of God, or the place of worship, and consequently branches of this tree were used to adorn the altar, and garlands of its leaves to decorate the Priest or Druid; and the mistletoe, being so seldom found on the oak, was considered so great and desirable an appendage, that no solemn festival, such as that held at the beginning of the new year, was to be without it. Hence, as the new year drew nigh, the inhabitants with their Priests at their head, marched with great solemnity to gather this plant, inviting all to assist at the ceremony in these words, "The new year is at hand, gather the mistletoe." The tree being found on which it grew, the Druid or Priest ascended in his sacerdotal robes, and with a golden hook or consecrated knife cut off the shrub which was received in a white sheet spread for that purpose underneath.

When the sacrifice was over, the berries of this plant were taken by the Ovate, the physician of the tribe, and converted to medical purposes. That these berries possessed medicinal virtues can hardly be doubted, like following passage respecting the mistletoe occurs in Bacon:

"Mistletoe groweth chiefly upon crab trees, apple trees, sometimes upon hazles, and rarely upon oaks; the mistletoe whereof is counted very medicinal. It is ever green, winter and summer, and beareth a white glistering berry: And it is a plant utterly differing from the plant on which it groweth."

Sir John Colbach published a dissertation on the efficacy of the mistletoe in the year 1720. But in medicine, as in fashion, what is deemed of high value in one age is discontinued in the next, and thought nothing of. Such is the fate of the mistletoe in the present day as to any medical use that is made of it. But it is not improbable that it will have its day again.

The anonymous author of a little work entitled "Identity of the Hebrew and Druidical Religions, demonstrated from the nature and objects of their worship," suggests a new idea respecting the mistletoe, which may or may not be true.

"The Israelites looked for a Redeemer, who should come in future times: they typified his advent by the scape goat and a variety of emblems. The Druids did the same, they looked for some one who was typified under the emblem of the mistletoe. The Druids hold nothing more sacred than the mistletoe, and the tree on which it is produced provided it be the oak. They make choice of groves of oak on this account; nor do they perform any of their sacred rites without the leaves of those trees. And whatever mistletoe, grows on the oak they think is sent from heaven. They call it by a name which means the curer of all ills."—(Pliny)

"Virgil, speaking of the mistletoe, calls it the golden branch, and says, by its efficacious powers alone, man could return from the realms beneath. The Druids represented the Almighty by the oak, supposing that that tree exhibited in the liveliest manner the God of vegetative nature, eternal, omnipotent, and self existing, defying the assaults of a past eternity, and looking on the future as only similar to himself in duration.

From him came the branch so much spoken of by ancient prophets, the Curer of all our ills, who is indeed the resurrection and the life, without whose kind assistance we cannot return from the gloomy territories of the grave."

Without pledging ourselves to the belief of every sentiment contained in this passage, we beg to make one remark, that as it was a very general practice of the ancients to represent and convey their ideas by means of symbols taken from nature, especially by trees and plants, and their various parts;—that as trees in the garden of Eden were divinely pointed out, as emblematical of the most awful ideas—life and happiness, death and misery;—and that as the promised Saviour is repeatedly characterized in the sacred writings by the symbolical appellations of "Branch, Rod, Root of David, Tree of life, Plant of renown," we see no reason whatsoever for denying to the British Druids the right and propriety of making the mistletoe of the oak a symbol of the promised Saviour, and calling it the curer of all ills, to remind themselves and the people of the benefits which that Saviour would confer on them. And it is not a little singular, that among the several names by which the mistletoe is known in the Principality at the present day, one is, Olliach, All-heal. And no use seems to be made of it medicinally, though other Druidical herbs such as the vervain and cowslip are still in high repute.

Every part of the Mosaic dispensation was symbolical, and that not only with the consent, but by the appointment of God. And the Christian dispensation is not without its symbols, both in baptism and in the supper of the Lord. The Druids were consequently right in making use of symbols. And far be it from us to suppose that a custom of symbolizing did not originally prevail in the antediluvian world.

William Winwood Reade

Mysteries of the Druids

(from The Veil of Isis, or Mysteries of the Druids, 1861)

African explorer and popular journalist William Winwood Reade may seem like an unlikely author of books on the Druids, but several books on the subject came from his pen in intervals between the highly colored tales of African adventure that formed the mainspring of his literary career. Like David James, he drew extensively on earlier writings from the Druid Revival, but his approach to the Druid tradition had much more in common with Thomas Paine's than with the rector of Almondbury.

An atheist and rationalist, immersed in the gospel of willpower that had so many followers in the latter half of the nineteenth century, he pictured the Druids in terms partly drawn from his African experiences, and partly inspired by the same rejection of Christian ethics that inspired Nietzche. Ironically, given Masonry's traditional prohibition of atheists, Reade was also a Freemason, and drew many of his more colorful ideas about Druid initiation from the Masonic literature of the time.

Just as James' Druids were the ideal Anglican clergymen, Reade's Druids are the ideal Victorian adventurer-savants, masters of mechanics and gunpowder, tested and tempered by the ordeals of their initiation, and committed to the maintenance of their power and the subordination of the common people. He was among the first writers to give an explicit role to priestesses in Druidry; though his account of rituals involving naked virgins probably has much more to do with ordinary Victorian prurience than anything in his sources, it hinted at themes that would soon become central to one part of the Druid Revival tradition.

Further Reading:

W. Winwood Reade, *The Veil of Isis, or Mysteries of the Druids* (C.J. Skeet, 1861).

* * *

Druidism was a religion of philosophy; its high-priests were men of learning and science.

Under the head of the Ovydd, I shall describe their initiatory and sacrificial rites, and shall now merely consider their acquirements, as instructors, as mathematicians, as law-givers and as physicians.

Ammianus Marcellinus informs us that the Druids dwelt together in fraternities, and indeed it is scarcely possible that they could have lectured in almost every kind of philosophy and preserved their arcana from the vulgar, unless they had been accustomed to live in some kind of convent or college.

They were too wise, however, to immure themselves wholly in one corner of the land, where they would have exercised no more influence upon the nation than the Heads and Fellows of our present universities. While some lived the lives of hermits in caves and in hollow oaks within the dark recesses of the holy forests; while others lived peaceably in their college-home, teaching the bardic verses to children, to the young nobles, and to the students who came to them from a strange country across the sea, there were others who led an active and turbulent existence at court in the councils of the state and in the halls of nobles.

In Gaul, the chief seminaries of the Druids was in the country of the Carnutes between Chartres and Dreux, to which at one time scholars resorted in such numbers that they were obliged to build other academies in various parts of the land, vestiges of which exist to this day, and of which the ancient College of Guienne is said to be one.

When their power began to totter in their own country, the young Druids resorted to Mona, now Anglesea, in which was the great British university, and in which there is a spot called *Myrfyrion*, the seat of studies.

The Druidic precepts were all in verses, which amounted to 20,000 in number, and which it was forbidden to write. Consequently a long course of preparatory study was required, and some spent so much as twenty years in a state of probation.

These verses were in rhyme, which the Druids invented to assist the memory, and in a triplet form from the veneration which was paid to the number three by all the nations of antiquity.

In this the Jews resembled the Druids, for although they had received the written law of Moses, there was a certain code of precept among them which was taught by mouth alone, and in which those who were the most learned were elevated to the Rabbi.

The mode of teaching by memory was also practised by the Egyptians and by Lycurgus, who esteemed it better to imprint his laws on the minds of the Spartan citizens than to engrave them upon tablets. So, too, were Numa's sacred writing buried with him by his orders, in compliance perhaps with the opinions of his friend Pythagoras who, as well as Socrates, left nothing behind him committed to writing.

It was Socrates, in fact, who compared written doctrines to pictures of animals which resemble life, but which when you question them can give you no reply.

But we who love the past have to lament this system. When Cambyses destroyed the temples of Egypt, when the disciples of Pythagoras died in the Metapontine tumults, all their mysteries and all their learning died with them.

So also the secrets of the Magi, the Orpheans and the Cabiri perished with their institutions, and it is owing to this law of the Druids that we have only the meagre evidence of ancient authors and the obscure emblems of the Welsh Bards, and the faint vestiges of their mighty monuments to teach us concerning the powers and direction of their philosophy.

There can be no doubt that they were profoundly learned. For ordinary purposes of writing, and in the keeping of their accounts on the Alexandrian method, they used the ancient Greek character of which Cadmus, a Phœnician, and Timagines, a Druid, were said to have been the inventors and to have imported into Greece.

Both in the universities of the Hebrews, which existed from the earliest times, and in those of the Brachmans it was not permitted to study philosophy and the sciences, except so far as they might assist the student in the perusal and comprehension of the sacred writings. But a more liberal system existed among the Druids, who were skilled in all the arts and in foreign languages.

For instance, there was Abaris, a Druid and a native of the Shetland Isles who traveled into Greece, where he formed a friendship with Pythagoras and where his learning, his politeness, his shrewdness, and expedition in business, and above all, the ease and elegance with which he spoke the Athenian tongue, and which (so said the orator Himenius) would have made one believe that he had been brought up in the academy or the Lyceum, created for him as great a sensation as that which was afterwards made by the admirable Crichton among the learned doctors of Paris.

It can easily be proved that the science of astronomy was not unknown to the Druids. One of their temples in the island of Lewis in the Hebrides, bears evident signs of their skill in the science. Every stone in the temple is placed astronomically. The circle consists of twelve equistant obelisks denoting the twelve signs of the zodiac. The four cardinal points of the compass are marked by lines of obelisks running out from the circle, and at each point subdivided into four more. The range of obelisks from north, and exactly facing the south is double, being two parallel rows each consisting of nineteen stones. A large stone in the centre of the circle, thirteen feet high, and of the perfect shape of a ship's rudder would seem as a symbol of their knowledge of astronomy being made subservient to navigation, and the Celtic word for star, *ruth-iul*, "a-guide-to-direct-the-course," proves such to have been the case.

This is supposed to have been the winged temple which Erastosthenes says that Apollo had among the Hyperboreans—a name which the Greeks applied to all nations dwelling north of the Pillars of Hercules.

But what is still more extraordinary, Hecateus makes mention that the inhabitants of a certain Hyperborian island, little less than Sicily, and over against Celtiberia—a description answering exactly to that of Britain—could bring the moon so near them as to show the mountains and rocks, and other appearances upon its surface.

According to Strabo and Bochart, glass was a discovery of the Phcenicians and a staple commodity of their trade, but we have some ground for believing that our philosophers bestowed rather than borrowed this invention.

Pieces of glass and crystal have been found in the cairns, as if in honor to those who invented it; the process of vitrifying the very walls of their houses, which is still to be seen in the Highlands prove that they possessed the art in the gross; and the Gaelic name for glass is not of foreign but of Celtic extraction, being *glasine* and derived from *glas-theine*, glued or brightened by fire.

We have many wonderful proofs of the skill in mechanics. The *clacha-brath*, or rocking-stones, were spherical stones of an enormous size, and were raised upon other flat stones into which they inserted a small prominence fitting the cavity so exactly, and so concealed by loose stones lying around it, that nobody could discern the artifice. Thus these globes were balanced so that the slightest touch would make them vibrate, while anything of greater weight pressing against the side of the cavity rendered them immovable.

In Iona, the last asylum of the Caledonian Druids, many of these *clacha-brath* (one of which is mentioned in Ptolemy Hephestion's History, Lib. iii. cap 3.) were to be found at the beginning of this century, and although the superstitious natives defaced them and turned them over into the sea, they considered it necessary to have something of the kind in their stead, and have substituted for them rough stone balls which they call by the same name.

In Stonehenge, too, we find an example of that oriental mechanism which is displayed so stupendously in the pyramids of Egypt. Here stones of thirty or forty tons that must have been a draught for a herd of oxen, have been carried the distance of sixteen computed miles and raised to a vast height, and placed in their beds with such ease that their very mortises were made to tally.

The temples of Abury in Wiltshire, and of Carnac in Brittany, though less perfect, are even more prodigious monuments of art.

It is scarcely to be wondered at that the Druids should be acquainted with the properties of gunpowder, since we know that it was used in the mysteries of Isis, in the temple of Delphi, and by the old Chinese philosophers.

Lucan in his description of a grove near Marseilles, writes:—"There is a report that the grove is often shaken and strangely moved, and that dreadful sounds are heard from its caverns; and that it is sometimes in a blaze without being consumed."

In Ossian's poem of *Dargo the son of the Druid of Bel*, similar phenomenon are mentioned, and while the Celtic word lightning is *De'lanach*, "the flash or flame of God," they had another word which expresses a flash that is quick and sudden as lightning—*Druilanach*, "the flame of the Druids."

It would have been fortunate for mankind had the monks of the middle ages displayed the wisdom of these ancient priests in concealing from fools and madmen so dangerous an art.

All such knowledge was carefully retained within the holy circle of their dark caves and forests and which the initiated were bound by a solemn oath never to reveal.

The Derwydd, or Philosophers

I will now consider the Druids of active life—the preachers, the law-givers, and the physicians.

On the seventh day, like the first patriarchs, they preached to the warriors and their wives from small round eminences, several of which yet remain in different parts of Britain.

Their doctrines were delivered with a surpassing eloquence and in triplet verses, many specimens which are to be found in the Welsh poetry but of which these two only have been preserved by the classical authors.

The first in Pomponius Mela: "To act bravely in war, that souls are immortal, and there is another life after death."

The second in Diogenes Laertius: "To worship the Gods, and to do no evil, and to exercise fortitude."

Once every year a public assembly of the nation was held in Mona at the residence of the Arch-Druid, and their silence was no less rigidly imposed than in the councils of the Rabbi and the Brachmans. If any one interrupted the orator, a large piece of his robe was cut off—if after that he offended, he was punished with death. To enforce punctuality, like the Cigonii of Pliny, they had the cruel custom of cutting to pieces the one who came last. Their laws, like their religious precepts, were at first esteemed too sacred to be committed to writing—the first written laws being those of Dyrnwal Moelmud, King of Britain, about 440 B.C. and called the Moelmutian laws; for these were substituted the Mercian code or the laws of Martia, Queen of England, which was afterwards adopted by King Alfred and translated by him into Saxon.

The Manksmen also ascribe to the Druids those excellent laws by which the Isle of Man has always been governed.

The magistrates of Britain were but tools of the Druids, appointed by them and educated by them also; for it was a law in Britain that no one might hold office who had not been educated by the Druids.

The Druids held annual assizes in different parts of Britain (for instance at the monument called *Long Meg and her Daughters* in

Cumberland and at the *Valley of Stones* in Cornwall) as Samuel visited Bethel and Gilgal once a year to dispense justice.

There they heard appeals from the minor courts, and investigated the more intricate cases, which sometimes they were obliged to settle by ordeal. The rocking-stones which I have just described, and the walking barefoot through a fire which they lighted on the summit of some holy hill and called *Samh'in*, or the fire of peace, were their two chief methods of testing the innocence of the criminal, and in which they were imitated by the less ingenious and perhaps less conscientious judges of later days.

For previous to the ordeal which they named *Gabha Bheil*, or "the trial of Beil," the Druids used every endeavor to discover the real merits of the case, in order that they might decide upon the verdict of Heaven—that is to say, which side of the stone they should press, or whether they should anoint his feet with that oil which the Hindoo priests use in their religious festivals, and which enables the barefoot to pass over the burning wood unscathed.

We may smile at another profanity of the Druids who constituted themselves judges not only of the body but of the soul.

But as Mohammed inspired his soldiers with sublime courage by promising Paradise to those who found a death-bed upon the corpses of their foes, so the very superstitions, the very frauds of these noble Druids tended to elevate the hearts of. men towards their God, and to make them lead virtuous lives that they might merit the sweet fields of *Fla'innis*, the heaven of their tribe.

Never before since the world, has such vast power as the Druids possessed been wielded with such purity, such temperance, such discretion.

When a man died a platter of earth and salt was placed upon his breast, as is still the custom in Wales and in the North of Britain.

The earth an emblem of the corruptibility of the body—the salt an emblem of the incorruptibility of the soul.

A kind of court was then assembled round the corpse, and by the evidence of those with whom he had been best acquainted, it was decided with what funeral rites he should be honored.

If he had distinguished himself as a warrior, or as man of science, it was recorded in the deathsong; a *cairn* or pile of sacred stones was raised over him, and his arms and tools or other symbols of his profession were buried with him.

If his life had been honorable, and if he had obeyed the three grand articles of religion, the bard sang his *requiem* on the harp, whose beautiful music alone was a pass-port to heaven.

It is a charming idea, is it not? The soul lingering for the first strain which might release it from the cold corpse, and mingle with its silent ascent to God.

Read how the heroes of Ossian longed for this funereal hymn without which their souls, pale and sad as those which haunted the banks of the Styx, were doomed to wander through the mists of some dreary fen.

When this hymn had been sung, the friends and relatives of the deceased made great rejoicings, and this it was that originated those sombre merry-makings so peculiar to the Scotch and Irish funerals.

In the philosophy of medicine, the Derwydd were no less skilled than in sciences and letters. They knew that by means of this divine art they would possess the hearts as well as the minds of men, and obtain not only the awe of the ignorant but also the love of those whose lives they had preserved.

Their sovereign remedy was the missoldine or mistletoe of the oak which, in Wales, still bears its ancient name of *Oll-iach*, or all-heal, with those of *Pren-awr*, the celestial tree, and *Uchelwydd*, the lofty shrub.

When the winter has come and the giant of the forest is deserted by its leaves and extends its withered arms to the sky, a divine hand sheds upon it from heaven a mysterious seed, and a delicate green plant sprouts from the bark, and thus is born while all around is dying and decayed.

We need not wonder that the mistletoe should be revered as a heaven-born plant, and as a type of God's promise and consolation to those who were fainting on death's threshold in the winter of old age.

When the new year approached, the Druids beset themselves to discover this plant upon an oak, on which tree it grows less frequently than upon the ash-crab or apple tree. Having succeeded, and as soon as the moon was six days old, they marched by night with great solemnity towards the spot, inviting all to join their procession with these words: *The New Year is at hand: let us gather the mistletoe.*

First marched the Ovades in their green sacrificial robes leading two milk-white bullocks. Next caine the bards singing the praises of the Mighty Essence, in raiment blue as the heavens to which their hymn ascended. Then a herald clothed in white with two wings drooping down on each side of his head, and a branch of vervain in his hand encircled by two serpents. He was followed by three Derwydd—one of whom carried the sacrificial bread—another a vase of water—and the third a white wand. Lastly, the Arch-Druid, distinguished by the tuft or tassel to his cap, by the bands hanging from his throat, by the sceptre in his hand and by the golden crescent on his breast, surrounded by the whole body of the Derwydd and humbly followed by the noblest warriors of the land.

An altar of rough stones was erected under the oak, and the Arch-Druid, having sacramentally distributed the bread and wine, would climb the tree, cut the mistletoe with a golden knife, wrap it in a pure white cloth, slay and sacrifice the bullocks, and pray to God to remove his curse from barren women, and to permit their medicines to serve as antidotes for poisons and charms from all misfortunes.

They used the mistletoe as an ingredient in almost all their medicines, and a powder was made from the berries for cases of sterility.

It is a strong purgative well suited to the lusty constitutions of the ancient Britons, but, like bleeding, too powerful a remedy for modern ailments.

With all the herbs which they used for medicine, there were certain mummeries to be observed while they were gathered, which however were not without their object—first in enhancing the faith of the vulgar by exciting their superstitions—and also in case of failure that the patient might be reproached for blundering instead of a physician.

The *vervain* was to be gathered at the rise of the dog-star, neither sun nor moon shining at the time; it was to be dug up with an iron instrument and to be waved aloft in the air, the left hand only being used.

The leaves, stalks and flowers were dried separately in the shade and were used for the bites of serpents, infused in wine.

The *samulos* which grew in damp places was to be gathered by a person fasting—without looking behind him—and with his left hand. It was laid into troughs and cisterns where cattle drank, and when bruised was a cure for various distempers.

The *selago*, a kind of hedge hyssop, was a charm as well as a medicine. He who gathered it was to be clothed in white—to bathe his feet in running water—to offer a sacrifice of bread and wine—and then with his right hand covered by the skirt of his robe, and with a brazen hook to dig it up by the roots and wrap it in a white cloth.

Prominent among the juggleries of the Druids, stands the serpent's egg—*the ovus anguinum* of Pliny—the *glein neidr* of the ancient Britons—the *adderstone* of modem folk-lore.

It was supposed to have been formed by a multitude of serpents close entwined together, and by the frothy saliva that proceeded from their throats. When it was made, it was raised up in the air by their combined hissing, and to render it efficacious it was to be caught in a clean white cloth before it could fall to the ground—for in Druidism that which touched the ground was polluted. He who performed this ingenious task was obliged to mount a swift horse, and to ride away at full speed pursued by the serpents from whom he was not safe till he had crossed a river.

The Druids tested its virtue by encasing it in gold, and throwing it into a river. If it swam against the stream it would render it possessor superior to his adversaries in all disputes, and obtain for him the friendship of great men,

The implicit belief placed in this fable is curiously exemplified by the fact of a Roman Knight of the Vocontii, while pleading his own cause in a law suit was discovered with one of these charms in his breast and was put to death upon the spot.

Their reverence for the serpent's egg has its origin in their mythology. Like the Phoenicians and Egyptians, they represented the creation by the figure of an egg coming out of a serpent's mouth, and it was doubtless the excessive credulity of the barbarians which tempted them to invent the above fable that they might obtain high prices for these amulets, many of which have been discovered in Druidic barrows, and are still to be met with in the Highlands, where a belief in their power has not yet subsided; for it is no uncommon thing when a distemper rages among men or beasts, for the *Glass-physician* to be sent for from as great a distance as fifty miles.

These eggs are made of some kind of glass or earth glazed over, and are sometimes blue, green, or white, and sometimes variegated with all these colors intermixed.

For mental disorders and some physical complaints they used to prescribe pilgrimages to certain wells, always situated at a distance from the patient, and the waters of which were to be drunk and bathed in. With these ablutions, sacred as those of the Mussulmen, were mingled religious ceremonies with a view to remind them of the presence of that God who alone could relieve them from their infirmities. After reaching the wells, they bathed thrice—that mysterious number—and walked three times round the well, *deis'iul,* in the same direction as the course of the sun, also turning and bowing from East to West.

These journeys were generally performed before harvest, at which time the modern Arabs go through a series of severe purgings, and when English laborers, twenty years ago, used systematically to go to the market town to be bled.

The season of the year—the exercise—the mineral in the water—above all the strong faith of the patients effected so many real cures that in time it became a custom (still observed in Scotland with the well of Strathfillan and in many parts of Ireland) for all who were afflicted with any disorder to perform an annual pilgrimage to these holy wells.

Caithbaid, an Irish historian, speaks of the Druid Trosdan who discovered an antidote for poisoned arrows, and there are many instances on record of the medicinal triumphs of the Druids.

They were more anxious to prevent disease than to cure them, and issued many maxims relating to the care of the body, as wise as those which appertained to the soul were divine.

Of these I will give you one which should be written in letters of gold: Cheerfulness, temperance and early rising.

The Bardd, or Musicians

As there were musicians among the Levites, and priests among the Phcenicians who chanted bare-foot and in white surplices the sacred hymns, so there were bards among the Druids, who were divided into three classes:

I. The *Fer-Laoi,* or Hymnists, who sang the essence and immortality of the soul; the works of nature; the course of the celestial bodies; with the order and harmony of the spheres.

II. The *Senachies* who sang the fabulous histories of their ancestors in rude stanzas, and who with letters cut from the bark of trees inscribed passing events and became the historians of their nation.

The *Fer-Dan* who were accustomed to wander through the country, or to be numbered in the retinues of kings and nobles, who not only sang encomiums upon the great warriors of the age, but who wrote satires upon the prevailing vices, worthy of a Juvenal or a Horace.

I can best give the reader some idea of the style and power of their conceptions, by quoting some of their axioms which have descended to us traditionally.

They are in the form of Triads, of which the subjects are, language—fancy and invention—the design of poetry—the nature of just thinking—rules of arrangement—method of description—e.g.:

The three qualifications of poetry—endowment of genius, judgment from experience, and happiness of mind.

The three foundations of judgment—bold design, frequent practice, and frequent mistakes.

The three foundations of learning—seeing much, studying much, and suffering much.

The three foundations of happiness—a suffering with contentment, a hope that it will come, and a belief that it will be.

The three foundations of thought—perspicuity, amplitude, and preciseness.

The three canons of perspicuity—the word that is necessary, the quantity that is necessary, and the manner that is necessary.

The three canons of amplitude—appropriate thought, variety of thought and requisite thought.

How full of wisdom and experience! What sublime ideas in a few brief words!

These poets were held in high honor by the Britons, for among a barbarous people musicians are angels who bring to them a language from the other world, and who alone can soften their iron hearts and fill their bold blue eyes with gentle tears.

There is an old British law commanding that all should be made freedmen of slaves who were of these three professions. A scholar learned in the languages—a bard—or a smith. When once the smith had entered a smithy, or the scholar had been polled, or the bard had composed a song, they could never more be deprived of their freedom.

Their ordinary dress was brown, but in religious ceremonies they wore ecclesiastical ornaments called *bardd-gwewll*, which was an azure robe with a cowl to it—a costume afterwards adopted by the lay monks of Bardsey Island (the burial-place of Myrrddin or Merlin) and was by them called *Cyliau Duorn*, or black cowls; it was then borrowed by the Gauls and is still worn by the Capuchin friars.

Blue which is an emblem of the high heavens and the beautiful sea had always been a favorite color with the ancient Britons, and is still used as a toilet paint by the ladies of Egypt and Tartary. Blue rosettes are the insignia of our students in the twin universities, and for the old Welsh proverb, "True blue keeps its hue," one of our proverbial expressions may be traced.

The harp, or lyre, invented by the Celts had four or five strings, or thongs made of an ox's hide, and was usually played upon with a plectrum made of the jaw-bone of a goat. But we have reason to believe that it was the instrument invented by Tubal which formed the model of the Welsh harps.

Although the Greeks (whom the learned Egyptians nicknamed "children," and who were the most vain-glorious people upon the earth) claimed the harp as an invention of their ancient poets, Juvenal in his third satire acknowledges that both the Romans and the Greeks received it from the Hebrews, This queen of instruments is hallowed to our remembrance by many passages in the Bible. It was from the harp that David before Saul drew such enchanting strains that the monarch's heart was melted and the dark frown left his brow. It was on their harps that the poor Jewish captives were desired to play, on their harps which swayed above them on the branches of the willow trees while the waters of Babylon sobbed past beneath their feet.

And it was the harp which St. John beheld in the white hands of the angels as they stood upon the sea of glass mingled with fire, singing the song of Moses, the servant of God, and the song of the lamb.

The trunks of these harps were polished and in the shape of a heart; they were embraced between the breast and the arm; their strings were of glossy hair. In Palestine they were made from the wood of the Cedars of Lebanon; in Britain of *Pren-masarn*, or the sycamore.

In their construction, the same mysterious regard was paid to the number three. Their shape was triangular; their strings were three in number, and their turning keys had three arms.

In later times the Irish, who believe that they are descended from

David, obtained an European fame for their skill in the making of this instrument. Dante mentions the circumstance, and the harp is still a mint-mark upon Irish coin.

The Bards from what we can learn of them, neither debased their art to calumny nor to adulations but were in every way as worthy of our admiration as those profound philosophers to whom alone they were inferior.

We learn that, (unlike the artists of later times) they were peculiarly temperate, and that in order to inure themselves to habits of abstinence they would have all kinds of delicacies spread out as if for a banquet, and upon which having feasted their eyes for some time they would order to be removed.

Also that they did their utmost to stay those civil wars which were the bane of Britain, and that often when two fierce armies had stood fronting each other in array of battle, their swords drawn, their spears pointing to the foe and waiting but for the signal from their chieftains to begin the conflict, the Bards had stepped in between and had touched their harps with such harmony, and so persuaded them with sweet thrilling verses, that suddenly, on either side soldiers had dropped their arms and forgotten the fierce resentment which had been raging in their breasts.

The Ovades, or Novitiates

In writing of the Derwydd, or philosophers, I have written also of the high priests, or magicians—for *magus* is but another name for priest, and in the Chinese and various hieroglyphical languages, the same sign represents a magician and a priest.

I have now to describe the lower order of *sacrificers* who, under the direction of their masters, slew the victims upon the altar, and poured out the sacramental wine.

The Ovades were usually dressed in white, while their sacerdotal robes were of green, an ancient emblem of innocence and youth, still retained in our language, but debased and vulgarized into slang.

They are generally represented with chaplets of oak-leaves on their brows, and their eyes modestly fixed on the ground.

Having been carefully trained in the Druidic seminaries, their memory being stored with the holy triads, and with the outward ceremonies of their religion, they were prepared for initiation into the sublime mysteries of Druidism.

During a period of probation, the Ovade was closely watched; eyes, to him invisible, were ever upon him, noting his actions and his very looks, searching into his heart for its motive, and into his soul for its abilities.

He was then subjected to a trial so painful to the body, so terrible to the mind, that many lost their senses for ever, and others crawled back to the daylight pale and emaciated, as men who had grown old in prison.

These initiations took place in caves, one of which still exists in Denbighshire. We have also some reason to believe that the catacombs of Egypt and those artificial excavations which are to be found in many parts of Persia and Hindostan were constructed for the same purpose.

The Ovade received several wounds from a man who opposed his entrance with a drawn sword. He was then led blind-folded through the winding alleys of the cave which was also a labyrinth. This was intended to represent the toilsome wanderings of the soul in the mazes of ignorance and vice.

Presently the ground would begin to rock beneath his feet; strange sounds disturbed the midnight silence. Thunder crashed upon him like the fall of an avalanche, flashes of green lightning flickered through the cave displaying to his view hideous spectres arrayed against the walls.

Then lighted only by these fearful fires a strange procession marched past him, and a hymn in honor of the Eternal Truth was solemnly chanted by unseen tongues.

Here the profounder mysteries commenced. He was admitted through the North Gate or that of Cancer, where he was forced to pass through a fierce fire. Thence he was hurried to the Southern Gate or that of Capricorn, where he was plunged into a flood, and from which he was only released when life was at its last gasp.

Then he was beaten with rods for two days, and buried up to his neck in snow.

This was the baptism of fire, of water, and of blood.

Now arrived on the verge of death, an icy chill seizes his limbs; a cold dew bathes his brow, his faculties fail him; his eyes close; he is about to faint, to expire, when a strain of music, sweet as the dis¬tant murmur of the holy brooks, consoling as an angel's voice, bids him to rise and to live for the honor of his God.

Two doors with a sound like the fluttering of wings are thrown open before him. A divine light bursts upon him, he sees plains shining with flowers open around him.

Then a golden serpent is placed in his bosom as a sign of his regeneration, and he is adorned with a mystic zone upon which are engraved twelve mysterious signs; a tiara is placed upon his head; his form naked and shivering is clothed in a purple tunic studded with innumerable stars; a crozier is placed in his hand. He is a king; for he is initiated; for he is a Druid.

Priestesses

The Druids had many rites of divination—from the entrails of their victims—from the flight of birds—from the waves of the sea—from the bubbling of wells—and from the neighing of white horses.

By the number of criminal causes in the year they formed an estimate of the scarcity or plenty of the year to come.

They also used divining rods, which they cut in the shape of twigs from an apple tree which bore fruit, and having distinguished them from each other by certain marks, threw them promiscuously upon a white garment. Then the Diviner would take up each billet or stick three times, and draw an interpretation from the marks before imprinted on them.

The ordering of these divinations were usually placed in the hands of women who formed an order of Sibylls among these ancient prophets.

It has been the belief of every age that women are more frequently blessed with the gifts of inspiration, and that the mists of the future hang less darkly before their eyes than before those of men.

And thus it was that women were admitted to those holy privileges which none others could obtain except with the learning and struggles of a lifetime, thus it was that even the commonest women was admitted to that shrine from which the boldest warriors were excluded.

There is, however, a tradition that at one period both in Gaul and Britain, the women were supreme, that they ruled the councils of state, that they led the armies of war. That the Druids by degrees supplanted them, and obtained the power for themselves. But to propitiate these women who had the blood of Albina in their veins, they admitted them into their order, and gave them the title of Druidesses.

They were eventually formed into three classes.

I. Those who performed the servile offices about the temple, and the persons of the Druids, and who were not separated from their families.

II. Those who assisted the Druids in their religious services, and who, though separated from their husbands, were permitted to visit them occasionally.

III. A mysterious sisterhood who dwelt in strict chastity and seclusion, and who formed the oracles of Britain.

Such is the origin of Christian nunneries. In all important events the Britons repaired to their dwelling. Not even a marriage was consummated among them without consulting the Druidess, and her *purin*, the seic seona of the Irish, viz., five stones thrown up and caught on the back of the hand, and from which she divined.

There are several instances recorded in classical history of predictions from these priestesses which came true.

Alexander Severus had just set out upon an expedition when he was met by a Druidess, "Go on, my Lord," she said aloud to him as he passed, "but beware of your soldiers."

He was assassinated by his soldiers in that same campaign.

My next example is still more peculiar. When Diocletian was a private soldier he had a Druidess for hostess, who found him every day reckoning up his accounts with a military exactitude to which the army in those days was a stranger.

"You are niggardly," she said.

"Yes," he answered, "but when I become an Emperor I will be generous."

"You have said no jest," replied the priestess, for you will be Emperor when you have killed a wild boar—*cum aprum occideris*."

In our language this prophecy loses its point, for there is a play upon the Latin word which cannot be translated. *Aper* means both the name of a man and a wild beast, and thus the prediction was wrapped in that wise ambiguity which has been the characteristic of all human prophecy.

Diocletian, whose ambition gave him faith, was much perplexed with the double meaning of the word, but hunted assiduously till he had killed so many wild boars, that he began to fear he had taken the word in its wrong acceptation.

So he slew Aper, his stepfather, the assassin of Numerianus, and shortly afterwards, sat upon the imperial throne.

In marble, as well as in ink, there are memorials of the sect of Druidesses. The following inscription was discovered at Metz in Normandy:

SILVANO
SACR
ET NYMPHIS LOCI
APETE DRUIS
ANTISTITA
SOMNO MONITA.

Of Druidic oracles we know only of one at Kildare in Ireland; of one at Toulouse which ceased when Christianity was introduced there by St. Saturnins; of one at Polignac dedicated to Apollo, or Belenus, or Baal; and most celebrated of all that in the island of Sena (now Sain) at the mouth of the River Loire.

This island was inhabited by seven young women who were beautiful as angels, and furious as demons.

They were married but their husbands might never visit them. The foot of man was not permitted to set foot upon their isle.

When the mantle of night had began to descend upon the earth, seven dusky forms might be seen gliding to the shore, and springing into their wicker boats, which were covered with the skins of beasts, would row across to the main-land, and fondle with their husbands, and smile upon them as if with the sweet innocence of youth.

But when the streaks of light began to glimmer in the East, like restless spirits summoned back to their daylight prison, strange fires would gleam from their eyes, and they would tear themselves from their husband's arms.

To them came the sailors who fished and traded on the seas, and entreated them for fair winds. But as they came and as they spoke, they shuddered at the sight of these women whose faces were distorted by inspiration, whose voices seemed to be full of blood.

When Christianity began to prevail in the north, it was believed that these women, by culling certain herbs at various periods of the moon, transformed themselves into winged and raging beasts, and attacking such as were baptized and regenerated by the blood of Jesus Christ, killed them without the visible force of arms, opened their bodies, tore out their hearts and devoured them; then substituting wood or straw for the heart, made the bodies live on as before and returned through the clouds to their island-home.

It is certain that they devoted themselves chiefly to the service of the Moon, who was said to exercise a peculiar influence over storms and diseases—the first of which they pretended to predict, the latter to cure.

They worshipped her under the name of Ked or Ceridwen, the northern name for the Egyptian Isis.

They consecrated a herb to her, called *Belinuncia,* in the poisonous sap of which they dipped their arrows to render them as deadly as those malignant rays of the moon, which can shed both death and madness upon men.

It was one of their rites to procure a virgin and to strip her naked, as an emblem of the moon in an unclouded sky. They then sought for the wondrous *selago* or golden herb. She who pressed it with her foot slept, and heard the language of animals. If she touched it with iron, the sky grew dark and a misfortune fell upon a world. When they had found it, the virgin traced a circle round it, and covering her hand in a white linen cloth which had never been before used, rooted it out with a point of her little finger—a symbol of the crescent moon. Then they washed it in a running spring, and having gathered green branches plunged into a river and splashed the virgin, who was thus supposed to resemble the moon clouded with vapors. When they retired, the virgin walked backwards that the moon might not return upon its path in the plain of the heavens.

They had another rite which procured them a name as infamous and as terrible as that of the Sirens of the South, who were really Canaanite priestesses that lured men to their island with melodious strains, and destroyed them as a sacrifice to their Gods.

They had a covered temple in imitation probably of the two magnificent buildings which the Greek colonists had erected at Massilia. This it was their custom annually to unroof, and to renew the covering before the sun set by their united labors.

And if any woman dropt or lost the burden that she was carrying, she was immediately torn to pieces by these savage creatures, who daubed their faces and their white bosoms with their victim's blood, and carried her limbs round the temple with wild and exulting yells,

It was this custom which founded the story told at Athens and at Rome, that in an island of the Northern seas there were virgins who devoted themselves to the service of Bacchus, and who celebrated orgies similar to those of Samothrace.

For in those plays, performed in honor of Dionusus, there was always a representation of a man torn limb from limb. And in the Island of Chios, as in Sena, this drama was enacted to the life.

Robert Stephen Hawker
The Quest of the Sangraal
(published 1864)

As the nineteenth century went on and the Druid Revival tradition became a fixture in British culture, it attracted to itself many other themes and traditions connected in one way or another to nature, esoteric spirituality, or romanticism. One of the most influential of these was the body of legend and lore surrounding the figure of King Arthur. The Arthurian legends had largely fallen out of popularity in the eighteenth century, but the Victorian era saw a dramatic revival of interest in the old stories of the Round Table and its knights, and these in turn found their way into the Druid traditions of the late nineteenth and early twentieth centuries.

Yet another Anglican clergyman with scholarly interests, Robert Stephen Hawker was one of many literary figures of the Victorian era who contributed to the Arthurian revival. He came from an ecclesiastical family with deep roots in southwestern Britain. Born in 1803 in the vicarage of Charles Church, Plymouth, and educated at Oxford, he was ordained in the Church of England in 1831 and, in 1834, became the vicar of Morwenstow, Cornwall, where he spent the rest of his life, dying there in 1875. An indefatigable student of the history, antiquities, and traditions of Cornwall, and a noted local eccentric, Hawker also became widely known in his own time as a poet, though he has been largely forgotten outside of Cornwall in recent years.

The Quest of the Sangraal, which appears below in its entirety, is widely considered his best poetic work. A narrative poem of the Grail quest, it weaves together theology, legend, social criticism, Cornwall's own deeply rooted Celtic traditions, and an intriguing cosmology that echoes the Druid Revival tradition in many ways. The fourfold symbolism traced out by Hawker's questing knights, in particular, and the mysterious "first element" of Numyne, will be immediately familiar to students of Druid Revival teachings. Less representative of the Revival, though equally revealing of the complex social and intellectual currents of the time, are the echoes of contemporary prejudices against Judaism and Pagan religion to be found in the poem, reminders that Hawker was inevitably a man of his own era.

Hawker's own involvement in the Revival is an open question—so far, at least, no evidence one way or the other has surfaced—but the parallels between his ideas and Revival teachings are striking, and his influence on later Druids is not in question; several twentieth-century Druid authors, including Ross Nichols (one of whose works also appears in this collection) cited him approvingly at length as an example of symbolic verse with deep relevance to the Druids of a later time.

Further Reading:

J.G. Godwin, ed., *The Poetical Works of Robert Stephen Hawker* (C. Kegan Paul, 1879).

* * *

The name Sangraal is derived from San, the breviate of Sanctus or Saint, Holy, and Graal, the Keltic word for Vessel or Vase. All that is known of the Origin and History of this mysterious Relique will be rehearsed in the Poem itself. As in the title, so in the Knightly Names, I have preferred the Keltic to other sources of spelling and sound.—R.S.H.

Ho! for the Sangraal! vanish'd Vase of Heaven!
That held, like Christ's own heart, an hin[1] of blood!
Ho! for the Sangraal! . . .
        How the merry shout
Of reckless riders on their rushing steeds,
Smote the loose echo from the drowsy rock
Of grim Dundagel, thron'd along the sea!

"Unclean! unclean! ten cubits and a span,[2]
Keep from the wholesome touch of human-kind:
Stand at the gate, and beat the leper's bell,
But stretch not forth the hand for holy thing,--
Unclean, as Egypt at the ebb of Nile!"
Thus said the monk, a lean and gnarlèd man;

His couch was on the rock, by that wild stream
That floods, in cataract, Saint Nectan's Kieve:[3]
One of the choir, whose life is Orison.
They had their lodges in the wilderness,
Or built them cells beside the shadowy sea,
And there they dwelt with angels, like a dream:
So they unroll'd the volume of the Book,
And fill'd the fields of the Evangelist
With antique thoughts, that breath'd of Paradise.

Uprose they for the Quest--the bounding men
Of the siege perilous, and the granite ring--
They gathered at the rock, yon ruddy tor;[4]
The stony depth where lurked the demon-god,
Till Christ, the mighty Master, drave him forth.

There stood the knights, stately, and stern, and tall;
Tristan, and Perceval, Sir Galahad,
And he, the sad Sir Lancelot of the lay:
Ah me! that logan[5] of the rocky hills,
Pillar'd in storm, calm in the rush of war,
Shook, at the light touch of his lady's hand!

See! where they move, a battle-shouldering kind!
Massive in mould, but graceful: thorough men:
Built in the mystic measure of the Cross:--
Their lifted arms the transome: and their bulk,
The Tree, where Jesu stately stood to die--
Thence came their mastery in the field of war:--
Ha! one might drive battalions--one, alone!

See! now, they pause; for in their midst, the King,
Arthur, the Son of Uter, and the Night,
Helm'd with Pendragon, with the crested Crown,
And belted with the sheath'd Excalibur,[6]
That gnash'd his iron teeth, and yearn'd for war!
Stern was that look (high natures seldom smile)

And in those pulses beat a thousand kings.
A glance! and they were husht: a lifted hand!
And his eye ruled them like a throne of light.
Then, with a voice that rang along the moor,
Like the Archangel's trumpet for the dead,
He spake--while Tamar sounded to the sea.

"Comrades in arms! Mates of The Table Round!
Fair Sirs, my fellows in the bannered ring,
Ours is a lofty tryst! this day we meet,
Not under shield, with scarf and knightly gage,
To quench our thirst of love in ladies' eyes:
We shall not mount to-day that goodly throne,
The conscious steed, with thunder in his loins,
To launch along the field the arrowy spear:
Nay, but a holier theme, a mightier Quest--
'Ho! for the Sangraal, vanish'd Vase of God!'

"Ye know that in old days, that yellow Jew,
Accursèd Herod; and the earth-wide judge,
Pilate the Roman--doomster for all lands,
Or else the Judgment had not been for all,--
Bound Jesu-Master to the world's tall tree,
Slowly to die. . . .
        Ha! Sirs, had we been there,
They durst not have assayed their felon deed,
Excalibur had cleft them to the spine!

Slowly He died, a world in every pang,
Until the hard centurion's cruel spear
Smote His high heart: and from that severed side,
Rush'd the red stream that quencht the wrath of Heaven!

"Then came Sir Joseph, hight of Arimathèe,
Bearing that awful Vase, the Sangraal!
The Vessel of the Pasch, Shere Thursday night,
The selfsame Cup, wherein the faithful Wine

Heard God, and was obedient unto Blood.
Therewith he knelt and gathered blessèd drops
From his dear Master's Side that sadly fell,
The ruddy dews from the great tree of life:
Sweet Lord! what treasures! like the priceless gems
Hid in the tawny casket of a king,--
A ransom for an army, one by one!

"That wealth he cherisht long: his very soul
Around his ark: bent as before a shrine!

"He dwelt in Orient Syria: God's own land:
The ladder foot of heaven--where shadowy shapes
In white appparel glided up and down.
His home was like a garner, full of corn,
And wine and oil; a granary of God!
Young men, that no one knew, went in and out,
With a far look in their eternal eyes!
All things were strange and rare: the Sangraal,
As though it clung to some ethereal chain,
Brought down high Heaven to earth at Arimathèe.

"He lived long centuries and prophesied.
A girded pilgrim ever and anon,
Cross-staff in hand, and, folded at his side,
The mystic marvel of the feast of blood!
Once, in old time, he stood in this dear land,
Enthrall'd--for lo! a sign! his grounded staff
Took root, and branch'd, and bloom'd, like Aaron's rod:
Thence came the shrine, the cell; therefore he dwelt,
The vassal of the Vase, at Avalon!

"This could not last, for evil days came on,
And evil men: the garbage of their sin
Tainted this land, and all things holy fled.
The Sangraal was not: on a summer eve,
The silence of the sky brake up in sound!

The tree of Joseph glowed with ruddy light:
A harmless fire, curved like a molten vase,
Around the bush, and from the midst, a voice:
Thus hewn by Merlin on a runic stone:--
Kirioth : el : Zannah : aulohee : pedah :

"Then said the shuddering seer--he heard and knew
The unutterable words that glide in Heaven,
Without a breath or tongue, from soul to soul--

"'The land is lonely now: Anathema!
The link that bound it to the silent grasp
Of thrilling worlds is gathered up and gone:
The glory is departed; and the disk
So full of radiance from the touch of God!
This orb is darkened to the distant watch
Of Saturn and his reapers, when they pause,
Amid their sheaves, to count the nightly stars.

"'All gone! but not for ever: on a day
There shall rise a king from Keltic loins,
Of mystic birth and name, tender and true;
His vassals shall be noble, to a man:
Knights strong in battle till the war is won:
Then while the land is husht on Tamar side,
So that the warder upon Carradon
Shall hear at once the river and the sea--
That king shall call a Quest: a kindling cry:
'Ho! for the Sangraal! vanish'd Vase of God!'

"'Yea! and it shall be won! A chosen knight,
The ninth from Joseph in the line of blood,
Clean as a maid from guile and fleshly sin--
He with the shield of Sarras;[7] and the lance,
Ruddy and moisten'd with a freshening stain,
As from a sever'd wound of yesterday--
He shall achieve the Graal: he alone!'"

"Thus wrote Bard Merlin on the Runic hide
Of a slain deer: rolled in an aumry chest.

"And now, fair Sirs, your voices: who will gird
His belt for travel in the perilous ways?
This thing must be fulfilled:--in vain our land
Of noble name, high deed, and famous men;
Vain the proud homage of our thrall, the sea,
If we be shorn of God. Ah! loathsome shame!
To hurl in battle for the pride of arms:
To ride in native tournay, foreign war:
To count the stars; to ponder pictured runes,
And grasp great knowledge, as the demons do,
If we be shorn of God:--we must assay
The myth and meaning of this marvellous bowl:
It shall be sought and found:--" Thus said the King.

Then rose a storm of voices; like the sea,
When Ocean, bounding, shouts with all his waves.
High-hearted men! the purpose and the theme,
Smote the fine chord that thrills the warrior's soul
With touch and impulse for a deed of fame.

Then spake Sir Gauvain, counsellor of the King,
A man of Pentecost for words that burn:--

"Sirs! we are soldiers of the rock and ring:
Our Table Round is earth's most honoured stone;
Thereon two worlds of life and glory blend,
The boss upon the shield of many a land,
The midway link with the light beyond the stars!
This is our fount of fame! Let us arise,
And cleave the earth like rivers; like the streams
That win from Paradise their immortal name:
To the four winds of God, casting the lot.
So shall we share the regions, and unfold
The shrouded mystery of those fields of air.

"Eastward! the source and spring of life and light!
Thence came, and thither went, the rush of worlds,
When the great cone of space[8] was sown with stars.
There rolled the gateway of the double dawn,
When the mere God shone down, a breathing man.
There, up from Bethany, the Syrian Twelve
Watched their dear Master darken into day.
Thence, too, will gleam the Cross, the arisen wood:[9]
Ah, shuddering sign, one day, of terrible doom!
Therefore the Orient is the home of God.

"The West! a Galilee: the shore of men;
The symbol and the scene of populous life:
Full Japhet journeyed thither, Noe's son,
The prophecy of increase in his loins.
Westward[10] Lord Jesu looked His latest love,
His yearning Cross along the peopled sea,
The innumerable nations in His soul.
Thus came that type and token of our kind,
The realm and region of the set of sun,
The wide, wide West; the imaged zone of man.

"The North! the lair of demons, where they coil,
And bound, and glide, and travel to and fro:
Their gulph, the underworld, this hollow orb,
Where vaulted columns curve beneath the hills,
And shoulder us on their arches: there they throng;
The portal of their pit, the polar gate,
Their fiery dungeon mocked with northern snow:
There, doom and demon haunt a native land,
Where dreamy thunder mutters in the cloud,
Storm broods, and battle breathes, and baleful fires
Shed a fierce horror o'er the shuddering North.

"But thou! O South Wind, breathe thy fragrant sigh!
We follow on thy perfume, breath of heaven!
Myriads, in girded albs, for ever young,

Their stately semblance of embodied air,
Troop round the footstool of the Southern Cross,
That pentacle of stars: the very sign
That led the Wise Men towards the Awful Child,
Then came and stood to rule the peaceful sea.
So, too, Lord Jesu from His mighty tomb[11]
Cast the dear shadow of his red right hand,
To soothe the happy South--the angels' home.

"Then let us search the regions, one by one,
And pluck this Sangraal from its cloudy cave."

So Merlin brought the arrows: graven lots,
Shrouded from sight within a quiver'd sheath,
For choice and guidance in the perilous path,
That so the travellers might divide the lands.
They met at Lauds, in good Saint Nectan's cell,
For fast, and vigil, and their knightly vow:
Then knelt, and prayed, and all received their God.

"Now for the silvery arrows! Grasp and hold!"

Sir Lancelot drew the North: that fell domain,
Where fleshly man must brook the airy fiend--
His battle-foe, the demon--ghastly War!
Ho! stout Saint Michael shield them, knight and knave!

The South fell softly to Sir Perceval's hand:
Some shadowy angel breathed a silent sign,
That so that blameless man, that courteous knight,
Might mount and mingle with the happy host
Of God's white army in their native land.
Yea! they shall woo and soothe him, like the dove.

But hark! the greeting--"Tristan for the West!"
Among the multitudes, his watchful way,
The billowy hordes beside the seething sea;

But will the glory gleam in loathsome lands?
Will the lost pearl shine out among the swine?
Woe, father Adam, to thy loins and thee!

Sir Galahad holds the Orient arrow's name:
His chosen hand unbars the gate of day;
There glows that heart, fill'd with his mother's blood,
That rules in every pulse, the world of man;
Link of the awful Three, with many a star.
O! blessèd East! 'mid visions such as thine,
'Twere well to grasp the Sangraal, and die.

Now feast and festival in Arthur's hall:
Hark! stern Dundagel softens into song!
They meet for solemn severance, knight and king,
Where gate and bulwark darken o'er the sea.
Strong men for meat, and warriors at the wine,
They wreak the wrath of hunger on the beeves,
They rend rich morsels from the savoury deer,
And quench the flagon like Brun-guillie[12] dew!
Hear! how the minstrels prophesy in sound,
Shout the King's Waes-hael, and Drink-hael the Queen!
Then said Sir Kay, he of the arrowy tongue,
"Joseph and Pharaoh! how they build their bones!
Happier the boar were quick than dead to-day."

The Queen! the Queen! how haughty on the dais!
The sunset tangled in her golden hair:
A dove amid the eagles--Gwennivar!
Aishah! what might is in that glorious eye!

See their tamed lion[13] from Brocelian's glade,
Couched on the granite like a captive king!
A word--a gesture--or a mute caress--
How fiercely fond he droops his billowy mane,
And wooes, with tawny lip, his lady's hand!

The dawn is deep; the mountains yearn for day;
The hooting cairn[14] is husht--that fiendish noise,
Yelled from the utterance of the rending rock,
When the fierce dog of Cain barks from the moon.[15]

The bird of judgment chants the doom of night,
The billows laugh a welcome to the day,
And Camlan ripples, seaward, with a smile.

Down with the eastern bridge! the warriors ride,
And thou, Sir Herald, blazon as they pass!
Foremost sad Lancelot, throned upon his steed,
His yellow banner, northward, lapping light:
The crest, a lily, with a broken stem,
The legend, Stately once and ever fair;
It hath a meaning, seek it not, O King!

A quaint embroidery Sir Perceval wore;
A turbaned Syrian, underneath a palm,
Wrestled for mastery with a stately foe,
Robed in a Levite's raiment, white as wool:
His touch o'erwhelmed the Hebrew, and his word,
Whoso is strong with God shall conquer man,
Coil'd in rich tracery round the knightly shield.

Did Ysolt's delicate fingers weave the web,
That gleamed in silken radiance o'er her lord?
A molten rainbow, bent, that arch in heaven,
Which leads straightway to Paradise and God;
Beneath, came up a gloved and sigilled hand,
Amid this cunning needlework of words,
When toil and tears have worn the westering day,
Behold the smile of fame! so brief: so bright.

A vast archangel floods Sir Galahad's shield:
Mid-breast, and lifted high, an Orient cruse,
Full filled, and running o'er with Numynous[16] light,

As though it held and shed the visible God;
Then shone this utterance as in graven fire,
I thirst! O Jesu! let me drink and die!

So forth they fare, King Arthur and his men,
Like stout quaternions of the Maccabee:
They halt, and form at craggy Carradon;
Fit scene for haughty hope and stern farewell.
Lo! the rude altar, and the rough-hewn rock,
The grim and ghastly semblance of the fiend,
His haunt and coil within that pillar'd home.
Hark! the wild echo! Did the demon breathe
That yell of vengeance from the conscious stone?

There the brown barrow curves its sullen breast,
Above the bones of some dead Gentile's soul:
All husht--and calm--and cold--until anon
Gleams the old dawn--the well-remembered day--
Then may you hear, beneath that hollow cairn,
The clash of arms: the muffled shout of war;
Blent with the rustle of the kindling dead!

They stand--and hush their hearts to hear the King.
Then said he, like a prince of Tamar-land--
Around his soul, Dundagel and the sea--

"Ha! Sirs--ye seek a noble crest to-day,
To win and wear the starry Sangraal,
The link that binds to God a lonely land.
Would that my arm went with you, like my heart!
But the true shepherd must not shun the fold:
For in this flock are crouching grievous wolves,
And chief among them all, my own false kin.
Therefore I tarry by the cruel sea,
To hear at eve the treacherous mermaid's song,
And watch the wallowing monsters of the wave,--
'Mid all things fierce, and wild, and strange, alone!

"Ay! all beside can win companionship:
The churl may clip his mate beneath the thatch,
While his brown urchins nestle at his knees:
The soldier give and grasp a mutual palm,
Knit to his flesh in sinewy bonds of war:
The knight may seek at eve his castle-gate,
Mount the old stair, and lift the accustom'd latch,
To find, for throbbing brow and weary limb,
That paradise of pillows, one true breast:
But he, the lofty ruler of the land,
Like yonder Tor, first greeted by the dawn,
And wooed the latest by the lingering day,
With happy homes and hearths beneath his breast,
Must soar and gleam in solitary snow.
The lonely one is, evermore, the King.
So now farewell, my lieges, fare ye well,
And God's sweet Mother be your benison!
Since by grey Merlin's gloss, this wondrous cup
Is, like the golden vase in Aaron's ark,
A fount of manha for a yearning world,
As full as it can hold of God and heaven,
Search the four winds until the balsam breathe,
Then grasp, and fold it in your very soul!

"I have no son, no daughter of my loins,
To breathe, 'mid future men, their father's name:
My blood will perish when these veins are dry;
Yet am I fain some deeds of mine should live--
I would not be forgotten in this land:
I yearn that men I know not, men unborn,
Should find, amid these fields, King Arthur's fame!
Here let them say, by proud Dundagel's walls--
'They brought the Sangraal back by his command,
They touched these rugged rocks with hues of God:'
So shall my name have worship, and my land.

"Ah! native Cornwall! throned upon the hills,
Thy moorland pathways worn by Angel feet,
Thy streams that march in music to the sea
'Mid Ocean's merry noise, his billowy laugh!
Ah me! a gloom falls heavy on my soul--
The birds that sung to me in youth are dead;
I think, in dreamy vigils of the night,
It may be God is angry with my land,
Too much athirst for fame, too fond of blood;
And all for earth, for shadows, and the dream
To glean an echo from the winds of song!

"But now, let hearts be high! the Archangel held
A tournay with the fiend on Abarim,
And good Saint Michael won his dragon-crest!

"Be this our cry! the battle is for God!
If bevies of foul fiends withstand your path,
Nay! if strong angels hold the watch and ward,
Plunge in their midst, and shout, 'A Sangraal!'"

He ceased; the warriors bent a knightly knee,
And touched, with kiss and sign, Excalibur;
Then turned, and mounted for their perilous way!

That night Dundagel shuddered into storm--
The deep foundations shook beneath the sea:
Yet there they stood, beneath the murky moon,
Above the bastion, Merlin and the King.
Thrice waved the sage his staff, and thrice they saw
A peopled vision throng the rocky moor.

First fell a gloom, thick as a thousand nights,
A pall that hid whole armies; and beneath
Stormed the wild tide of war; until on high
Gleamed red the dragon, and the Keltic glaive
Smote the loose battle of the roving Dane!

Then yelled a fiercer fight: for brother blood
Rushed mingling, and twin dragons fought the field!
The grisly shadows of his faithful knights
Perplext their lord: and in their midst, behold!
His own stern semblance waved a phantom brand,
Drooped, and went down the war. Then cried the King,
"Ho! Arthur to the rescue!" and half drew
Excalibur; but sank, and fell entranced.

A touch aroused the monarch: and there stood
He, of the billowy beard and awful eye,
The ashes of whole ages on his brow--
Merlin the bard, son of a demon-sire!
High, like Ben Amram at the thirsty rock,
He raised his prophet staff: that runic rod,
The stem of Igdrasil[17]--the crutch of Raun--
And wrote strange words along the conscious air.

Forth gleamed the east, and yet it was not day!
A white and glowing horse outrode the dawn;
A youthful rider ruled the bounding rein,
And he, in semblance of Sir Galahad shone:
A vase he held on high; one molten gem,
Like massive ruby or the chrysolite:
Thence gushed the light in flakes; and flowing, fell
As though the pavement of the sky brake up,
And stars were shed to sojourn on the hills,
From grey Morwenna's stone to Michael's tor,
Until the rocky land was like a heaven.

Then saw they that the mighty Quest was won!
The Sangraal swoon'd along the golden air:
The sea breathed balsam, like Gennesaret:
The streams were touched with supernatural light:
And fonts of Saxon rock, stood, full of God!
Altars arose, each like a kingly throne,
Where the royal chalice, with its lineal blood,

The Glory of the Presence, ruled and reigned.
This lasted long: until the white horse fled,
The fierce fangs of the libbard in his loins:
Whole ages glided in that blink of time,
While Merlin and the King, looked, wondering, on.

But see! once more the wizard-wand arise,
To cleave the air with signals, and a scene.

Troops of the demon-north, in yellow garb,
The sickly hue of vile Iscariot's hair,
Mingle with men, in unseen multitudes!
Unscared, they throng the valley and the hill;
The shrines were darkened and the chalice void:
That which held God was gone: Maran-atha!
The awful shadows of the Sangraal, fled!
Yet giant-men arose, that seemed as gods,
Such might they gathered from the swarthy kind:
The myths were rendered up: and one by one,
The Fire--the Light--the Air--were tamed and bound
Like votive vassals at their chariot-wheel.
Then learnt they War: yet not that noble wrath,
That brings the generous champion face to face
With equal shield, and with a measured brand,
To peril life for life, and do or die;
But the false valour of the lurking fiend
To hurl a distant death from some deep den:
To wing with flame the metal of the mine:
And, so they rend God's image, reck not who!

"Ah! haughty England! lady of the wave!"
Thus said pale Merlin to the listening King,
"What is thy glory in the world of stars?
To scorch and slay: to win demoniac fame,
In arts and arms; and then to flash and die!
Thou art the diamond of the demon-crown,
Smitten by Michael upon Abarim,

That fell; and glared, an island of the sea.
Ah! native England! wake thine ancient cry;
Ho! for the Sangraal! vanish'd Vase of Heaven,
That held, like Christ's own heart, an hin of blood!"

He ceased; and all around was dreamy night:
There stood Dundagel, throned: and the great sea
Lay, a strong vassal at his master's gate,
And, like a drunken giant, sobb'd in sleep!

Author's Notes

1. The hin was a Hebrew measure, used for the wine of the sacrifice.

2. The distance at which a leper was commanded to keep from every healthy person.

3. Or cauldron.

4. Routor, the red hill, so named from the heath which blossoms on the hill-side.

5. Logan, or shuddering stone. A rock of augury found in all lands, a relic of the patriarchal era of belief. A child or an innocent person could move it, as Pliny records, with a stalk of asphodel; but a strong man, if guilty, could not shake it with all his force.

6. A Hebrew name, signifying "champer of the steel."

7. The city of "Sarras in the spiritual place" is the scene of many a legend of mediaeval times. In all likelihood it was identical with Charras or Charran of Holy Writ. There was treasured up the shield, the sure shelter of the Knight of the Quest. The lance which pierced our blessed Saviour's side was also there preserved.

8. Space is a created thing, material and defined. As time is mensura motus [the measure of motion], so is space mensura loci [the measure of place]; and it signifies that part of God's presence which is measured out to enfold the planetary universe. The tracery of its outline is a cone. Every path of a planet is a curve of that conic figure: and as motion is the life of matter, the whirl of space in its allotted courses is the cause of that visible movement of the sun and the solar system towards the star Alcyone as the fixed centre in the cone of space.

9. The "Sign of the Son of Man," the signal of the last day, was

understood, in the early ages, to denote the actual Cross of Calvary; which was to be miraculously recalled into existence, and, angel-borne, to announce the advent of the Lord in the sky.

10. Our Lord was crucified with His back towards the east: His face therefore was turned towards the west, which is always, in sacred symbolism, the region of the people.

11. Our Lord was laid in His sepulchre with His head towards the west: His right hand therefore gave symbolic greeting to the region of the south; as His left hand reproached and gave a fatal aspect to the north.

12. The golden-hill, from brun, "a hill" and guillie, "golden:" so called from the yellow gorse with which it is clothed.

13. This appropriate fondling of the knights of Dundagel moves Villemarque to write, "qui me plaise et me charme quand je le trouve couché aux pieds d'Ivan, le mufle allongé sur ses deux pattes croisées, les yeux à demi-ouvert et revant." ["It pleases me and charms me when I find it [the lion] lying at the feet of Yvain, its muzzle stretched out upon its crossed paws, its eyes half open and dreaming.]

14. See Borlase, bk. iii, ch. iii for "Karn-idzek:" touched by the moon at some weird hour of the night, it hooted with oracular sound.

15. Cain and his dog: Dante's version of the man in the moon was a thought of the old simplicity of primeval days.

16. When the cone of space had been traced out and defined, the next act of creation was to replenish it with that first and supernatural element which I have named 'Numyne.' The forefathers called it the spiritual or ethereal element, coelum; from Genesis i. 2. Within its texture the other and grosser elements of light and air ebb and flow, cling and glide. Therein dwell the forces, and thereof Angels and all spiritual things receive their substance and form.

17. Igdrasil, the mystic tree, the ash of the Keltic ritual. The Raun or Rowan is also the ash of the mountain, another magic wood of the northern nations.

Owen Morgan

The Gods and Goddesses of the Druids

(from The Light in Britannia, 1890)

The seeds planted by Iolo Morganwg gave rise to many remarkable growths in the century following his time, but none was so exotic as the Druidry of the Pontypridd Gorsedd under the leadership of Owen Morgan, also known by his bardic name, Morien. Few Druids of the late nineteenth and early twentieth centuries studied a wider range of sources, or challenged the habitual thinking of the Victorian age more ruthlessly. His impact on the Druid tradition was comparable; in his own time, he had a substantial following in Wales and America, and much of the Neopagan revival of the following century bears an unacknowledged debt to Morgan's thinking. His book *The Light in Britannia,* from which the following excerpt is drawn, is among other things the first detailed account in the modern Western world of a fertility religion centered on the sexual relationship of one all-encompassing god and goddess—a formula that would later be central to Gerald Gardner's new "old religion" of Wicca.

Scholarship on the origins of Pagan mythology had come a long way since the Helio-Arkite theory championed by Edward Davies back in 1809. In Morgan's time, two principal theories had become central to scholarship on the subject. One, usually called the "Solar Theory of Religion," argued that the myths of the ancient Pagan faiths were allegorical descriptions of the seasonal cycle and the relations between the sun, the moon, and the earth. The other, usually called the "Phallic Theory," suggested that the worship of what Victorian writers primly called "the generative powers," expressed through symbols derived from the genitals of both sexes, had been the foundation of Pagan mythology.

Morgan, familiar with the scholarship on both sides, saw no contradiction between these two theories. For him, the divine life force expressed itself with equal clarity in the seasonal cycle and the process of human reproduction. Nor did he restrict the fusion between the two to Pagan religions. For him, Christianity was equally an expression of the primal religion of the life force, and he identified solar and phallic symbolism and the corresponding terrestrial and vaginal imagery throughout the Christian Bible and the traditions of the church.

The selection that follows, the second and third chapters of Morgan's first book of Druid theology, sketches out the fundamental concepts of his vision of Druidry. His debt to Edward Davies and Iolo Morganwg is clear; so, however, is the originality of his theories, and his willingness to push well beyond anyone's orthodoxy in pursuit of a Druidry he still believed could be traced in the distant past.

Further Reading:

Owen Morgan, *The Light in Britannia* (Daniel Owen and Co., 1890).

-----, *The Winged Son of Avebury* (Daniel Owen and Co., 1921).

* * *

It should be borne in mind by the reader that the Druids, in their enquiries after the Divine nature, while tracing it by the light of nature, passed beyond the boundary of the material world. They supposed, as already mentioned, the Divine nature consisted of two principles, the active and the passive, and that those principles were intellectual, omnipotent, and eternal. Beyond them no mind could go, hence to the Almighty the Druids gave the name Celi, or Keli (Concealing), and to the passive principle the name Cêd (Aid). In course of time, it appears, the Druids gave the name Cêd to that constellation (Cetus) in which the sun, between 8,000 and 10,000 years ago, appeared in the south at the winter solstice, or on December 20th, in exact Druidism. The Latins called a whale, Cetus; and the Greeks named it Der Ketos; and the world, corrupting Druidism, came to suppose a whale to be the mother of the sun, because the Druids had taught that Cêd was the Consort of the Celi Almighty. How other nations came to confound Cêd with a whale, with Cetus and Ketos, or dolphin, we know not. It is evident the Druids believed in the eternity of matter in an atomic condition, and also in the eternity of water; and that the passive, that is, the feminine, principle of the Divine nature pervaded both from eternity. Theorising as to the origin of the universe, they, like St. Paul, believed, "the invisible things of Him, from the beginning of the world, are clearly seen, being understood by the things that are made; even His eternal power;" the Druidic Philosopher took in his hand the lamp of Nature, and sought to explore the mysteries of the eternal Celi and Cêd, by its light. He imagined a period before creation began, when darkness and silence pervaded illimitable space, and when only the Celi, Cêd, and the atomic elements and water existed. Employing the figure of the relation of husband and wife to each other, to the Celi and Cêd to each other, the Druidic Philosopher theorised, that, at some inconceivable distant period, the active principle of Celi concentrated its energy in the passive principle of Cêd, and as the result of contact, as in electricity, a ball of dazzling brilliancy, called the Sun (Son) of God, bounded into space, from the nature of Cêd, and illuminated the awful gloom. Immediately after, under the sun's influence, the atomic elements began to evolve into solidity, and to it, as plastic chaos, the Druids gave the name Calen. To this day a formless mass of anything, such as a lump of butter, soap, etc., is called "Calen" in the Welsh language.

The moment after the active work of the creation of the universe had commenced by the Celi and Cêd, the Celi was named Iôn (Leader Lord); his spirit in the sun was called Iona (Dove); and Cêd (Aid)'s emanation pervading matter was named Anian (Anima Mundi). Cêd was supposed to be black, and as the consort of the Celi, but afterwards mother of the Sun, she was called y Vorwyn Ddu (the Black Virgin), mother of Venus. She was called also Latona, or Moon—Lloer in Welsh. Latona is simply another name for the great mother-goddess Cêd, the Cetus of the Latins, and the Ketos of the Greeks. The moon, six days old, is meant, resembling in shape a boat, which was used as one of the symbols of Cêd, because it was supposed she pervaded the waters of eternity before the sun and earth were "born" of her. This is the reason why the moon came to be called the Queen of Heaven, Consort of Almighty Celi. The sun itself was represented as the son of Cell and Cêd; but the High Priest of the Sun on earth, the Archdruid, was the symbol of the incarnating power of the sun and earth in spring, and the Druidic "Church" was Morwyn or Mary, the incarnated "Sister-Spouse" of the Archdruid, called Gwyddon or Odin. All seeds in the concrete were the gift of Cêd, but their fructification was performed in the spring time of the year. It seems, as said before, exceedingly probable that the Latin name for seed, Satus (Cetus), is due to this most ancient idea that all seeds came from Cêd, the Consort of the Most High God, whom the Greeks called Der Ketos.

In the description of the sanctuary of the Hebrews, which, owing to its vast importance in dealing with the origin of religious beliefs, we shall examine at some length, there appears to be a very curious mixing of figures or symbols. We have their goat's hair and ram's skin brought into curious juxtaposition. At the winter solstice the sun is in the sign of the Goat (Capri); at the vernal equinox the sun is in the sign of the Ram. It appears as if the Jews symbolised the earth at the vernal equinox, or spring, by the emblem of a goat, and the sun, at the same time, by the emblem of a Ram or Aries, which was the symbol of Jupiter Amon (Iu Hidden Father). The ancients, when the sun was in the sign of the Goat (December 22nd) would naturally symbolise the earth's Anima by the figure of a she-goat, and the Hebrews by the goat's hair of the *membrum virginalis* of the Eastern (March 21st) entrance into the Holy of Holies, seem to have dragged the goat's hair symbol from its proper place, at the winter solstice, and used it to symbolise the appendages of the *membrum virginalis* of Venus, or the earth's conceiving power in the springtime, instead, and thereby making the She-Goat to be the consort of the Ram (Aries)!

The Druids held that the passive principle of the first feminine cause, personified as Cêd, operated through her conceiving attribute, personified as Venus Geneterix, and influenced the material earth from below the earth. Cêd bears the same relation to Venus as the Almighty does to Apollo (the sun). One is regarded as agent of the great Mother, and the other of the great Father. Cêd's influence from below was supposed to be exercised by exhalations— the breathings, as it were, of the great Mother. God's influence, from above, through the sun, was supposed to be exercised by the agency of warm dew or humidity. This agent of the Father was personified by the Druids and named Nevydd Nâv Neivion. Nevydd (Heavenly), Nâv (Constructor), Neivion (Volatile or buoyant), Iôn (Leader Lord). The name, therefore, signifies: Iôn, Heavenly-Constructor-by-the-Agency-of-Humidity. As a poetical personification, Nevydd Nâv Neivion is identical with Neptune, otherwise Oceanus, the second person of the Latin trinity, and implies the sun as the transmitting cause, as warmth in dew, on June 21st.

The Cave and the Pythoness seated on the tripod astride the Cave, at Delphi, symbolised both the navel and Cêd's conceiving power, personified as Venus Geneterix. Both Apollo and Jupiter are names of the sun in spring, but the name Apollo refers to the sun as the Son of the Creator, who is referred to by the Druids as the higher Sun of the Circle of Infinitude, above the Zodiacal sun; and Jupiter is the expression of the Creator's inner and hidden creating fatherhood or Pater. The sun, in his old age at the winter solstice, described as Saturn, is often confounded with the Almighty, and Saturn, in consequence is said to be the father of Jupiter, Neptune and Pluto. The Cave at Delphi, underneath the tripod, symbolised the matrix of Cêd, herself influencing her daughter, Venus, seated on the tripod. The Priapian or middle staff of the tripod caused conception; the umbilicus, or navel, from the mother to the child or seed, continued the nourishing work until the birth. The Greek poem *Eumolpia* states the navel symbol at Delphi was sacred to the earth (Venus) and to Neptune. That signifies the warm humidity at night caused by the sun's heat in summer, nourishes, in combination with the feminine principle, the growing seeds of the earth, as the navel attached to the mother transmits by her own agency nourishment to the growing babe in her womb. Therefore, the root of each seedling is compared to an umbilicus, or navel, and it and the matrix of the seedling are agents of Venus Geneterix.

Now, the round surface of the earth above the rational horizon is the belly of Cêd, and she is the Druidic circular "church." Her centre surface to the womb is the navel and vulva symbols of the goddess Venus Geneterix, or the conceiving and nourishing powers of the earth personified. In the Welsh language the navel is called Bogel. It is compounded of Bo(d), existence, and Cêl (mutated to Gêl), concealed—concealed existence—referring to the concealed living seedling of the earth, and the living child in the womb of the mother. The centre of a wheel is likewise called Bogel, or navel, in that language. The form of the word "Navel" leads us to believe it is a Welsh word, and that it is a compound of Nâv (God constructor) and El (Haul, or Sun), and not derived from the Sanscrit *Nabhi* as scholars suppose. Celi and Cêd are one, and co-operate in the work of creation. Another figure under which the centre of the Druidic circle went was garden; the garden of the sun—the garden which the Lord himself planted. Venus, as the personified conceiving surface of the earth, is called the garden of Adonis; and the Roman Catholic Church, borrowing the figure, and substituting the Virgin Mary for Venus, describes the Virgin Mary as a garden; as a Mystical Rose; and as the Ark of the Covenant: and confounding her with Cêd describes her as the Mother of God (sun of the new year—December 25th in Julius Caesar's Calendar), and with the crescent moon, six days old, as a symbol of Cêd under the figure of a boat, describes her as the Queen of Heaven. Thus the Virgin Mary is confounded with both Cêd and with her daughter, Morwyn or Venus Marina, otherwise Venus Geneterix.

The great Druidic temple of Avebury (Ab and Rhi; God the Father—sun and Son) is a vast circle, with a very lofty bank sloping back all round the circle. At the base of the bank inside is a deep trench for holding water. Running round the outer edge of the vast arena, enclosed by the deep and broad trench, were one hundred great stones placed endways in the earth, and fixed at regular intervals from each other. This vast enclosure symbolised the round earth above the rational horizon, and the hundred stones and the circular fosse full of water symbolised the sea, and illimitable space around and beyond it. The centre of the enclosure was a symbol of the earth as the garden of Arthur (the sun), otherwise Adam (Ad Hama is Persian for the sun), Noah, &c., the gardener of the Creator. Thebes, the celebrated Egyptian city, was a similar symbol of Venus as a garden, but instead of Venus it was said to be sacred to the holy Tebah, which, it will be remembered in the Egyptian language, signifies cow. Afterwards, the cow was substituted by a second Isis, the first being Isis the great mother, precisely as Cêd is the mother of Venus. Most writers confound the two Isises—mother and daughter—with each other. We remind the reader that the enclosed garden commenced to be sacred to the cow about 4619 B.C., when the sun in spring commenced rising in the sign of the Bull of the Zodiac, and the sun, therefore, came to be regarded as a bull himself. No doubt the "hundred gates" of the City of Thebes were really one hundred stones like those at Avebury, encircling the "city," otherwise, the Garden of the Sun, the Gardener of the Almighty Celi and of Cêd.

"The voice of God," states the Druidic adage, "is heard in the voice of Anian," which is another title to Venus. We are told the Pythonic priestess sitting on the tripod which was astride the Cave at Delphi, delivered oracular utterances while under the influence of the exhalation rising from the cave. This implied the exhalation came from Cêd, the mother of Venus, whom (Venus) the priestess symbolised, and that it 'met the masculine principle of the Deity coming through the sun on the threshold of her own person, and that, as the active and passive principles, they asserted themselves intellectually in her matrix, and the fraudulent priest listened with his ear to her navel,' pretending to hear "the voice of God" in the matrix of the wife of Apollo (the sun), represented by the priestess seated, on the tripod astride the Cave, which symbolised the entrance into the vulva of Cêd (Cetus), herself the wife of Iôn, the two being the parents of both Venus and Apollo, or of the conceiving function of the earth, and the masculine principle symbolised by the middle Pryapian rod and the two others, or tripod, in contact with the person of Venus's representative. It will be seen it was Apollo, as regent, and not his father, the Most High, that was pretended to whisper in the body of the young Pythoness on the tripod at Delphi. Still, he was the Word of the Creator himself, and while the Pythoness was Venus incarnate, the priest who heard the Word was the Word incarnate, and interpreted to mortals the Divine utterances of Apollo heard in Venus incarnate. In a similar manner the Hebrew High Priest was supposed to receive from the Oracle, in the sanctuary, the oracular utterances of Jehovah, which was the Word of God, and not the Almighty Himself. Whether the Almighty did thus in ancient times speak to mortals the reader will judge for himself.

It is said of the Cave in the Temple of Apollo at Delphi that it was on the middle of the whole earth. The same thing was said of the Ark of the Covenant in the Temple at Jerusalem. All the ancient churches of Christendom are built east and west, and all the worshippers turn their faces towards the east when repeating the Creed; towards the point of the heavens from where, in spring, the sun transmits into the earth his fertilising influence as the consort of Venus (Gwen-y-Môr, otherwise Mor'wyn). The Priest and the Church are now incarnate son and daughter of Apollo and Venus, and the priest interprets what both the Church invisible and the visible are saying. Indeed, the message comes to the priest through the visible Church, the Bath-Kol, or the daughter's voice, as the Divine words came to the Delphic priest through the agency of Venus, and to the Hebrew high Priest through the agency of the Ark of the Covenant.

To each of the ancient churches there is a door facing the south, where, on December 20th, the great mother Cêd (Cetus, otherwise Der Ketos) was supposed to be stationed in the sea to receive the old sun's Divinity into her own body to shield his Divinity, represented as a flying white dove, from the Power of Darkness, which was said to have shattered the old sun's body in the heavens at noon on December 20th.

And the old sun received each year a new body in his mother, and he reappeared after forty hours, rejuvenated, as explained elsewhere. Inside, beyond the southern porch of the church is the baptismal font, which is the matrix symbol of Cêd, the personified invisible church. There the spiritual regeneration, by water and the Spirit, takes place in baptism, precisely as the old sun was supposed to be regenerated from Cêd, in the sea, on the morning of December 22nd, by the spirit of Celi, or the Creator, co-operating with his consort Cêd in the water. Outside, and directly opposite to the porch, is a cross on the top of a pyramid. On the top of the cross, called Tau, is a loop. Both cross and loop are plentiful on most ancient Egyptian monuments. That loop is the symbol of the open vulva of Cêd, prepared to receive the sun in his escape from the cross of his murderous enemy in the heavens, and through which he returns "renewed." The porch, and the cross on the pyramid opposite to it, are the said cross with the loop called Tau, and are to be understood as one figure. The middle part of a church is called the nave. Pollux states the belly of a ship is called Ketos (Cêd or Cetus) in' Greek.[5] Nave is from Navis, a ship or Ark, and implies also navel. The central mast is the navel, and it communicates with the hold, emblem of Cêd (Ketos). Cêd (earth) as a belly was represented roaming in the sea, and so does a ship with her navel in her centre. It is evident the Druids sometimes represented Cêd lying with her head westward; her belly, the round earth, above the rational horizon; her navel personified as Venus Geneterix (she that produces or causes—a mother). Her feet were represented, open like a triangle, towards the sun rising at the summer solstice and winter solstice respectively; the apex of the fork would be on the equinoctial line, opposite the virile sun in spring rising due east.

In the language spoken by the Druids, namely, the Welsh, a grave is called *Beddrôd*, which signifies, literally, circular grave. The English *Bed* seems to be derived from the first word in the Welsh compound. In Welsh, coffin is still called *Arch* (ark), and no doubt it was originally given to the stone kist (which also is Welsh), in which, anciently, the Druids placed the remains of the dead low down in the centre of the *Beddrôd*. The primitive meaning of the word *Arch* (Ark) in Welsh, is command, order, or bidding; it is also used in the sense of request or supplication;

[5] Dr. Potter's *Archaeologica Graeca*. Vol. ii, p. 128.

"Archav *arch* im' *Nav y* Dewin doethaf," (I'll supplicate a request to the Divine Constructor, the wisest diviner). It will appear, from the above, the Druids applied the name Arch to a kist or coffin to imply that death was the result of the will or command of the.Creator. The word, too, came to be employed to describe supplication, from the suppliant condition of the dying. The round tumulus is the ancient *Beddrôdd* form of a Druidic grave. Each circular tumulus is the symbol of the round earth above the rational horizon, and that symbolised, as already stated, the female protuberance—the cavity in which 'the navel (Venus) communicates with the child in the womb of Cêd. It seems that, in the ancient world, the matrix of the personified mother of Nature was regarded in two ways. Those who buried the dead with their feet towards the south— the most ancient mode of burial, as the contents of stone kists indicate—regarded the grave as the matrix of Cêd (Aid), the mother of all; those who buried the dead with the feet towards the east, regarded the interior of the circular grave as the matrix of Venus Geneterix, or Morwyn, sometimes named Gwen-y-Mor (the Holy One of the Sea, signifying the exhalation of the earth), and that the resurrection would be in the springtime. We believe it is perfectly evident that the Druids favoured the former idea. And those who observed the old custom of burying in the Nave, &c., of churches, followed the example of those who entertained the former idea when burying with feet directed south. One of the old Bards compares Owen Glyndwr to a son of Cêd, and, therefore, brother of the sun and earth:

> "Ar *drydedd*, Cymmyredd Cêd,
> Wynedd wiw a aned."
> And the third, beloved, by Cêd,
> To North Wales was given.

Cêd in modern Welsh signifies gift; and a tribute is called *Teyrn-Gêd*, signifying a gift to the king.

It appears to have been a disputed question among the ancient Druids as to from what direction the life would return into the body at the resurrection of the dead. Those who buried their dead with the feet directed southward believed life would return from Annwn with the, or in the, sun. Others, who buried with the feet towards the east, believed that life would return from Gwynva (Heaven, spring) to be reunited with the body on earth. In Welsh a tumulus is called Tomen; Tom (soil) and En (principle of life) We find the same idea in the Welsh Gwrn (Urn) in which, anciently, the Druids deposited the burnt ashes of the dead. Gwrn is an abbreviated form of Gwr-en, which signifies the Source of Life of Man, clearly a reference to the reanimation of the dust in the Urn. The same hope of a reunion with the body after death is implied by Tomen, the round mound, called also Barrow, in which the Druids buried the dead. We have many references to Tomen as the sepulchre of the dead, as—

"A gasglo domen, a gaiff un car cywir"

(He who will gather a tumulus will have one faithful friend) meaning the grave.

"Tomen Elwyddan nis gwlych gwlaw—
Mae yma Odyn o danaw:
Dyn wnai Gynon ci gwynaw."

(The Tumulus of Elwyddan is not drenched with rain, for there is a kiln under it.)

The word "Odyn," which we have translated "kiln," seems to be used as a figure for Cêd, as the original source of the perpetual exhalation of the earth as a life-giving principle.

The Druid's ecclesiastical year commences at midnight on March 20-21. That is the time of the vernal equinox, and the sun was then—at the period with which we are dealing—in the sign of the Ram (Aries)—it is now in the Fishes,—hence the Ram-Sun, as the Father's agent in the heavens, between the invisible Creator or Father and the earth (Venus), and operating on the seeds in her, the sun was, himself, often called Father by some nations, whereas he was but the transmitter of the impregnating essence. Hence the sun in spring was mistakenly called Iu Pater (Jupiter) that is Iu Father. He is represented with the horns of a ram on his head, in reference to his being then in the sigu of the Ram of the Zodiac. At the same time of the year he is called Father Hermes, or Father of harmony, by some nations, in reference to the equal day and night and the comity existing at that period of the year between the rival forces of creation and destruction; in other words, between summer and winter, or, the Divinity in the sun, and the evil existing in the darkness. It was regarded as the period of a drawn battle between Arthur (Sun) and Avagddu (Pluto). Nennius and Geoffrey have substituted for Avagddu the "Saxons." Arthur, being the Druidic title of the sun, is represented as fighting the

"Saxons" in twelve battles, instead of saying that he annually fights the Power of Darkness through the twelve signs of the Zodiac. When the sun was in the Zodiacal Rain sign, March 21, the earth was opposite in the autumnal equinox in the west, and the earth then was called Virgin (Venus), being in the sign Vfrgo of the Zodiac, that name having been given to the constellation because the earth was in the west of the heavens when the sun rose in spring in the eastern heavens in the sign of the Ram. These figures or emblems have been borrowed to set forth Christ and his Church, and they are described as the Ram, or "Lamb," and the "Bride," "the Bride of the Lamb." In ancient days, as we have already said, when the sun rose in spring in the sign of the Bull, the earth was symbolised by a Sacred Cow. To be consistent the "Bride" of the Ram should have been a "Sheep"—and the Church is actually called Ewê, but spelt "yew," the Greeks, &c., having humanised Iu Pater and humanised Aphrodite (Venus), they alluded to ram-horned Jupiter as the Consort of the "Bride," or Venus, represented as a lovely woman.

In the following we give the signs of the Zodiac as they were about the beginning of the Christian era in their relation to the sun and the earth. On March 21 the sun was in the sign of the Ram and the earth in the sign of the Virgin; on June 21 the sun was in the sign of Cancer and the earth in the sign of the Goat; on September 23 the sun was in the sign of the Virgin and the earth in the sign of the Ram; on December 2-2, the sun was in the sign of the Goat and the earth in the sign of Cancer. At the season of September the earth casts forth her ripened fruits, and what is not gathered returns to her ovary, by which the Druids meant the soil, or the earth's loam. That season was sacred to the Virgin or earth. It appears the Druids paid more attention to the four seasons than to the twelve signs of the seasons and their constellations. No doubt they had a Zodiac of their own and that the names of their Zodiacal signs exist now among the various names or titles of God in the Welsh language, for those names are names of the Deity's various emanations which come to the earth through the sun. The vernal equinox the Druids named Eilir (second generation); the summer solstice Hevin—Hâvhin—(sunny temperature); autumnal equinox (Elved) —Hel Med(i)—(gathering fruit or harvest)-; winter solstice (Arthan) (Arthur's season?)

Arthan is puzzling. It seems to be made up of Arth (Bear) and man (place). We know Arthur, or Arddir, signifies gardener or husbandman.

But Arth is Welsh for Bear. The characteristic of Arthur (sun) at the winter solstice, or from November 20th to December 20th (Druidic Mythology), is Valour in Fighting the Power of Darkness. He is the sun as Archer, armed with a bow and arrow, engaging the enemy. It seems as if the Druids had given the name to the sun before they came to the northern latitudes, and that in reference to, Arthur's fighting and terrible qualities, displayed towards the close of the solar year when face to face with his enemy, the Druids afterwards gave his name to the bear, which no doubt was often seen in Britain in remote times. Volney states the name Typhon signifies a bear, and that it also signifies, in Arabic, Deluge or Anarchy. But the Orientals, at some very remote period, in personifying the characteristics of the sun at the winter solstice, gave him the devil character, and called him Typhon, or devil, which is the third person of the Egyptian and other trinities. In Druidism, the sun is called Arthur as one of his names throughout the year. Strange that the sun's personified third emanation at the winter solstice, discredited as Typhon, a destroyer, in Egypt, should signify the sun's said emanation and also bear in that country, while in Britain the sun's personified third emanation should imply, not etymologically, but poetically, both heroism as a divine attribute, and bear. It is a striking proof that the Egyptians borrowed of the Druids, and afterwards wrongly interpreted the character of Arthur at the winter solstice.

In concluding this chapter, we say the circular church of the Druids was sacred to Cêd and her three daughter goddesses, and to the Creator and his three son gods—Alawn, Plennydd and Gwron, or as usually given, Plennydd, Alawn and Gwron.

Rudolf Steiner

The Sun Initiation of the Druid Priests and their Moon Science
(from *Man in the Past, Present, and the Future*
Rudolf Steiner Press, 1966)

Until the late nineteenth century, the Druid Revival had developed in relative isolation from the wider currents of esoteric spirituality in the Western world. Freemasonry and the mystical side of the Anglican tradition provided most of the Druid Revival's philosophical and spiritual content, while classical writings on the Druids, Welsh traditions (real and invented), and the slow evolution of a legacy of ritual and custom within the Revival movement itself, provided most of its organizational and ritual forms. By the dawn of the twentieth century, though, the resurgence of esoteric traditions in the Western world shattered that isolation and offered access to a wealth of inner perspectives that the Druids of that time were not slow to adopt.

One of the many currents drawn upon by twentieth-century Druidry was Anthroposophy, the tradition of spiritual science created by the Austrian philosopher and mystic Rudolf Steiner in the first half of the twentieth century. Steiner's work spans a remarkable range of subjects, from esoteric philosophy and practices of spiritual development through innovative approaches to education, medicine, the arts, and much more. His system of biodynamic agriculture, one of the central inspirations for modern organic farming, proved particularly attractive to Druids interested in more natural approaches to life in the world.

In several places in his voluminous writings, Steiner discussed the ancient Druids and their spiritual teachings. Intuitive perception guided by a distinctive set of spiritual disciplines provided the raw material for his understanding of the Druids of the past; the differences between the resulting vision and the older Druid Revival picture of ancient Druidry will be clear, though important similarities can also be traced. The essay included here, which has been included with the permission of the Rudolf Steiner Press, gives a good sample of Steiner's views, as well as his philosophy and literary style. The footnotes to this essay are in the original text, and were added by Steiner's editors to help clarify some of his references and ideas.

Further Reading:

Rudolf Steiner, *The Druids* (Rudolf Steiner Press, 2001)

-----, *Man in the Past, Present, and the Future* (Rudolf Steiner Press, 1966).

-----, *How to Know Higher Worlds* (Anthroposophic Press, 1994).

* * *

We have been able to penetrate to some extent into Druid culture. With the means available today to external science, people will ask in vain as to what was the real soul constitution of these Druid priests. (I might just as well call them Druid sages, for both are expressions entirely suited to that age, although of course the terms did not exist then.) What was it that lived in the impulses by means of which these Druid priests guided their people?

What we are often told as history, and what indeed often sounds terrible, always refers to events which happened when an epoch was slipping into decadence and degeneration. What I am going to describe here always refers to what preceded such an epoch of degeneration and was active when the civilization was at its height. For these *cromlechs*, these sun circles, refer in their true meaning to what existed in the epoch when the Druid mysteries were in their prime. And with the methods given us by anthroposophical spiritual science we can in a certain way even today penetrate into the whole manner and mode of working of these Druid priests. It may be said that they were everything to their people, or rather their tribe. They were the authorities for the religious requirements, in so far as one can speak of religious requirements at that time. They were the authorities for the social impulses, and also for the healing methods of that time. They united in one all that later on was distributed over many branches of human civilization.

We obtain the right perspective on Druid culture—and it is quite correct to use this expression—only when we realize that its essence is to be found in an epoch preceding that which echoes to us from the mythological ideas of the North that are connected with the name of Wotan or Odin.[6] What is associated with the name of Wotan really lies

[6] *On Odin and his mastery of the runes,* see further Rudolf Steiner, *The Mission of Folk-souls,* pp. 133ff.

later in time than this epoch when Druid culture was in its prime. In the orbit of wisdom that points to the divine name of Wotan or Odin, we must recognize something that comes over from the East, proceeding initially from Mysteries in the proximity of the Black Sea. The spiritual content of these Mysteries flowed from the East towards the West, in that certain 'colonizing' Mysteries, coming from the Black Sea and proceeding westwards, were founded in a variety of ways.

All this, however, streamed into a culture that must be called elevated in a deeper sense into a primordial wisdom, Druid wisdom. This Druid wisdom was really an unconscious echo, a kind of unconscious memory of the sun and moon elements existing on earth before the sun and moon were separated from it.[7] Initiation in the Druid mysteries was essentially a sun initiation bound up with what was then able to become moon wisdom through the sun initiation.

What was the purpose of these *cromlechs,* these Druid circles? They were there essentially for the purpose of a spiritual observation of the relationship of the earth to the sun. When we look at the single dolmens, we find that they are really instruments by which the outer physical effects of the sun were shut off in order that the initiate who was gifted with seership could observe the effects of the sun in a dark space. The inner qualities of the sun element, how these permeate the earth and how they are again radiated back from the earth into cosmic space—this was what the Druid priest was able to observe in the single *cromlechs*. The physical nature of the sunlight was shut out; a dark space was created by means of the stones fitted into the soil with a roof stone above them. In this dark space it was possible by the power of seeing through the stones to observe the spiritual nature and being of the sun's light.

Thus the Druid priest, standing before his altar, was concerned with the inner qualities of the sun element to the extent that he needed

[7] Sun and Moon here denote former stages of cosmic evolution, of which the presently existing sun and moon are a kind of physical remnant. Steiner describes a primal planet which contains spiritually all that will unfold in our Solar System ('ancient Saturn'); after the Sun and Moon stages, there follows the emergence of the physical Earth. Others among the present planets are a kind of anticipation of future spiritual-cosmic states. The whole sequence of cosmic evolution can therefore be summed up in the terms: Saturn; Sun; Moon; Earth; Jupiter; Venus; Vulcan. See the lengthy account of cosmic evolution in Steiner, Occult Science (London 1969), pp. 102-221 (also available as *An Outline of Esoteric Science* (New York 1997). Ancient cosmologies and religions often reflect knowledge of these cosmic relationships from the standpoint of the ancient instinctive clairvoyance.

the wisdom that then streamed into him—streamed in such that the wisdom still had the character of a force of nature—for the purpose of directing and guiding his people. But we must always bear in mind that we are here speaking of an age when human beings could not look at the calendar to see when it was right to sow, when this or that seed ought to be put into the soil. In those ages human beings did not look at books in order to get information about the time of the year. The only book in existence was the cosmos itself. And the letters that formed themselves into words arose from the observations of how the sun worked on one or other contrivance that had been erected. Today, when you want to know something, you read. The Druid priest looked at the action of the sun in his cromlech, and there he read the mysteries of the cosmos. He read there when corn, rye, and so on were to be sown.

These are only examples. The impulses for all that was done were read from the cosmos. The greater impulses which were needed to complete the calendar were obtained from observation within the shadow of the Druid circle. So that in this age, when there was nothing that was derived from the human intellect, the cosmos alone was there. And instead of the printing-press, human beings had the *cromlech* in order to unravel from out of the cosmos the mysteries it contained.

Reading the cosmic book in this way, human beings were therefore concerned with the element of the sun. And in distinction to the sun element they perceived the moon element. The forces which were then concentrated in the moon were once united with the earth. These forces, however, did not wholly withdraw; they left something behind in the earth. If there had been sun forces alone, only rampantly growing cells would have been created, life elements always with the character of small or large cells. Diversity, the forming element, does not emanate from the sun forces but from the moon forces working together with the sun forces. When human beings exposed themselves to all that their circles, their *cromlechs* could reveal to them, the Druid priests did not receive the mere abstract impression which we today receive, quite rightly, when in our way—that is to say, in an intellectual way—we enter into the things of the spirit. For the forces of the sun spoke to them directly. In the shadow of the sun the spiritual nature of the sun worked into them directly, and it worked far more intensely than a sense impression does on us today for it was related to far deeper forces. As the priest stood before his place of ritual, observing the nature of the sun, his breathing changed even as he observed. It became lifeless, it was blunted, it went in waves so that the one breath merged into the other. He, with all that he was as a human being through his breath, lived in the influence of the sun. And the outcome was not abstract knowledge of some kind, but something that worked in him like the circulation of the blood, pulsating inwardly through him, kindling the human part of his being down to the physical level. Yet this penetration of the physical was spiritual at the same time, and the inner stimulation he experienced was really his knowledge.

We must think of this knowledge in a very living way, as a very intense, living experience. Moreover, the Druid priest received it at certain times only. At a lesser intensity, it could be brought to life in him every day at noon. But if the great secrets were to be revealed, the priest had to expose himself to these influences at the time which we now call the season of St. John. Then there arose what might be called the great wave of his knowledge as against the lesser daily waves. And as through the sun influences, which he thus captured on earth in a particular and artificial way, he experienced what he felt as his initiation—his sun initiation—he became able also to understand the forces that had remained behind as moon forces in the earth when the moon had left it. Those were the laws of nature which he learned about under the influence of sun initiation. What was revealed on the surface of things was unimportant to him, but what welled up from below as the moon forces in the earth was important. Through the principle of initiation, whose relics are preserved in these strange monuments today, he placed himself in a state to receive knowledge. And the knowledge he gained was of all that works in nature, especially when in the sky at night-time the stars stood over the earth, and the moon travelled across the heavens.

Sun initiation gave the Druid priest the spiritual impulses that provided him with his science of nature. Our science of nature is an earth science. His was a moon science. He felt the underlying moon forces as they ray forth in the plants from the depths of earth, as they work in wind and weather and so forth. He felt the forces of nature not in the abstract way that we do today with our earth science. He felt them in all their living characteristics.

And what was thus livingly revealed to him he experienced as the elemental beings living in the plants, in the stones, in all things. These elemental beings, having their dwellings in trees and plants and so forth, were enclosed in certain bounds. But they were not those narrow bounds that are set for human beings today. They were far wider. His science of nature being a moon science, the Druid priest perceived how the elemental beings can grow and expand into gigantic size. This is where his knowledge of the Jötuns, the giant beings, came from.[8] When he looked into the roots of a plant beneath the soil, where the moon forces were living, he found the elemental being in its true bounds. But these beings were always endeavouring to grow outwards, gigantically. When the kind of elemental beings who lived beneficially in the roots expanded into giants, they became the giants of the frost whose outward symbol is the frost and who live in all that sweeps over the earth as the destructive hoar frost and the other severe forces that are characterized by frost. The loosened root forces of the plants worked destructively when they lived within the frost as it swept with its giant forces over the earth, whereas in the root the same forces worked productively and beneficially. And what worked in the growth of the leaves too could grow to giant size. Then it lived as a giant elemental being in the murky storms that swept over the earth with all that they contained in certain seasons—the pollen of the plants, and so forth. And what lives gently, modestly, one might say, in the flower forces of the plants becomes all-destroying fire when it grows to giant size.

Thus in the weather processes the Druid priests saw the forces of beings expanded to giant size—the same forces that lived within their right limits in the kingdoms of nature. The chosen places where we find these old heathen centres of ritual show that what they received through the sun circles and the croinlechs was developed into earth knowledge. That is how such knowledge arose. They developed it so as to be able properly to observe the mysterious workings of wind and weather as they swept over the earth—the working together of water and air, the hoar frost oozing forth from the earth, the melting dew. It was through sun initiation and the knowledge of the moon beings that there arose this most ancient conception which we find at the very foundations of European culture.

[8] That which springs from the body of the earth,' says Steiner (in contrast to what comes down from the cosmos into earthly life), 'is described in Norse mythology as belonging to the realm of the giants.' Steiner, *The Mission of Folk-souls*, p. 171.

Thus the Druid priest read and deciphered the cosmic secrets which his institutions of the sun initiation enabled him to gain from the cosmos. Stimulated by the sun initiation, he thus gained his knowledge from his science of moon-related nature. All of social and religious life was closely related to this. Everything which the priest told the people was based on the spiritual foundations of this element in which they lived. We see it best of all in what the Druid priests possessed as a science of healing. They saw on the one hand the elemental beings contained within their bounds in the various growths and products of the mineral and especially of the plant kingdom. Then they observed what happened to the plants when these were exposed to frost, exposed to the influences which the giants of the storm and wind carry through the airy spaces, or exposed to the seething fire-giants. They studied what the giants of frost and hoar frosts, the giants of the storm, the fire-giants would do to plants if released and set free. At length they came to the point of taking the plants themselves, and imitating within certain limits all that was indicated in outer nature as the influence of the giants. They subjected the plants to certain processes, to the freezing process, the process of burning, the process of binding and solution. The Druid priests said to themselves: 'Observing this world of nature, we see the destructive working of the giants, of frost and storm and fire. But we can take from these giants, from the Jötuns, what they spread so awkwardly and clumsily over the world; we can wrest it from them; we can harness once more within narrow limits these liberated forces of the moon.'

This they did. They studied what takes place in the thawing earth, in storm and wind, in the fierce, seething heat of the sun. All this they applied to the sun characteristics which lived in the plants and which they themselves received in their initiation. And in so doing they created their remedies, their healing herbs and the like, all of which were based upon the fact that the giants were reconciled with the gods. In those times each single remedy bore witness to the reconciliation of the opponents of the gods with the gods themselves.

What human beings received under the direct influences of sun and moon in the form offered by nature itself was food. A medicine, on the other hand, would be something that human beings themselves created by continuing nature beyond itself, harnessing the giant force to place it in the service of the sun.

We must imagine Druid civilization spread out over a great part of northern and central Europe about 3,000 or 3,500 years ago. There was nothing remotely similar to writing. There was only the cosmic script. Then this was infused from the East—to begin with from a Mystery centre in the region of the Black Sea—with what ordinary consciousness now considers as an insoluble riddle of Norse mythology associated with the name of Wotan. For what is Wotan? The Mystery from which the Wotan culture proceeded was a Mercury Mystery, a Mystery that supplemented the impulses of sun and moon with the impulse of Mercury. We might say that that old civilization existed in the innocence and simplicity radiated by sun and moon, untouched by what was imparted to human beings through the Jupiter impulses. Only away in the East these Jupiter impulses were already present. From there they now spread in a colonizing influence towards the West. Wotan-Mercury carried his influence westwards.

This also throws light upon the fact that Wotan is described as the bringer of runes, of the runic art of writing. He was the bringer of what human beings expressed at a base primitive level of intellectual thinking as a way of deciphering the universe. The Wotan impulse is the very first appearance of intellectual thinking. Thus one might say that the character of Mercury, of Wotan, was now added to the characters of sun and moon.

Wherever the Wotan impulse came fully to expression, it influenced everything that was present from earlier experiences. Everything received a certain impulse from the Wotan element. For Druid culture has a special secret. We know that everywhere things arise that do not belong there, just like weeds grow on cultivated land. We might say that Druid culture only recognized the sun and moon qualities as the good plants of civilization, and if, leaping forward as it were to a later time, the intellectual element began at that time already, they treated it as a weed.

Among the many remedies the Druids had, there was one against the Mercury quality of deep thought and introspection. Strange as it may seem to us today, they had a remedy against this habit of sinking into one's inner being, or, as we say, of reflecting on one's own salvation. The Druids wanted human beings to live with nature and not to sink into themselves, and they regarded as sick and ill anyone who even attempted to express anything in symbols or the like unless it was merely to imitate the things of nature in a primitive form of art. Anyone who made symbols was diseased and had to be healed. Yes, my dear friends, if we with all our present knowledge were transposed into Druid culture, we should all be sent to hospital to be cured.

And now the Wotan civilization brought this very illness from the East. The Wotan civilization was indeed felt as an illness. But with a power grown truly great and gigantic, it also brought what had formerly appeared as an abnormality, an unhealthy introspection. Into the midst of what had formerly been taken only from the cosmic script, it introduced the rune. So that human beings now transferred their intellectual element into the symbols they made. The Wotan civilization introduced everything that was experienced as Mercury culture. Thus it is no surprise that what proceeded from the Wotan culture—distilled from the best forces it contained, namely, the being of Baldur, the sun being—was perceived as something not linked with life but with death. Baldur had to go to Hel, into the dark forces of death, the dwelling-place of death.[9] Moreover, as we can see from the traditions of the *Edda*, human beings to begin with reflected most not on the question of how Baldur, son of the Wotan forces, should be freed from Hel—for this is really a later idea—but on the question of how he should be healed. And finally they said: we have many means of healing, but for Baldur, the intelligence proceeding from the runes of Wotan, there are no remedies and it can only lead to death.

Thus we see once more what I have described from so many different aspects in the study of human evolution. In ancient times, human beings in their instinctive knowledge knew nothing of the significance of death; human beings remembered their pre-earthly life and knew that death is only a transformation. They did not feel death as an incision any deeper than this. Above all, there was no such thing as the tragedy of death.

This only entered with the Mystery of Golgotha, which became, indeed, redemption from the fear of death. In the Baldur legend, one can see most clearly how, with the entry of the intellectual element, there arises that mood of soul which expects death; and one can see what thus entered into human evolution. What was therefore experienced with the

[9] See further *The Mission of Folk-souls*, pp. 148ff.

death of Baldur, who could not rise again, was only healed again in soul and spirit when the figure of Christ, who could rise from death, was set against that.

It is wonderful how an understanding of the Christ impulse was prepared in the North through the influence of the Mercury forces on the sun and moon forces. In Baldur, the god who falls into death and cannot rise again, we see the forerunner in the North of Christ, who also falls victim to death but who can rise again because he comes directly from the sun. Baldur, on the other hand, the sun force coming from Wotan, is the sun force reflected back by Mercury, shining out from the symbols which human beings create with their intellect.

Thus we see how all these things evolved in the northern regions, where human beings lived in and read the script of the cosmos, seeking their religious, social and medical ideas in the cosmos, until at a later stage they passed over to live with the earth forces. From his stone of sacrifice, the Druid priest observed the configuration of the shadow of the sun and read what appeared in the shadow, representing the spiritual aspect of the sun. Then we approach the time when the sun being that had been caught up, we might say, in the *cromlechs* is drawn in abstract lines called rays. We approach the time when the relationship of what lives in root and leaf and blossom with what lives in frost and wind and fire is recognized at most in a chemical sense. Both giants and elemental beings are transformed into 'forces of nature'. And yet our forces of nature are no more than the giants of ancient times. Only, we are not aware of the fact and feel immensely superior. It is a straight line of development from the giants to the forces of nature. These are their latter-day children. Human beings, who today live in a highly artificial—that is, an unoriginal—civilization, cannot but be deeply moved when they look at these scant relics of the Druid age. It is like seeing the ancient ancestors of our present time.

Lewis Spence

Druid Teachings and Initiations

(from *The Mysteries of Britain*, 1928)

A poet of some popularity and a recognized authority on Native American mythology, Lewis Spence was also for many years one of the most influential writers in the Western revival of esotericism and occult traditions. Where Rudolf Steiner influenced the Druid Revival from outside its ranks, Spence was a participant in the Revival, and his insights into Druidry drew on an extensive knowledge of the older literature of the Revival. Edward Davies, Iolo Morganwg, and Owen Morgan are among the most significant influences on his work.

The form of Spence's Druidry is thus familiar to anyone who reads the literature of the last century and a half of the Revival. The content, though, had changed. Spence was actively involved in the same Western esoteric revival that helped shape Rudolf Steiner's career; like Steiner, he was for some years a member of the Theosophical Society, the organization that jumpstarted the rebirth of Western occultism, and like Steiner he withdrew from the Society as that organization turned toward Asian traditions.

Unlike Steiner, whose innovative spirituality combined German Rosicrucian teachings with his own intuitive insights, Spence in his latter years found the basis for his spiritual practice and vision in the traditions of the Druid Revival. The results included three influential books on Druidry that remained standard reading in many Revival circles straight through the twentieth century. *The History and Origins of Druidism* provided an overview of the tradition; *The Magic Arts in Celtic Britain* explored the records of magical practice, and offered raw material for practical occultists interested in reinventing a Druid magic; while *The Mysteries of Britain* drew an appealing picture of Druidry as an initiatory path suited to modern people.

In many ways the selection that follows, chapters 8 and 9 from Spence's *The Mysteries of Britain*, sums up the heritage of the Revival as it had been handed down to Spence's time. That heritage remained committed to the claim that the spirituality of the Revival reflected the original practices of the ancient Druids, and wields Spence's considerable powers of scholarship and rhetoric in the service of that claim. It remained for another generation of Druids to take the next step, and recognize that a Druid spirituality of nature could draw its validity from its relevance to the present and future, rather than on any claim concerning the past.

Further Reading:

Lewis Spence, *The History and Origins of Druidism* (Rider and Co., 1947)
-----, *The Magic Arts in Celtic Britain* (Rider and Co., 1945)
-----, *The Mysteries of Britain* (Rider and Co., 1928)

* * *

The Teachings

It is now necessary to turn to the higher aspects of the Secret Tradition of Britain as enunciated in its most distinguished document, that Barddas already described in a former chapter, only the superficial philosophy of which was touched upon. In the first place it will be necessary to satisfy ourselves regarding the notion of deity as there set forth.

God, we are told, is three things, and cannot be otherwise: coeval with all time; co-entire with all essence; and co-local with all mental purpose. He is inconceivable and incomprehensible, the greatest and the most immeasurable of all that are together in place.

But of what god are these statements made? It seems probable that the Welsh bards of later times recognized the God of Christianity as the supreme divinity, but there are not wanting allusions to a certain Hu whose nature has already been touched upon.

Now concerning this Hu there is a considerable diversity of opinion. "The meaning of Hu," explains a note to Barddas, "is that which is apt to pervade, or to spread over. It is used as an epithet of the Deity, in reference to His omniscience, and is not unfrequently to be met with as such in the works of the Bards." The bard Cynddelw identifies him with Jesus, and the annotator ventures the opinion that he was identical with the Heus of Lactantius and the Hesus of Lucan, described as a god of the Gauls.

Canon MacCulloch regards him as probably "an old culture-god of some tribes," and adds that the triads referring to him are of later date. Rhys speaks of him as a "British Hercules", and thinks that he was superseded by Arthur. In fact, very little notice has been taken of him by the official mythologists. But it is obvious from the constant reference to him in the triads that he was a personage of importance, a culture-god, skilled in the arts of husbandry, a law-giver, probably of solar origin. He is alluded to as the "supreme proprietor of the isle of Britain," and as "a bull dwelling in a sacred stall," a statement which seems to equate him with Osiris. Undoubtedly he is the individual alluded to in the poem of "The Spoils of Annwn" as "the brindled ox with the thick head-band, having seven-score knobs in his collar." That such an animal was kept by the Druids as a symbol of this deity in the same manner as the priests of Egypt kept the Apis bull as the representative of Osiris, is proved by a passage in the same poem "They know not what animal they (the Druids) keep of the silver head." The name of this bull or ox seems to have been Elzen, judging from a poem by Merlin, and its slaughter by the pagan Saxons is deplored by that magus.

This not only equates Hu to some extent with Osiris, but associates his worship with that of Mithraism and the bull-cults of the Mediterranean area. Now the Gaulish god Esus, or Hesus, mentioned previously and alluded to by Lucan, is depicted on an altar found at Paris as a woodman cutting down a tree, and on the same altar a bull is represented. There is a similar altar at Trèves. Pre- Roman bronze bulls have been found at Hallstadt in Austria, and at La Tène. "Many place-names in which the word Laruos occurs, in Northern Italy, the Pyrenees, Scotland, Ireland, and elsewhere," says Canon MacCulloch, "suggest that the places bearing these names were sites of a bull-cult." He adds that possibly the animal tended to become the symbol of a god, a tendency perhaps aided by the spread of Mithraism, and states that "a later relic of the bull-cult may be found in the carnival procession of the Boeuf Gras at Paris." We will also recall the sacrifice of bulls at Gairloch and elsewhere in Britain in later times.

That Hu was a culture-god symbolized by the bull (as was Osiris) is therefore clear enough, and that he had a common origin with the Egyptian god in North-West Africa is also extremely probable. Frazer, in a note to the Golden Bough, mentions the discovery of a Druidic grave in North Africa, complete with implements, and Westermarck provides many evidences of the survival in Morocco of the rite of Bealtainn, a ceremony for the annual purification of cattle by passing them through the sacred fire or smoke.

Now we are informed in Barddas that God alone can endure the eternities of Ceugant, and as we know the three circles of the Keltic psychic progression to have been depicted in solar form, as shown on the early British coins, and, according to some, in the stone circles at Avebury and elsewhere, Ceugant, the dwelling of the Most High Hu, was probably regarded as the sun itself, Gwynvyd, the happy dwelling of immortal beings, as its outer rim, and Abred, as the outer darkness. But the drawing of the psychic scheme in Barddas shows Abred as the central figure, Gwynvyd as the outer, and Ceugant as corresponding to the rays of the luminary. It may thus be that Abred or Annwn was regarded as a fiery solar abyss wherein all things germinated, a torrid and burning alembic of life. But as Abred is obviously the earth-plane, some confusion may have taken place between it and Annwn in the mind of the draughtsman of this plan. In all probability the three psychic planes of man were Annwn, the place of germinal existence, Abred, the earth-plane, and Gwynvyd, the plane of justified spirits. Ceugant, the plane of God, was unapproachable and reserved for deity alone. That some confusion certainly did exist is clear from two statements in the Book of Derwyddiaeth, placed side by side, one of which bears out that the three states of existence of living beings are "the state of Abred in Annwn; the state of liberty in humanity, and the state of love, that is Gwynvyd in Heaven." While the other lays down as the three necessities of all animated existence, "beginning in Annwn; progression in Abred; and plenitude in Gwynvyd".

The three necessary obligations of man are set forth as suffering, change, and choice, and his equiproportions as Abred and Gwynvyd, necessity and liberty, evil and good, to which he has the power of attaching himself as he pleases. This is no philosophy of fatalism, and as such is differentiated from the Eastern systems and marks the growth and acceptance of the Western doctrine of human freewill, which, indeed, is insisted on. Yet there are obvious associations with the doctrine of escape, as observed in the Oriental systems, for we are told that Man does "escape" from Abred and Cythraul (evil) to Gwynvyd through forgetfulness and death. Thus former states cannot be recalled in the happier sphere, although elsewhere it is explicitly set forth that it is essential for perfectitude that they should be.

There are thus the three planes and no others in our early British mystical philosophy, not seven as in the Eastern. Nor does it seem to have been assumed that man has numerous psychic bodies, as in the Eastern philosophies, although, as has been shown, he is composed of various "materials," or elements.

In the triads of Bardism is an interrogatory which throws considerable light on the early British notions concerning the faculties of the soul. To the question "What is conscience?" the reply is "The eye of God in the heart of man, which sees everything that is perceptible in its right form, place, time, cause, and purpose." Reason is explained as the revolving of the conscience, whilst it contemplates by means of sight, hearing, and experience whatever comes before it, and understanding is described as the working of the conscience whilst it exercises its energies and might for the purpose of acquiring knowledge.

In this questionary God is described as the life of all lives, the spirit of God as the power of all powers, and the providence of God as the order of orders and the system of systems. Truth is the science of Wisdom preserved in memory by conscience, and the soul is the breath of God in a carnal body, while Life is the might of God.

In *The Sentences of Bardism*, written by Ieuan ab Hywel Swrdwal, a poet who flourished about 1450, a good deal of insight is given into the Bardic philosophy of existence. It is indeed strange to find in the Wales of this particular era so much of profound thought as is contained in these sentences, sentiments indeed, which, if they had been known to the doctors of Elizabethan London, might have caused them to revise their opinions of contemporary Keltic civilization! Let us glance briefly at a few of these aphorisms.

That does not but exist, we are told, from which a greater amount of good than evil can be produced, since it cannot be otherwise in virtue of God's power, wisdom, and love. Of that which is neither good nor bad, neither the existence nor non-existence is safe for man, for nothing in reason is known of it. Others say that it is the material of everything. However, there is only God that knows its good and evil, its utility and inutility, whether the good or evil be the greater. Where a great good to all, without harm to anyone, can be comprehended, it cannot be but that it is in existence, since otherwise the three principal attributes of God, namely, knowledge, wisdom, and mercy, would not stand without being opposed by distress and necessity "therefore Bardism is true."

Truth cannot be had from that in which every truth cannot consist, and which will not consist in every truth, for truth cannot be had from what will contradict or withstand that which is true. The very power of God, we are further informed, is a guarantee that the best of all things are in existence.

"The Ten Commandments of the Bards" found in the Blue Book have obviously been interpenetrated by Christian thought. For example, we are told to keep Sunday religiously and to beware of worshipping idols, which shows that the tendency to worship idols was actually present. But certain passages betray the Keltic mentality. That, for example, concerning the three deliverances—'there will be no transgression which will not be set right, no displeasure which will not be forgiven, and no anger which will not be pacified, and thence will be obtained the three excellences: first, there will be nothing ill-favoured which shall not be adorned; secondly, there will be no evil which shall not be removed; thirdly, there will be no desire which shall not be attained. And from reaching this mark: in the first place, there can be nothing which shall not be known; there can be no loss of anything beloved which shall not be regained; thirdly, there can be no end to the Gwynvyd which shall be attained. And it is not necessary that there should be an understanding might and love other than these things, with the careful performance of what is possible."

These latter sentiments particularly display a Keltic bias. Possibly there is nothing Biblical about them, and there is certainly nothing of the hard, dry theology of the Teuton in the yearning beauty they contain. The core of their philosophy seems to imply that, the struggle of the soul notwithstanding, all will be well in the end. They reiterate the age-long cry of the poet that beauty cannot die, that somewhere, even though occluded by clouds, it awaits the spirit at the end of its journey, and that despite human agony, there is certainty of gain at the conclusion of the struggle. This is not fatalism, nor has it anything to do with the ugly philosophy of punishment which seems to have a peculiarly Judaic origin and to have arisen through a survival of early barbarous beliefs. It is indeed the philosophy of joy, which shines through all Keltic art, however shadowed it may seem in places.

Wherefore, then, the struggle of man? It seems to me that in our native British mysticism the idea of struggle, of evolution, is stressed more as a natural and necessitous course than as a series of phases through which the human soul must pass, almost, indeed, as an act of psychic growth, rather than a definite rule which it must observe. The Oriental philosophies seem to indicate that it is necessary for man, if he would develop in psychic stature, to tread a certain path definitely laid out for him, a path which may take him aeons of ages ere it lead him to the ultimate. At practically every step of this path choice is afforded him to tread rightly or wrongly; but the mysticism of our fathers, or so it seems to me, lays less of stress on choice. Man must progress whether he would or not. True, he may fall back into Abred time and again, but ultimately he must gain Gwynvyd. True, there is a belief associated with the Eastern philosophies that in the end all life must return to God, but not only does the process seem to be very much more prolonged, but it does not seem to be so mechanical. To my way of thinking Barddas postulates a species of evolutionary machine in which, from a low form of existence, the soul is slowly raised to the heights of Gwynvyd, rather than a specific scheme to which the conduct of man is chiefly contributory. Not that in the British system it is not contributory, but rather that man appears, in virtue of it, to receive more assistance from supernatural powers. It is, as I have said, rather that he seems to be slowly born through the planes of being into the light of Gwynvyd, than that he arrives there entirely through his own volition and conduct.

It is obvious, too, that enormous stress is laid upon the value to the soul of man of scientific knowledge in this development, that it is indeed the lever by which he raises himself from one plane to another. This alone is proof, in its practical thrust, of a Western origin. Good deeds doubtless assist man, but without a knowledge of the secret sciences he may be retarded. It looks, indeed, as if the process were hastened through such knowledge, and therein probably lay the desire for initiation, that is, it would appear that, given this initiation, man would be assured of entrance into the plane of Gwynvyd, and that without it he might possibly fall back into Abred. This scheme of things notably resembles the Egyptian idea that without a knowledge of The Book of the Dead the human soul could not hope to gain paradise.

So loosely are the tenets of our ancient mysticism set down that it is extremely difficult to systematize them. They are, for the most part, cast into Triads or groups of three, after the manner of the Welsh bards, and frequently in an arbitrary fashion though never altogether incoherently. The juxtaposition of some of these aphorisms, too, is often irrelevant. It is therefore necessary to cull from the mass that which seems important and to the point.

The three laws of man's actions are set forth as necessity, choice, and judgement, according to what is possible, for ever in the circle of Gwynvyd. There are three things, we are told, which are to be found everywhere: God, truth, and the Circle of Gwynvyd, and to know this is to be united with them and to have deliverance from Abred. There are again three things the magnitude of which cannot be known, the Circle of Ceugant, the plane of the existence of God alone, the length of eternity, and the love of God.

The three principal vigours of man are set forth as Awen, affection, and intellect, from which triad all goodness proceeds. All the, efforts of man should be in unison with that which is in the Circle of Gwynvyd. There are three grades of animation:

God in Ceugant, spiritualities in Gwynvyd, that is "Heaven", and corporalities in Abred, that is in water and earth. Here we have the Circle of Gwynvyd absolutely identified with the Christian Heaven, and Abred with earth rather than Annwn. A note to this passage states that: "Some persons profess to discover indications of the doctrine of Abred or the metempsychosis in the Holy Scriptures, thus they say that the passage in Job (cli. xxxiii, v. 29-30): 'Lo, all these things worketh God oftentimes with Man, to bring back his soul from the Pit, to be enlightened with the light of the living,' ought, according to the Hebrew, to be rendered: 'Lo, all these things worketh God with Man, and thrice to bring back his soul from the Pit'." This may be so, yet still, as I have said, I find nothing of the doctrine of transmigration in our ancient mysticism, rather that of evolution, or psychic development.

We come next to the three conditions to which the nature of existence and animation is subject efficient, as with God and His powers; effected, as is the case with finite vitalities and mixed beings; and non-effective, that is what was not made "and will not make", as space, absolute time, mortality, and darkness. These conditions are postulated in another way as follows: "What has not been made, that is God; what has been made, that is the living and motion; what has not been made, that is the motionless dead." It is curious to find the theory of relativity introduced into these ancient triads, where the existence of absolute time and space are denied—another instance in which, I take it, the Welsh bards were greatly in advance of thought of contemporary Europe.

The three stabilities of oneness are given as universality, for there can be no two kinds of one universality, infinity, for there can be no limits to one whole, nor can anything be whole which is not universal nor omnipresent, for that is not one whole which is not all-comprehensive; and immutability, for it is impossible that there should be one conjunctive, universal, entire and all-existent, otherwise than they are; therefore there can be no God but from fundamental and universal oneness.

The manner in which the end of Abred or the earth-plane will be accelerated is set forth not so much prophetically as with an air of scientific exactitude. Three things, we are told, will accelerate its conclusion: diseases, fighting, and becoming eneidvaddeu, which has already been explained as a state of being legally punished for offence. But "eneidvaddeu" in this instance implies a state of punishment which has been justly and reasonably brought about, for example, by war or conflict carried out in a just cause. We are told that it was for the benefit of and out of mercy to living beings that God ordained the mutual fighting and slaughter which takes place among them, a doctrine which, we will remember, was stressed with no little weight by Wordsworth. However the modern mind recoils from such a belief, it seems to have commended itself to our British ancestors as a short cut from the miseries of the plane of Abred, and this strengthens my theory that the philosophy set forth in Barddas by no means found its origin in any of the Oriental systems, which not only prohibit slaughter and regard the taking of life as blasphemy, but rather look upon life as a painful experience to be overcome more by a good train of thought than anything else. Moreover the doctrine in question shows most distinctly its Druidic origin, for the Druids, although at times they seem to have intervened in tribal wars, at others certainly inspired their people to combat. But before we blame them for the creation of a doctrine which appears to us barbarous and inhuman, let us remember that even within our own times it has been, preached, and not without effect.

The basic foundations of Abred, we are told, are the predominance of opposition and Cythraul over prosperity and amendment, necessary lawlessness and death ensuing from the mastery of Cythraul and from the system of deliverance which is according to the love and mercy of God. Here we find the state of Abred set forth as a dreadful necessity, a part of a psychic evolution which must be borne. It is clear that from this philosophy man is expected to realise that life on the earth-plane can never be a happy experience, that he must be resigned to it. This might seem at the first glance similar to the Eastern idea of bearing existence with resignation, but this is rather belied by the preceding statement that such a condition may be shortened by strife and slaughter.

The three necessities of the state of Gwynvyd, the spiritual plane, are the predominance of good over evil, memory reaching from Annwn, and hence perfect judgement and understanding without the possibility of doubting or differing, and lastly superiority over death. This consists in power derived from knowing the whole of its cause and the means of escaping it, and hence everlasting life. It has often seemed strange to commentators on ancient dogma that the idea of the survival of memory in the last phase of psychic existence should be so greatly stressed. One wonders precisely what the value of such recollection might be, unless it is to render the soul more perfect by providing it with the lessons of experience in full. I am inclined to think that it signifies that there can be no real happiness without perfect knowledge and experience, that happiness in a higher state is actually relative to the suffering endured in lower phases of existence. Again, the spell, so to speak, by aid of which man escapes from death, triumphs over it, consists in power derived from knowing the whole of its cause. That is, the secrets of death must be plumbed and accurately understood before the soul can triumph over it. This throws some light on the allegory of the descent of Hu, or his other form Arthur, into the depths of Annwn. Not only did he penetrate thither for the purpose of seeking the cauldron of inspiration, the source of life, which was naturally located in the gloomy abyss whence life in its early forms was thought to have sprung, but he also sought to gauge the secrets and mysteries of death, the opposite of life, and that this knowledge was part of the initiation of the brotherhood of the Secret Tradition we can scarcely doubt.

We have little data to assure us that the belief in such a secret was held by other ancient brotherhoods. As regards the Osirian tradition, Osiris was certainly Lord of the Dead, but that the priests of his cult regarded it as essential to probe into the mysteries of death I can discover no evidence. The same holds good of the Eleusinian mysteries and others. The place of death, the Underworld, was to the hierophants of these cults also the place of the beginning of life, at least of cereal life, to which they likened that of mankind. At the same time the initiates must pass through the place of death to reach life. The embalmers of Egypt were wont to imitate the hues and colours of life in the corpse by painting its face red and by giving it artificial eyes. However, the early Osirian alchemy appears to have excogitated a system of thought by which out of dead metals and earths a species of psychic elixir was developed. In some religions, too, we observe the idea that life may emanate from death. The idea of resurrection was known to the Egyptians and is still upheld by the Christian religion, and although this is by no means the same thing as the conquest of death by the discovery of its secrets, it is nevertheless an assertion that death can be conquered.

But we find in both the Egyptian and Christian religions the powers of death definitely overcome by Osiris and Christ, and in at least one Central American religion, that of the Quiches of Guatemala, a similar allegory exists. Death and Hell are overcome by these champions, it is implied, either by material or spiritual weapons. In the allegory of Arthur's descent into Annwn we have a similar instance of the Harrying of Hell. The heroes descend into Annwn and some even do not return. Annwn, in the allegory, was therefore conquered by force of arms, material or spiritual, and this also, we may take it, formed part of the theatric pantomime of initiation through which the neophyte must pass when he became a member of the Brotherhood of the Secret Tradition.

On the whole, then, we cannot deny a veridically British character to the philosophy set forth in Barddas. Although certain of its principles appear to have much in common with the mystical philosophies of the East, there is assuredly contained in it a strong leaven of Western thought and idealism, which renders it worthy of the consideration of British mystics as enshrining much that is of extraordinary value to the race from a psychological point of view, and which should not be lightly cast aside.

Why, indeed, should we not strive to study and preserve the mysticism of our early ancestors rather than seek in the records of the East for guidance in things hidden and secret? Are the tenets set forth in the records and chronicles of our own island less lofty or less worthy of consideration, are they not more in consonance with the tendency and genius of British mentality than the mystic systems of the Orient? Are we not carried away in this regard by the hallucination of a specious Oriental glamour heightened by spurious imagination and sham romance? The attitude is on the same plane as that which prefers Continental musical talent to our own, and which has resulted in the decay and almost the death of British music, formerly a flourishing institution. Is there not something weakly, supine, and unimaginative in the fashion which strains for a distant enchantment and can discover none at its own portals? Wherefore has British mysticism been permitted to languish for generations to the behoof of an exotic tradition which is not superior to it and is of no prior authority?

Let the reproach be removed, let us address ourselves to the serious consideration and rehabilitation, the rescue and restoration of the noble Secret Tradition of our fathers. I do not mean to infer that we should entirely neglect other traditions. That would be as foolish as to despise our own. But I emphatically believe that it would be eminently for our psychic advantage to restore and rebuild the ruined edifice of British mysticism, as rendered conformable to Christian belief by the bards, who were the conservators of the ancient Secret Tradition. In its tenets, as purified by them, is little of the barbarous which only too plainly reveals itself in the systems of the East, and which has, therefore, rendered them unacceptable to thousands of British people as suspect of diabolism and the horrors of the lower cults which indubitably cling to them. As set forth in Barddas there is nothing in our native mysticism which the most orthodox Christian could not accept. It is, in a word, the native British mystical thought applied to the Christian ideal. The scattered stones are to our hands. Some, indeed, are lost, but search, can assuredly restore them. Let them be unearthed, and the Temple of the British Secret Tradition be reedificated. These are days of restoration, when men in every land, tired of the cosmopolitan with its wearisome affectations, are inquiring into the foundations and origins of those things which have developed their own particular environment. "Far fowls have fair feathers," says the old proverb, illustrating a human infirmity which enlightened men are beginning to realize only too well.

As a patriotic Scotsman and Briton, I would appeal to English,

Scottish and Welsh mystics not to let that die easily which must inevitably be to us all of the utmost value. We Britons are a "peculiar people," rapt and divided from our Continental neighbours by tendencies of thought exceptionally remote and individual. In that lies our greatness. And so it was in the beginning. This sacred isle constituted a laboratory of thought and mystery recognized by the races of the Continent as unspeakably hallowed and inscrutable. Can we, if we admit and encourage alien and by no means harmless esoteric systems, do so without damage unspeakable to the psychical integrity of our island? We assuredly cannot. The system to our hands is not only of British origin, but it is more susceptible of response to British mentality than any exotic system, it is capable of such a degree of restoration as may render it of much greater opportunity to British mystics as a gateway to the universalities by reason of a more native, more kindly and more familiar aspect than any alien portal reveals.

It may be that in the higher existence there is neither Greek nor Jew, Syrian nor Ethiopian, bond nor free. But in this of Abred we are so much the creatures of our immediate environment, that only by a realization of and agreement with its properties can we hope to accomplish anything, whether material or spiritual. And surely a system which has already sounded and comprehended these properties is of all systems the most fitting and natural for us to adopt as a groundwork of psychic advancement.

The Secret Tradition of Britain! Does not the very name stir the heart and appeal to the imagination of the true son of Albion with a thrill more mysterious and romantic than any allusion to the magics of Egypt or Hind? I need no Thebes or Benares, no Vedic Hymns, no Book of the Dead, for I am heir to a lore as exalted, as sublime as these, inherited from Druid sires, and in the main restored by pious searching. And in this Tradition restored I believe the future germ of British Mysticism to reside, that from its ash and cinder the phoenix of a marvellous rebirth shall arise on invincible wing:

Like that self-begotten bird
In the Arabian woods embost,
That no second knows, nor third,
And lay erewhile a holocaust,

From out her ashy womb now teemed,
Revives, reflourishes, then vigorous most
When most unactive deemed,
And though her body die, her fame survives
A secular bird, ages of lives!

The Initiations

From the evidence already placed before the reader it is possible in some measure to reconstruct the rites of initiation of the Secret Tradition. It is not claimed that it is here competent to divulge them in their entirety, as the gaps and lacunae in the evidence are only too obvious, but an outline at least can be supplied, and there is no doubt in the mind of the writer that adequate research would succeed in the recovery of still further evidence, the lost links of the chain.

Caesar tells us that the Druids were in the habit of making their initiates undergo a very long course of preparation before they reached what may be described as adeptship. He also states that they were extremely jealous lest their rites and ceremonies should be observed or overlooked by the vulgar herd. Now this can in no sense apply to public rites. It cannot but signify those more secret ceremonies associated with magic or initiation. That an arcane brotherhood, the Pheryllt, actually existed we have already seen, and doubtless it was to them that the business of initiation was entrusted. That this was associated with the Cauldron is manifest not only from numerous Welsh poems, but also from the allegory itself, which makes it plain that the draught of inspiration was the last, or one of the last, steps in the ceremony of initiation.

Now we have the authority of a poem of Taliesin entitled "The Chair of Taliesin," for describing certain of the apparatus and ceremonial associated with initiation. As it is important, I make no apology for quoting it in full after the translation of Davies:

> I am he who animates the fire, to the honour of the god Duvydd, in behalf of the assembly of associates qualified to treat of mysteries—a bard with the knowledge of a *Sywedydd*, when he deliberately recites the inspired song of the Western Cudd on a serene night amongst the stones.

As to loquacious, glittering bards, their encomium attracts me not when moving in the course; admiration is their great object.

And I am a silent proficient who address the bards of the land; it is mine to animate the hero; to persuade the unadvised; to awaken the silent beholder—the bold illuminator of kings!

I am no shallow artist, greeting the Bards of a household like a subtle parasite—the ocean has a due profundity!

The man of complete discipline has obtained the meed of honour in every knightly celebration, when Dien is propitiated with an offering of wheat, and the suavity of bees, and incense and myrrh and aloes from beyond the seas, and the golden pipes of Lleu, and cheerful precious silver and the ruddy gem, and the berries, and the foam of the ocean, and cresses of a purifying quality, laved in the fountain, and a joint contribution of wort, the founder of liquor, supplied by the assembly, with a raised load, secluded from the moon, of placid, cheerful vervain.

With priests of intelligence to officiate on behalf of the moon, and the concourse of associated men under the open breeze of the sky, with the maceration and sprinkling and the portion after the sprinkling, and the boat of glass in the hand of the stranger, and the stout youth with pitch, and the honoured *Segyrffyg*, and medical plants from an exorcised spot.

And Bards with flowers and perfect convolutions, and primroses and leaves of the *Briw*, with the points of the trees of purposes, and solution of doubts, and frequent mutual pledges; and with wine which flows to the brim, from Rome to Rosedd, and deep standing water, a flood which has the gift of Dovydd, on the tree of pure gold, which becomes of a fructifying quality when that Brewer gives it a boiling who presided over the cauldron of the five plants.

Hence the stream of Gwion and the reign of serenity and honey and trefoil, and horns flowing with mead—Meet for a sovereign is the lore of the Druids.

Now it is impossible to credit, whatever the date of this manuscript, that it has not actually come down to us as evidence of the former existence of an ancient system of initiation. For what possible purpose, indeed, could it have been otherwise invented? Its details are too closely associated with what we know of Druidical practice and, indeed, of the rituals of other and similar mysteries not to have had an actual background in reality. Let us examine them a little more closely. The first four paragraphs are obviously prefatory. The name Sywedydd is the first hint we receive that we are dealing with something out of the common, something occult and mysterious. It implies mystagogue, or revealer of mysteries, and the word Cudd which follows it signifies "the Place of the Dark Repository".

The paragraph which follows these relates to the herbs and other materials which were seethed together in the Cauldron of Inspiration. The "gold pipes of Lleu" obviously allude to some yellow flower, and the "cheerful precious silver" seems to mean the fluxwort, which in Wales is known as *ariant Gwion*, or ''Gwion's silver,' which in itself proves that it was associated in Cambrian lore with the mystical cauldron. The "ruddy gem" is perhaps the hedge-berry, which was also known as *eirin Gwion*, the Borues of Gwion. The cresses allude to the *Fabairia*, called *berwi Taliessin*, or "Taliessin's Cresses," and on vervain the Druids set particular store, casting lots by its use and employing it in divination. It was usually gathered at the rise of the Dog-star "Without being looked upon either by the sun or moon." In gathering it the earth was propitiated by a libation of honey and it was dug up with the left hand.

The Boat of Glass was a crescent shaped like a half-moon and in all probability was the vessel from which the draught of inspiration was quaffed. Primroses ranked highly among the mystical apparatus and the briw was probably also vervain, which was known by the name of *briw'r March*.

The poem states that the same rite of libation prevailed from Rome to Rosedd. This seems to point to a date for its composition when the Britons were acquainted with the Romans, but while Rome itself was yet pagan. The "deep water" seems to signify the bath for the immersion of the neophyte, and the gift of Duvydd was the Selago or hedge-hyssop, which in modern Welsh is known as gras Duw. Pliny says of this plant: "Similar to savin is the plant called Selago. It is gathered without using iron and by passing the right hand through the left sleeve of the tunic, as though in the act of committing a theft. The clothing must be white, the feet washed and bare and an offering of wine and bread made before the gathering. The Druids of Gaul say that the plant should be carried as a charm against every kind of evil and that the smoke of it is good for diseases of the eye."

These, then, were the mystical plants, the ingredients of the Cauldron of Keridwen which produced the stream of Gwion, to which is ascribed the beginning of genius, the power of inspiration and the reign of serenity.

Now we find that these rites, far from falling into desuetude, were actually employed so late as the twelfth century, when Hywel, Prince of North Wales, was initiated into the lesser mysteries of Keridwen in 1171, and that he longed for admittance to the greater mysteries conducted by Gwyddnaw and his son. In a song supposed to be sung by Hywel he addresses Keridwen as the moon, lofty and fair, slow and delicate in her descending course, and requests her to attend his worship in the mystical grove. "I love the place of the illustrious lady near the pleasant shore," sings Hywel, "for the severe discipline which I experienced in the hall of the mysterious god, I have obtained her promise—a treasure of high privilege. . . . I shall long for the proud-wrought place of the Gyvylchi till I have gained admittance. Renowned and enterprising is the man who enters there." "If we may judge from these strains of Hywel," says Davies, "and from many similar passages in the works of his contemporaries, the Cambrian bards were as zealously devoted to the worship of Keridwen in the twelfth century as they had been in the sixth, or in any earlier age of heathen superstition."

Now "the proud-wrought enclosure in the Gwvylchi, in the desert of Arvon in Eryri," or Snowdon, and near the shore, was the Caer or sanctuary of Keridwen and her daughter Llywy. "The topography of this temple is so minutely pointed out," says Davies, "that the spot cannot be mistaken...Dwy-Gyvylchi is still known as the name of a parish in the very spot where the Cambrian prince fixed his Caer Wen Glaer, or sanctuary of the illustrious lady, in the deserts of Arvon in Eryri and towards the sea: and here the remains of the Caer are still to be found." Camden's annotator, Gibson, has described a strong fortress "seated on the top of one of the highest mountains which lies towards the sea," and gives the following account of this ancient temple. "About a mile from this fortification stands the most remarkable monument in all Snowdon, called *Y Meineu Hirion* upon the Plain Mountain within the parish of Dwy-Gyvycheu, above Gwddw Glas. It is a circular entrenchment about twenty-six yards diameter; on the outside whereof are certain rude stone, pillars, of which about twelve are now standing, some twoi~ yards and others five foot high: and these are again encompassed with a stone wall. It stands upon the Plain Mountain as soon as we come to the height, having much even ground about it; and not far from it there are three other large stones pitched on end in a triangular form."

Gibson, the annotator of Camden, also informs us that at the distance of about three furlongs fromi this monument are several huge heaps or cairns and also several cells constructed of huge stones fixed in the ground, each cell being covered with one or two stones of great size.

Bearing in mind the words of Hywel relative to the locality, there can surely be no question that these stones are the remains of the open-air temple of Keridwen, and that the cells alluded to by Gibson were the secret places in which the neophyte was prepared for initiation. I do not propose to enter into the welter of controversy concerning the question as to whether the Druids actually employed the stone-circles of this island for purposes of worship or not That they did not raise many of them is obvious but it is odd that those who have argued so fiercely against their use by the Druids should not have been able to discover the many evidences in literature where they are spoken of as using them for that purpose and of which I shall give some account towards the end of this chapter.

The reader will recollect that the Pheryllt, or priests of the Pharaon, had a city or temple on Snowdon known as Dinas Emrys, which has already been described. Now it seems to me not at all unlikely that this Temple of Keridwen, only about a mile away from the site of Dinas Emrys, must have been under the auspices of the Pherylit, and this leads to the supposition that they were flourishing in Hywel's time—that is in the twelfth century.

An ancient poem in the Welsh Archaiology supplies us with an old formula in obscure language which appears to have been employed on occasions of initiation as an introduction for approaching the gate of the sanctuary. Arthur and Kai are represented as coming to the portal, which is guarded by a hierophant, and the following dialogue takes place:

> Arthur: What man is he that guards the gate?
>
> Hierophant: The severe hoary one with the wide dominion—who is the man that demands it?
>
> Arthur: Arthur and the Blessed Kai.
>
> Hierophant: What good attends thee, thou blessed one, thou best man in the world? Into my house thou canst not enter unless thou wilt preserve.
>
> Kai: I will preserve it and that thou shalt behold; though the birds of wrath should go forth and the three attendant ministers should fall asleep, namely the son of the Creator Mabon, the son of Mydron, attendant upon the wonderful supreme Ruler, and Gwyn, the Lord of those who descend from above.
>
> Hierophant: Severe have my servants been in preserving their institutes. Manawyddan, the son of Llyr, was grave in his counsel, Manawyd truly brought a perforated shield from Trevryd, and Mabon, the son of Lightning, stained the straw with clotted gore: and Anwas the winged and Llwch Llawinawg (the ruler of the lakes) were firm guardians of the encircled mount. Their Lord preserved them and I rendered them complete. Kai! I solemnly announce though all three should be slain, when the privilege of the grove is violated, danger shall be found.

The rest of this obscure dialogue describes the adventures of Arthur and Kai after their initiation, but it is clear that in the part of it I have quoted the neophyte engaged before the hierophant to preserve the laws of the sanctuary, even though assaulted by enemies or deserted by friends. The hierophant in his turn denounces the fate of those who violate the sacred engagement. It is plain, too, from the text that the hierophant was attended by three assistant ministers, each of whom seems to have impersonated a god, and in this the usage seems to have been the same as that prevailing in the Eleusinian mysteries, in which four priests officiated, the hierophant, who represented the Creator, the torch-bearer, who personated the sun, the herald, who took the part of Mercury, and the minister of the altar, who represented the moon.

We must now return for enlightenment to the myth of Keridwen and her Cauldron. This Cauldron cannot but have been one and the same with the Cauldron of Inspiration alluded to in the myths of Annwn, to which Arthur or Hu penetrated. It has precisely the same character and is described in the same manner, and when we learn that Keridwen was a goddess of the Underworld, the identity of the vessel seems complete. She is also styled Ogyrven Amhad, "the goddess of various seeds," a statement which equates her with Ceres, and indeed she appears to have been the British Ceres.

We will recollect that when Gwion unwittingly tasted the virtue of her Cauldron of Inspiration she pursued him, that he transformed himself into a hare, when she became a greyhound, turned him, and chased him toward a river. He leapt into the stream and became a fish, but as she pursued him as an otter, he took the form of a bird. Transforming herself into the guise of a sparrowhawk, she was gaining upon him, when he perceived a heap of wheat upon a floor, dropped into the midst of it, and assumed the form of a single grain. Keridwen then changed herself into the shape of a black, high-crested hen, descended into the wheat, scratched him out, and swallowed him, and, as the history relates, he was born of her in due time as the beautiful babe Taliesin, who was found in the fishing weir of Elphin.

Now the whole myth certainly bears allusions to the rite of initiation. Keridwen first transforms herself into a female dog. Virgil, in the sixth book of his Aeneid, describing all that it was lawful to reveal of the Eleusinian mysteries, says that one of the first things observed by his hero as the priestess conducted him toward the mystic river were a number of female dogs, and Pletho in his notes upon the Magical Oracles of Zoroaster, remarks that it is the custom in the celebration of the mysteries to exhibit to the initiated certain phantoms in the figures of dogs. The dog was, indeed, the guardian of the Underworld, and it seems probable that, as the initiate was supposed to enter this gloomy region when undergoing his ordeal, the presence of dogs may have entered symbolically into the ceremony. Indeed, Diodorus, dealing with the mysteries of Isis, mentions that the whole solemnity was preceded by the presence of dogs, and he even terms the priests of mysteries "dogs," although he believes that the Greeks mistook the Hebrew word *cohen,* a priest, for their own word *kune,* dog. However, the dog of Gwyn ap Nudd, the British Plato, is named Dormarth, "the gate of sorrow," so it would seem that the animals represented in the British mysteries somewhat resembled the classical Cerberus, and that they had a similar significance—that they were, indeed, of the same character as the Proserpine Lànen which Apuleius approached in the course of his initiation.

Then we find that the aspirant was converted into a hare, a sacred animal among the Britons, as we learn from Caesar, but perhaps here symbolizing the great timidity of the novice. This hare is turned and driven toward a river. The first ceremony in the Greek mysteries was that of purification, which was celebrated upon the banks of rivers. The Athenians, for example, performed this ceremony at Agra on the Ilissus, a river of Attica, whose banks were called "the mystical," and whose stream itself was named "the divine."

According to the myth, the aspirant now plunges into the stream, and the otter here seems to symbolize the priest who attended to his lustrations. His form then changes into that of a bird, probably the dryw, which means both a wren and a Druid, and, indeed, elsewhere Taliesin informs us that he had once taken that form. His adversary becomes a hawk, reminiscent of Egyptian mythology. At last he takes the shape of a grain of pure wheat, mixing with an assemblage of the same species, and thus assumes a form eminently sacred to Ceres or Keridwen, who receives him into her bosom, whence he is re-born. The meaning of this statement probably resides in the fact that the initiate remained for a season in one of the mysterious cells or caves of the Druidic cult, where he was subjected to a rigid course of discipline, and where he studied the rites and imbibed the secret doctrines of Keridwen, lastly emerging "re-born" into the outer world.

But this description probably applies to the lesser or initial mysteries only. The greater were still to follow. After the initiate had completed his course of discipline in the cell and had been born again of Keridwen, the goddess enclosed him in a coracle covered with skin and cast him into the sea. Now if we compare this procedure with that known to have been followed in the Greek mysteries, we discover a close resemblance between the two. After passing through the lesser mysteries the herald summoned the initiates to the sea-shore. The name of the day on which this took place was entitled "Novitiates to the Sea," after the summons of the herald. The aspirants on this occasion embarked upon the sea in certain vessels, and it was in these mysteries, we are told, that the whole truth was to be revealed. Now we will recall that in the myth of Taliesin he was, while yet a babe, albeit a learned one, launched by Keridwen in a coracle which took him to the weir of Gwyddno, where he was discovered by Gwyddno's son Elphin. He prophesied the future renown of Elphin and his own as well. Elphin bore the babe to the castle, where Gwyddno demanded of Taliesin whether he was a human being or a spirit. The infant Taliesin replied in a mystical song, in which he described himself as a general primary bard who had existed in all ages and was in some measure identified with the sun. "Thrice have I been born," sang Taliesin, the Radiant Fronted one, "I know how to meditate. It is pitiful that men will not come to seek all the sciences of the world which are treasured in my bosom, for I know all that has been and all that will be hereafter."

Now Davies (whom I have closely followed as regards these latter passages, and who was, indeed, very much more competent to speak on these matters than some of the modern mythologists who have rather cruelly sneered at him, owing to his rather tiresome theory that the whole of British myth is to be referred to what he calls "Arkite" theology), believed that Gwyddno and his son were the husband and son of Keridwen. This seems not improbable, when we remember that Gwyddno was the lord and Keridwen lady of Annwn. Gwyddno's surname was Garanhir, or the "long, or high crane," or "Stalking Person," to which allusion has already been made in the chapter on the Grail and elsewhere, where it was stated that the bull god of the Continental Kelts was styled Trigaranos, because he carried three cranes. Elsewhere Taliesin alludes to Elphin as "The sovereign of those who carry ears of corn," and later in his life he was to liberate him from a strong-stoned tower in which he had been imprisoned by Maelgwn. Elphin has certainly some solar significance.

One of the poems attributed to Gwyddno appears to have an

application to the enclosing of the aspirant in the coracle. The novice is about to be plunged into the waves and he sings: "Though I love the sea-beach I dread the open sea. A billow may come undulating over the stone." To this the hierophant replies: "To the brave, to the magnanimous, to the amiable, to the generous who boldly embarks, the ascending stones of the Bards will prove the harbour of life. It has asserted the praise of Heilyn, the mysterious impeller of the sky. Until the doom shall its symbol be continued." Still the novice is not reassured. "Though I love the strand," he cries, "I dread the wave. Great has been its violence— dismal the overwhelming stroke. Even to him who survives, it will be the subject of lamentation." Once more endeavouring to reassure him, Gwyddno says: "It is a pleasant act, to wash in the bosom of the fair water. Though it fill the receptacle it will not disturb the heart. My associated train regard not its overwhelming. As for him who repented of his enterprise, the lofty wave has hurried the babbler far away to his death; but the brave, the magnanimous, will find his compensation in arriving safe at the stones. The conduct of the water will declare thy merit."

But to the timid or rejected candidate he addressed himself thus: "Thy coming without external purity is a pledge that I will not receive thee. Take out the gloomy one! From my territory have I alienated the rueful steed. My revenge upon the shoal of earth-worms is their hopeless longing for the pleasant place. Out of the receptacle which is thy aversion did I obtain the rainbow."

Davies believed this ceremony to have taken place in Cardigan Bay, at the mouth of the Ystwyth. The ceremony was intended to test the constancy and purity of mind of the neophyte. "The old bards," he says, "speak in magnificent terms of the benefits which were derived from these mysterious rites. They were viewed as most important to the happiness of human life. They imparted sacred science in its greatest purity and perfection; and he who had completed his probation was called *Dedwydd*, 'one who has recovered intelligence,' or rather has been brought back into the Presence. It is nearly equivalent to the Greek term *Epoptes*, which describes a person who had been initiated into the greater mysteries." By the course of the tide it was to be discovered whether or no the initiate was worthy to survive, as in the case of Taliesin himself.

Taliesin, in a poem recited immediately after he had gone through the concluding ceremony, describes himself as "thrice-born," that is, once of his natural mother, once of Keridwen, and lastly of the mystic coracle. As a consequence of this regeneration he tells us that he "knew how to think rightly of God," and that all the sacred science of the world was treasured in his bosom.

In a poem immediately following this, Taliesin sings: "I was first modelled into the form of a pure man in the hall of Keridwen, who subjected me to penance. Though small within my chest and modest in my deportment, I was great. A sanctuary carried me above the surface of the earth. Whilst I was enclosed within its ribs the sweet Awen rendered me complete, and my law, without audible language, was imparted to me by the old giantess, darkly smiling in her wrath." In the concluding verse he says: "I fled in the form of a fair grain of pure wheat. Upon the edge of a covering cloth she caught me in her fangs. In appearance she was as large as a proud mare, which she also resembled—then was she swelling out like a ship upon the waters. Into a dark receptacle she cast me. She carried me back into the sea of Dylan. It was an auspicious omen to me when she happily suffocated me. God the Lord freely set me at large." This obviously applied to a course of penance, discipline and mystical instruction undergone by the initiate, and must have consisted in scenic or symbolical representation, as language does not seem to have been employed. It appears to have taken place in the Temple of Keridwen, and the goddess seems to have taken various shapes, just as did Diana in the mysteries described by the author of the Orphic Argonautics. She transformed herself into the shapes of a dog, a horse, and a lion, according to the particular knowledge she desired to impart.

One of the most remarkable poems connected with Keridwen is that in which her priest deals with certain passages in her history. He tells us that in the dead of night and at the dawn, the lights of the initiates have been shining, and that as to Avaggdu, her son, the correcting god has formed him anew for happiness. In the contention of the mysteries, indeed, his wisdom has exceeded her own, and he has become the most accomplished of beings. His bride is a woman composed of flowers, whom, by his exquisite art, Gwydion created.

"When the merit of the presidencies shall be adjudged," says Keridwen through the mouth of her priest, "mine will be found the superior amongst them—my chair, my cauldron and my laws and my pervading eloquence meet for the presidency." "This poem," says Davies, "was evidently intended to be sung or recited by a priest or priestess who personated Keridwen."

Davies concludes his rather rambling criticisms of these ceremonial poems by certain remarks which, whatever one may think of his general method, have a good deal of cogency behind them. He says it is scarcely to be wondered at that the ancient Britons should have pertinaciously adhered to the rites of the British Ceres as lately as the sixth century, especially during the period between the dominion of the Romans and the coming of the Saxons. "There seems," he says, "to have been several parts of Wales into which Christianity as yet had scarcely penetrated; or where, at least, it had not prevailed. Hence Brychan is commended 'for bringing up his children and grand-children in learning, so as to be able to show the faith in Christ to the Cymry where they were without the faith'." He goes on to say that the Welsh princes, to the latest period of their government, not only tolerated but patronized the old rites, and that the mysteries of Keridwen were celebrated in Wales as late as the middle of the twelfth century. They influenced the writings of the bards, and the princes were induced by national prejudice to regard these as innocent and to fancy that they might be good Christians enough without wholly relinquishing their heathenish superstitions. The ministers of Christianity thought otherwise, and sometimes refused Christian burial to these Gentile priests, and there are numerous instances of the bards themselves promising a kind recantation some time before their death.

We must now turn to the question as to whether the stone circles commonly attributed to the Druids were ever employed by them for religious or mystical purposes. That they were first raised by the Druids, as Druids, is, as we have seen, out of the question. The cult which was responsible for them may have been proto-Druidic, that is, it may have held the early germs of Druidism, although there is no evidence to countenance such a theory. But that they were actually employed by the later Druids is undoubted, whatever recent arguments may have been brought against this belief.

In the first place, we have early Christian evidence on the matter. Pope Gregory in his famous Bull, and in his instructions to the Abbot Melitus when he dispatched him to Britain, advised him not to destroy the British temples or fanes, but only the idols they contained, as they might be suitable to the worship of the true God. William Thorn, the monk of Canterbury, speaks of a fane towards the east of that city where King Ethelbert was accustomed to celebrate heathen worship.[1] This fane, we are told by another chronicler, was built "in the British manner". The twentieth Canon of the Council of Nantes, promulgated about A. D. 658, provides that stones in ruinous places and woods raised to the worship of demons shall be destroyed, and a similar fulmination against standing stones is given in the Liber Poenitentialis of Archbishop Theodore, of Canterbury (A.D. 602—690). "If any may have vowed or paid a vow at trees, or at fountains, or at stones, whether at the balusters, or anywhere else, excepting in the Church of God." The word "balusters" here means "encompassing rails" or stone balustrade. In Ireland, St. Patrick is said to have incised the name of Christ on three lofty stones on the Plain of Magh Slecht which were associated with heathenish rites.

We know that St. Samson, Bishop of Dol in Brittany, when travelling in Britain actually surprised certain "Bacchanalians" while worshipping an idol on the top of a mound within a stone circle. He endeavoured to dissuade them from the practice, and they were disputing him, when a certain youth passing in a chariot was thrown therefrom and broke his neck. This was taken as a sign that God was displeased with the idolatry, and the pagan congregation broke up.

There is plenty of evidence that in Scotland courts were held at stone circles as late as the fourteenth century. One was convened in 1349 by William, Earl of Ross, Justiciary of Scotland, at the standing stones of Rayne in Garioch, and another by Alexander Stewart, Lord of Badenoch, the King's Lieutenant, in the year 1380 at the standing stones of Easter Kyngucy in Badenoch. This is eloquent of very ancient custom.

Davies provides a lengthy and in some ways a useful disquisition on the question of Druidic circles. He believes that the circle named Caer Sidi was the Temple of Keridwen, and that its prototype was the locality of Caer Sidi in Annwn. Of this Chair Taliesin was the president. "Is not my chair protected by the Cauldron of Keridwen?" sings Taliesin, "therefore let my tongue be free in the sanctuary of the praise of the goddess." Davies believed that this sanctuary was modelled on the great circle of the Zodiac. "I have presided in a toilsome Chair over the circle of Sidin whilst that is continually revolving between three elements. Is it not a wonder to the

[1] According to accounts received while this volume was in press, this "fane" has only recently been unearthed.

world that men are not enlightened?" These words of Taliesin, Davies translates as signifying that the sun is the visible president. Taliesin, or "Radiant Front," was his earthly representative in that sanctuary, which typified the abode of the god.

Now Davies further believed that these "Caer Sidis" were none other than the stone circles. He drags the Ark into his elucidations, but if we discount this, we arrive at some not invaluable conclusions, for, despite his notions regarding "Arkite philosophy," Davies was logical enough.

He shows, for example, that when the mystical Bards treat of history and the rites of Keridwen, that they almost invariably allude to the completion of the year and the return of a particular day. He thought that the stones in the circles represented the various constellations, with the sun and the moon in the centre. Now Caer Sidi, as he has said, means the Circle of Revolution, and he notes that at least one Druidic grove, the *Cylch Baich Nevwy*, was known as the "magnificent celestial circle." He also proves that Aneurin, Taliesin and Merlin in their mystical poems mention the particular stones which composed certain circles.

Then he reverts to the poem of Prince Hywel in the Desert of Arvon in Snowdon, where stood the sanctuary of Keridwen, visited by the prince as lately as the twelfth century. This was composed of a circle of twelve stones, and like other circles found in Britain, was, he believed, "constructed upon astronomical principles. In short, it represented either the Zodiac itself, or certain cycles and computations deduced from the study of astronomy. Hence the frequent repetition of twelve, nineteen, thirty, or sixty stones which has been marked in the circles of these monuments." He indicates that the number twelve is twice repeated in the circle at Avebury, in the circle of Classernish, in the western islands of Scotland, and in certain Cornish monuments.

Lastly, after a long dissertation on Stonehenge, which has been superseded by recent research, he states that the personage or prince known as Seithin Saidi is called "the guardian of the gate of Godo" or "the uncovered sanctuary," which he believes alludes to the typical stone circle.

Now when one recalls the philosophy set forth in Barddas, with its cosmography of the universe described in circles, it does not seem at all improbable that the stone circles may have had some bearing upon it. It seems likely that Druidism in these islands mingled with a much older religion, which had as its basis the circular cosmography above alluded to. On the other hand, it may have adapted the stone circles to this cosmography, likening the outer circle to Abred and the inner to Gwynvyd. I hasten to say that I do not dogmatize on the subject, for where all is so vague it would, indeed, be rash to do so. Moreover, it would be necessary to prove that a similar course was adopted in Gaul and elsewhere. We know that other cults in other countries employed the ancient stone circles built by their predecessors. Thus it was only in the age of Zoroaster, some five hundred years before our era, that the Persians adopted covered temples, having formerly worshipped in open-air circular structures, and even the Greeks themselves, according to Pausanius, are not free from the suspicion of having done so in the early days of the Hellenic religion.

We know that the Druids worshipped in circular groves. What, then, is more likely that, finding stone groves ready erected and to their hand, they employed these for a worship which had probably much in common with the cult which had originally been practised within them? At that I leave the question. A great deal more requires to be known concerning the cult of those who raised these circles before we can speak more definitely upon it. But Mr. Kendrick has given it as his opinion that although the Druids certainly did not build Stonehenge, they employed it as a temple, aud on the whole I also conclude that this was actually the case.

One of the most pregnant statements on the use to which certain stone monuments were put is that of Mr. Bernard H. Springett on *Traces of Mithraism and Early Masonic Resemblances in the Stone Remains of South Brittany*, a copy of which he was kind enough to send me in 1924. The remarks in it might with equal reason apply to stone remains in Britain. Many of the stone monuments in Brittany struck Mr. Springett when he visited them as having been erected—for something beyond the usual reason assigned, that of sun worship, and so forth. In inspecting the dolmens, by which name the Bretons call those stones covered by a large slab, he noted that they were frequently found in the centre of a tumulus, whereas certain stone chambers or cells were invariably underground. In describing these underground chambers, he says:

> You descend a varying number of steps to the entrance of a passage, the steps being so arranged, with a curve or an angle in them, that it is impossible from the first step to look along the passage. This is roughly lined with upright slabs like the chambers themselves, with appearances of having originally had the interstices filled with chips of stone, or merely earth, perhaps. This central passage... leads direct to the largest chamber of a series of three, two others on the right of the passage having entrances from it, but no intercommunication. On the left of the central passage is a long, somewhat narrower passage running right alongside it, almost to the end chamber, so that anyone could pass direct into this end chamber without traversing, except at each end, the main central passage.

Mr. Springett asked a Masonic friend who accompanied him if the plan of these chambers had suggested anything to him, and he replied that they reminded him of the rooms used by Masons in the Rose Croix Degree. "Then," writes Mr. Springett, "we pictured together the whole ceremony, crude enough, no doubt, most probably terrifically awe-inspiring to the ancient candidates, conducted by a Deacon down the steps, along the central passage, first into one side chamber, to be shown some terrible and fearsome object, perhaps then into the second chambe; finally into the larger chamber at the end, no doubt for an Obligation, and then admission. Meanwhile, officiating priests, on the other side of the left hand wall of the central passage, were probably producing 'stage effects'."

Mr. Springett believes that the cult which made use of these underground initiation chambers was that of Mithraism. There are, he says, two legendary periods for the erection of these stones in Brittany. One tradition asserts that they were erected by Druids, who came from Britain for this express purpose and imitated the structures used by them for religious ceremonies in their own country. The other is that they were erected by a people who came from the East.

It seems to me, however, that these cells of initiation were Druidic. Mr. Springett gives as an evidence of the existence of Mithraism in Brittany the legend of St. Comely, the patron saint of Carnac, who is always represented as accompanied by two bulls—the symbolic beast of Mithraism; but this animal, as we have seen, was also symbolic of Druidism. He thinks that the smaller underground chambers were used for outer degrees, while the interiors of the tumuli were employed for the more arcane rites of higher degrees. Many of these latter were not employed for sepulchral purposes, and the bones of burnt cattle were discovered within them. Moreover, on the walls of these chambers are rude carvings of serpents and ears of corn, both accompaniments of Druidism as well as of Mithraism. On an ancient covering stone of a tomb reclining against the south wall of Plouharnel Church Mr. Springett observed a carving which seemed to him to represent an initiate before an altar which supports a volume and a square. Behind the altar stands the Master's Light, which, like the chalice behind the candidate, springs from a base supporting cones of increasing size, symbolizing the three stages to be passed through before reachjng the vault below, from which the cope-stone is removed. Beneath are the skull and cross-bones, the level and twenty-four inch gauge. Mr. Springett takes care to mention that certain stones in Britain gave him much the same impression as these Breton monuments, the cells associated with which seem to me to be similar to, if not identical in form with, those alluded to by Camden's annotator as occurring at the Circle of Keridwen in Arvon. In all probability they were the cells in which the lesser mysteries were revealed to the initiates, a conclusion which it will be seen Mr. Springett shares with Davies and other writers on the subject.

Ross Nichols

An Examination of Creative Myth

(from *The Cosmic Shape*, 1946)

Over the course of two and a half centuries, the Revival had created a remarkable body of ritual, teaching, and symbolism; the only difficulty with this creation, as it turned out, was that it had only the most distant connection with the ancient Celtic Druids. By the middle of the twentieth century, Revival groups faced the critical question of finding a new basis on which their traditions could rest. More than any other Druid of his time, Ross Nichols helped point the way to an answer. By his time, archeological and historical research into Celtic antiquity had progressed far enough that many claims that had long been made by the Druid Revival about the ancient Druids could no longer be justified by the facts. Revival groups that insisted they had rediscovered the secrets of the ancient Druids—or worse still, were directly descended from the ancient Druids, as some branches of the Revival did by then—found their claims forcefully challenged by scholars whose command of the facts could not easily be gainsaid.

Poet, painter, teacher, and Druid, Philip Ross Nichols played a crucial role in the twentieth century transitions of the Druid Revival. His response to those transitions had three intertwined aspects. First, he argued forcefully for the continuity of the modern Druid tradition as a significant presence in the spiritual life of Britain from the eighteenth century onward. Second, he stressed the real extent to which the Druid Revival tradition drew on the traditions of the medieval Celts and, through them, on archaic spiritual traditions that could be traced over much of the ancient world.

The third aspect was the most crucial, and forms the central theme of "An Examination of Creative Myth," the essay that follows. Relating to nature through the archaic tools of poetry, vision, and myth, Nichols proposed, was not simply a luxury of the past that present-day romantics might choose to imitate. It was a crucial necessity in a society that desperately needed a more meaningful connection with the natural world that sustains human life. The mythic vision that could create that connection need not come intact from the past, he argued, and in some sense could not do so; though roots in the past experience of a people were essential, so was the creative freedom to adapt traditional images to the needs of a new time.

Perhaps the most interesting thing about this essay is that it was written before he became an active participant in Druidry. In his essay, and even more in "Cosmic Legend," the poetic exploration that appears in it, Nichols sketched out the rough framework of the kind of tradition that might use a creative and poetic grasp of mythology to heal the breach between humanity and nature. He later found that tradition in Druidry. His major work on the latter subject, *The Book of Druidry*, restates many of the themes of the essay presented here from a Druid perspective, and with the additional resources provided by the long tradition of which he had become one of the custodians.

"An Examination of Creative Myth" was originally published in *The Cosmic Shape*, a book which included the essay, a statement of intention by Nichols and his fellow-poet James Kirkup, Nichols' poem-cycle "Cosmic Legend," and two extensive poems by Kirkup, "The Glass Fable" and "The Sleeper in the Earth." The essay and Nichols' poem-cycle appear here by permission of the Order of Bards Ovates and Druids.

Further Reading:

Philip Carr-Gomm, *Journeys of the Soul: The Life and Legacy of a Druid Chief* (Oak Tree Press, 2010).

Ross Nichols, *The Book of Druidry* (Aquarian, 1990).

-----, *Prophet, Priest and King: The Poetry of Philip Ross Nichols*, ed. Jay Ramsay (Oak Tree Press, 2001).

* * *

Some Definitions and Objectives

The recall of the shapeliness of myth-forms and their appropriate symbols to the modern poetic copsciousness has long been overdue. Here and there attempts and spasmodic movements have occurred which seem to show that the need is felt. On the whole however we cannot be said to have progressed very far on the road either to defining what myth can mean to this century or to practising effectively the evocations that myth commonly requires. A further examination and attempted definitions are clearly needed, if only as a basis for further discussion.

Myth, as found in the classical lands of Europe and in the lands of the Scandinavian tradition, is firstly a social belief in an imaginative drama incarnating the forces of nature and having definite social purpose. It has a certain comprehensive quality distinguishing it from legend, which is the weaving of imagination around the doings of beings essentially human, however dimly recognizable. Again, it is distinct from symbol and image; these on reflection appear to be lesser devices almost invariably comprehended within the myth texture. The social content of myth perhaps needs stressing because the Apocalyptic group have used the ward as the equivalent of personal symbolism. "The projection of the self into the world at large" is Henry Treece's definition, following J. W. Dunne; but that surely is just what myth is not; rather is it a canalization of the feelings of a group towards certain phenomena reccurent in the world and its heavens; only the elements common between the selves, that is, can form the substantives of myth. In its effect myth has a dynamic quality, moreover, to which the metaphor of a canal is inadequate; it forms rather the very lever whereby the minds of earlier men obtained some purchase upon the universe. Marx clearly recognizes this. "Mythology," he says, "masters and dominates nature in and through the imagination." A recent critic echoes the idea: "Myths...control and organize the feeling, thought and action of a people," declares Michael Roberts.

One primary conception of myth, then, is the active projection of certain shapes, superhuman or semi-human, by a race or group endeavouring to understand; and in the process to humanize, its surroundings. To label this process anthropomorphism and leave it at that is the negation of thought. Men herein are not merely making nature in man's likeness; they are doing the essential first task of a civilization, to make the early pastoral or agricultural man feel at home in his often grim natural precincts. Even the fearsome lightning, if seen as the weapon of the locally worshipped Zeus, is not so terrifying; it is the same fire as that which burns on the hearth, that which Prometheus the friend of man had obtained for him from heaven.

Mankind may have grown out of myths simply as explanations of the universe; but its need for myth as dramatization of nature's processes, as shapes to feed the imagination, as foci for seasonal activities, is probably as great as ever. It is true historically, as Marx says, that "mythology disappears as soon as man gains mastery over the forces of nature"; true, too, that the disappearance leaves a yawning gap in the common man's attunement to nature; which the utter bewilderment and even fear shown by adult evacuees from town to country has lately illustrated.

Now the social responsibility of the writer lies in his ability to condition mental attitudes, at first in a few minds, eventually in very many. To those of us who believe in the need for a more reverent, more co-operative approach by men to the earth, the forward line for writers seems plain; it is no less than to essay to change an inadequate attitude towards the soil processes. Necessarily starting with a literary public, its eventual effect should be upon the whole public. To make a new approach to nature which shall satisfy minds aware of recent movements of thought we have to go as far beyond the romantic's self-absorption as beyond the intellectual eclectic's quarryings. Very broadly speaking, the isolationism of Wordsworth and the escapism of Shelley have eventually bred the weekender who has merely cultivated his own sensations; who, speeding about in a speed age, has imposed a feeling of static inferiority on the youth of the countryside and so increased the townward drift. What we need is to induce men to think of themselves as not outside the natural cycle but as active partners with nature in it. This is almost the opposite of wandering about in natural surroundings and dreaming. We need a functional approach, not a cult of pretty bits of indulgence in speed sensations.

The bringing back of average people to a land from which they have been divorced by industrial developments over which they have had little if any control is urgently necessary; indeed post-war conditions may well drive us back to the land whether we wish it or not. This means that we are again at the ground-plan of civilization; we have to consider the conditioning of the assumptions made by the average man, a man now strangely alien from the earth: doing in a new form the work done by the earlier myths. Only this time the actual facts of the universe do not need to be accounted for by fables; there is a much harder task, namely, to show those who think they already know that cheap-jack scientific explanations which may satisfy when thinking about nature in towns are not enough; that observation and attendance upon the moods of nature, something more akin to a cult than to the dogmatism of the laboratory, is necessary if any intensive soil cultivation which is to last is to be built up.

For this we plainly need to put back into the at present impersonal forces of nature some of the imaginative quality driven out by the necessarily ruthless dogmas of the early church and more recently by the equally ruthless dogmas of "scientific" cultivators. A useful counter-blow to these has been the important "Discipline of Peace" by K. B. Barlow. In this a factually-based philosophy of broad scope is expounded, a creed inculcating the urgent need for mankind to withdraw from the attitude of having a self-appointed lordship of creation and begin to regard its own function rather as that of a gardener than of a master.

Man is in action governed by emotive beliefs. If the weekender is merely living out the essentially selfish creed of the romantics, to bring about a different, humbler approach a different belief needs to be inculcated, quite dogmatically if necessary; and this is where myth enters. For the powerful magic of the Nazi race-and-war myth, we need to substitute a myth of the creative cycle. The rhythms of the seasons which formed the widespread early deificatioui that disciplined the subconscious are missing elements very necessary to any groping towards a more cooperative attitude to nature and away from egocentric romanticism. How generally at this date it is possible by incantation to evoke race-memories, and how far conventional poetic methods are still appropriate to the purpose, are indeed questions for critical debate.

"Pure incantation" was, it may be remembered, a definition of his art by the Symbolist post Mállarmé. One method applicable to the literary problem involved in these premises is a return to personification. Its equivalent in the world of objects is the symbol. "The psychological machine that transforms the energy is the symbol," says Jung (*Contributions to Analytical Psychology*). Whilst primitive shapes have brooded fosteringly over sculpture and to an extent over painting, in poetry few indeed have ex-pressed with symbol, legend or mythical figures the primitive life-schemes which are still basic mind patterns, however overlaid with more recent consciousness. The Surrealists, whilst they have opened the way to a franker call upon the unconscious, wherein such patterns reside, have not taken the full liberty of their programme.

Symbols and legends—the rich mine systematically opened up by Sir James Fraser, Jessie Weston and others—do, in fact, operate unconscious race memories—something halfway between the arbitrary elements of the unconscious exploited by Surrealists and the over-deliberate structures of intellect. To use their evocative power to induce in modern man a fresh sympathy with the vegetation cycle, something different in kind from the utilitarianism of business farmers and from the idler recreationists, to inculcate a recognition that the land is something with its own way of life, this is a full and worthy task for the writer and an aspect which in poetry has been sparely recognized so far. Although England is a land of country-lovers, it is a fact that the vast majority of English nature-poetry has consisted of mere sensitive reactions by cultured persons to superficial and obvious beauties, having no reference to processes of husbandry in any organic way; whilst romanticized local superstitions have through the gradual centuries taken the place of the fundamental shapes of legend that gave strength to much of the literature of the Romans—that race of farmers. Certain parts of D. H. Lawrence suggest an approach; but he was still too far the individualist rebel to attempt the task that Virgil in the *Georgics* did for Roman readers. Inability to point to a corresponding English exemplar in itself proves the need

Since practice is the soundest ground for theory, let us examine this great classical poetry of the seasons and the social background whence it arose.

The Gods and the Soil

The national circumstances in which Virgil wrote the Georgics are curiously parallel with certain aspects of our rural situation in the present century. Then, as now, there were two schools of thought about cultivation; the ranching school and the peasant-occupier school. The ranching was done largely by gang-slave-labour and its big estates, given over to cattle and sheep, were called "latifundia". Since the period of the Punic Wars they had been developing a disastrous social process which was constantly to spread and gradually to ruin the sounder Italian agriculture whose decay was perhaps the greatest single cause of the depopulation that overtook Rome's home territories, the south being worse than the north. The agitation of the Gracchi had been essentially the revolt of the small farmer against the latifundia system. As remedy, ex-soldiers were now being settled on the land in large numbers—the period of wars seemed temporarily to have ceased;—it was the common settlement process, in fact, which faces us after every peace treaty.

Virgil's intense feeling for the soil, the "pietas" attaching to it and the practicality of the owner's directions his *Georgics* give, cannot be understood without postulating that he was one of those who, in this process, had loved and lost, and then regained, so that both livelihood and sentiment were closely involved. His family was, so the traditional accounts say (and there is no particular reason to disbelieve them) expelled from its farm when the poet was about 29 years old, owing to the compulsory parcelling out of land to veteran legionaries by the Triumvirs in 41 B.C. The first of the *Eclogues* refers to these consfications. At some undefined later date it appears that Virgil, with the probable help of Maecenas, succeeded in inducing Augustus to compel the restitution of the precious Mantuan acres. Thus, during his adult formative years as poet, land hunger must have been a preoccupation with Virgil and his parents, and it must surely have conditioned his reactions to nature.

Virgil could have had no cause to love the new settlers, and there is probably no truth in the earlier notion, now pooh-poohed, that he wrote to instruct them in husbandry. Yet he did write with didactic purpose, and this as part of imperial policy. In the *Georgics* he speaks as a small owner to other owners. He writes for the farmer or the successful trader who had bought an estate, and his object is clearly to recommend and explain the cult of the soil; so much is plain from the poem itself. Land restoration was part of the governmental plans. Without imagining a definite command from Augustus, we may well surmise a hint from the helpful Maecenas. At the completion of the work Virgil was about 40 years old; and the *Georgics* were recited to Augustus and apparently approved.

Here then is a poet with as practical an exposition to make as had poet ever, and equipped with plenty of technical knowledge. Yet he knows better than to start by being prosaic. He begins on the contrary by firmly linking earth to heaven; he personifies every aspect of country life, so that each tree, animal or implement will recall some deity. The humanizing element, that which he expects to attract the reader, is the myth in each thing; that is his way of inculcating devotion to the land as a life, the seasons are the gifts of the stars; wheat, grapes, the art of the plough and the farm waggon, belong to Bacchus and Demeter who gave them to man; the winnowing-fan, also, belongs to Bacchus. Neptune gave men horses, Pan presides over flocks and herds; the olive-tree is Minerva's. And the whole hard rural scheme of life is ordained of Jove to stimulate man's invention and resourcefulness. The acceptance of all this scheme, collaboration with it, is "pietas."

So throughout; only on a background of supernatural forms does he paint his prosaic realism. The farmer harrows and golden Ceres regards him from heaven; she, above all, is to be worshipped. Sometimes in midnight stormclouds comes Jove, flashing thunderbolts. The moon is "flushed with her brother's' rays", clouds are "thin woolly fleeces" from Hercules' flock; kingfishers are "beloved of Thetis." In his technical second book about trees Virgil cries, how blessed are those who know Pan, Silvanus, the Nymphs: the farmer, he only, still leads the life of the golden age when Saturn dwelt on earth. After a sandy stretch in the third book about animals, wherein he merely rises to a few heroes,' Virgil evidently feels by the time he reaches bees—feeders of Jupiter in Crete—that we need enlivening, and he tells us a story—not the original one he wrote, which was struck out by higher authority, but a substitute. It is a strictly relevant legend, designed to counterbalance the materialism of the subject which immediately precedes it by again driving home the need for worship if things are to go aright. Aristaeus' bees failed because he had neglected to sacrifice to Ceres, and for no other reason. If in future he will do so in due form, all will certainly be well. So! there we are left, with the god-form dominant:—Virgil has steered a careful course with his mythology; he has neither proliferated legends, like Ovid, nor remained objective and scientific, like Lucretius the godless Epicurean; much as he owed in philosophy to Lucretius, who was almost the Godwin to his Shelley. Virgil's gods are benignant and an intimate part of the rural round; almost, to work is to pray. There is no determinism; place is left to man for self-perfection. Gods must be tended as lovingly as fields, and are the dominant partners in earth's welfare. The gods in fact are nature; the careful watching of weather signs for crops, the vigilance of good husbandry with harvests, implements, trees, animals all specially given by gods, is in itself a devotion to them. So understood, myths become a means of inducing the co-operation of man with nature, of activating Albert Schweitzer's "reverence for life".

The effect of the *Georgics* upon a rural situation wherein the gradual disappearance of the small man was causing public concern we can only tell by inference. In subsequent centuries tribute has again and again been paid to the value of the practical husbandry in this elegant and learned poem; and we know that the work at once took its place amongst the great books of literature. The Romans delighted in country poetry, and it was conned in the schools of rhetoric by the well-to-do young as part of their education. Sharp separation between town and country as yet was not, and the prosperous Roman was usually a farmer, even if he spent most of his time in Rome. A large part of Virgil's simple and beautiful creed, therefore, must have gone home to the right classes. It could not affect the ultimate decline of agriculture, but his idealism may very well have held it up awhile. We know that in the third century A.D. an attempt was made to revive the small settler ideal; it was a compromise, because it was an attempt to fit this into the frame of "big business"—the latifundia were run as groups of small farms, worked by settled slaves or by freemen who were tenants, not owners. The weakness of the scheme was seen when, in the next century, this absence of independent ownership left the door wide open to the binding to the soil of these tenants by imperial decree. This it was which set on foot the process resulting in the medieval manorial system of later centuries; part of a great cycle of economic changes over which mere poetry could have no jurisdiction. Too many evils had accumulated by the fifth and even by the fourth century for any poem to effect a cure of Roman civilization.

Myths and the Greater Faith

Myth is of its essence something that carries the impress of the past on into the present and future. And the myth of any present must still be rooted in group or racial feeling of the past, using their mold to some extent, however recent the figure or events giving rise to it.

Thus it was on a vast scale with the change over from classical to Christian beliefs. The past was carried over into the new faith to an extraordinary extent. The process whereby the local god or hero emerged into a suitable saint who took over some modified characteristics and a dedicated day is a commonplace among scholars, less known to average readers. A whole pagan-Christian calendar can be constructed, from the Christmas of the sun-god Mithra at winter solstice, through the forty-day Lenten propitiation of the winter gods, to the springtime resurrection of Attis at the vernal equinox. The sun-disk Horus slays the monster Set on St. George's Day; the midsummer Attis water-festival is that of St. John Baptist; the Osiris feast of lamps for the dead occurs about the time of

All Souls' Day. Between the fifth and the ninth centuries the age really is "dark" concerning the record of detailed events; but theocrasia is plain. Numerous traces of propitiatory sacrifices and Baal-worship in the British Isles bring the process home.

If one wishes one can make much of the "Paganism in our Christianity," as Arthur Weigall titled his brilliant popular study of the subject. Nevertheless, after the lapse of centuries one can broadly say it really was Christianity not paganism which dominated the admixture. The surviving paganism increasingly bore the aspect merely of old customs. The church gained her ends by flanking movements, and the life of the several myths was drained into the church's own central myth-truth of sacrifice and resurrection. All other figures and their fables were but echoes or pale foreshadowings of the Christ. Even at harvest-time, when the great cyclic vegetation myths reach apogee, when, therefore, they might be expected to survive at strongest, the tragic figure of the sacrificial god-king sinks into a John Barleycorn, by these days little more than a quaint fancy.

This adaptation of local cults by the church was in a way the symbol of the process whereby monasticism between the fifth and thirteenth centuries was to lay the foundations of European civilization. All over Europe bodies of monks, Benedictines, Cluniacs, Carthusians, Cistercians, were seeking out' remote valleys and inhospitable swamps. To seek out and reclaim or cultivate that which was waste was the effect of their search for devotional solitude. Once again agriculture was identified with' religion; hard physical work was inculcated by the rule of St. Benedict, although later heavy manual labour was largely left to lay brothers and peasants. The monks' improved methods spread to the countryside generally. The rotation of the manorial estates, decried during the enclosure period and in text-books since, but now recognized by many as in essentials sound for its period, seems to have been monastic in method. The growth of urbanism and of communications generally ruined the manorial system, the process being hastened by the Black Death. One cannot judge the efficiency of an agriculture in its declining period, denuded of labour and in the hands of absentee owners.

Thus the agricultural basis of the great medieval civilization was laid by those to whom the sepulture of Christ meant also the sowing of the grain in mortality—the Resurrection, the coming of the new grass and flowers, the fresh budding of trees. The apparatus of festivals and fasts, the attributes of saints, to a large extent satisfied the human desire for legendary variety, whilst deeper needs were met by the religion itself.

Meanwhile outside the Christian framework large obscure pockets of minority-cults continued the group-influence of pagan myths in debased forms. The mysterious shape of the Graal, most potent of symbols, for centuries haunted the church, which steadily refused to compromise with its apparently sexual content—it was left for ignorant poets of a later age to identify it with the eucharistic chalice. Of such ironies history is full. The fertility cult of Pan suffered a horrible change into the satanism of the diabolic goat and eventually emerged into the once formidable cult of black magic, still with us. Group-belief in such a myth has obviously lost all the life-giving properties found in the Virgilian usage.

Simultaneously, the materialism of the later middle ages added to the accuser of mankind, originally the djinn-like Hebrew Satan, the grosser Pan qualities. The mystics on the other hand developed a belief in good necessarily interlaced with evil; almost, in evil essential to the display of good. The devil, no longer merely autumn death or the innocent powers of fertility, but the power of darkness with his own realm and ministers, bulked large both in devotional writings and in popular sermons. This was the ultimate lodgement of one figure from cyclic myth under the tragic intensification of the Christian ethos.

The Social Functioning of Myth

The decline in the legendary content of the corporate belief which accompanied Protestant domination has slowly emptied the countryside of mythical meaning. If the officialization of Christianity by Constantine wrecked a mythology which was probably overblown, at least the new faith built up substitutes which humanized agriculture, under which, in fact, it was reconditioned. Protestantism and the commercialism which accompanied it may, again, have replaced a corrupted religious system—how corrupt; historians are likely to dispute for many years yet; but so far as myth or legend are concerned, during these centuries Protestantism has given nothing comparable with what it destroyed. Herein therefore lies our present problem: to find forms of expression for the time-spirit of the seasons in such a way as to enrich the spirit of devotion to the soil, to express and to intensify co-operation with nature. And this has to be done in ways that do not offend religious susceptibilities; though they may offend, even designedly offend, the business mentality to which the countryside means a profit-and-loss account and not a living way.

For the function of myth in a society shaped by Christianity obviously cannot be the revival of pagan deities. Nor can it pretend to explain to our generation the actions of natural forces when they are already expounded in scientific terms. The boy or girl who "knows" that lightning is the result of electrical discharges cannot be told simultaneously that it is Zeus' bolt, however little his "knowledge" really tells him and however much more powerful for imaginative purposes Zeus may be.

Yet from most of the Christian and especially from the Protestant sects seems to have died out the sense of a God immanent in creation: and scientific instruction normally omits to deal with the logic of causation. If popular Christianity, in its stress upon conduct, tends to lose the sense of the divine as constantly revealed in natural processes—if science, as rurally taught, has to confine itself to "how" and omit any essay at "why"—then surely there is place for the bringing back through myth of the sense of divine mystery, which most of the Christian bodies commonly fail, in fact, to make part of the sense of living and which the glib factuality of the laboratory is apt to kill.

Any myth that is to hope for more than the smallest of specialized audiences must now shed its merely fabulous, fanciful parts, so proliferated by Ovid. It must incarnate and display its central, unifying theme only, be more sparing even than Virgil of mythological figures in its variants upon the seasonal cycle whence the vast bulk of myth derives.

Moreover the variant used must be locally acceptable, maybe indigenous. In England it would be unnatural to attempt to present Greek mythology; Demeter and Persephone, however satisfying as South European incarnations of earth and summer, will remain exotic by Thames-side. The British Isles have their own rich and appropriate myths.

Two means may be tentatively suggested whereby in the urbanized country-dweller and in his offspring, taught everything except the lore and imaginations that should attach to their own countryside, some sense of the mystery and beauty that lie about them may be induced. One lies in festival drama; the other in using the sense of play-ritual in children.

Only in the presence of drama of some kind, on screen or stage, and when sensitized by music, does the self-conscious modern, in England at any rate, habitually relax his critical inhibitions. In festival drama is a possible technique whereby he may learn to partake of mass dramatic action and music without the entry of that paralysing sense of the ridiculous that checks the outward expression of any form of reverence. Russian experiments in the theatre have much to teach us concerning the extent to which audiences can become part of plays and truly experience them.

Living in this sense the presentation of the best-known native seasonal myth, that of Arthur, can certainly be made. Some hints may be found in Rutland Boughton's original Glastonbury presentation of part of the cycle. Boughton, however, did not appear to realize the seasonal character of the myth but was moved by its later Celtic story-forms; he was preoccupied with the Wagnerian music-drama idea, not with the renewal of the myth by a constant identification with natural processes.

The Arthurian myth clearly embodies the northern season cycle. The twelve knights are the heavenly star-signs whose flashing sword-dance induces fertility at the year's opening, frees the frozen waters for the coming of the spring (there are parallels in India and elsewhere). Arthur is the fisher—king whose coming is the rising of vegetation, for fishes are symbols of reproduction: Arthur catches the world-fish Gascoyne, who endeavours always to put his tail in his mouth. From the western isles—whence come the rain-bearing clouds—comes to him Güinevere, his Isis-like mate, and the Graal dwells in the land.

Then comes the desolation of the fallen leaf and the buried seed, when the king is smitten by the dolorous stroke. Excalibur is immovable in the stone, the Graal vanishes from the kingdom. Guinevere laments with her maidens, with all the bereaved mother-goddesses. Arthur sleeps, or is rowed away over the death-waters into the west.

The returning year or the springing seed comes back as Gawain the herb-healer, or Galahad the pure. He raises the king, draws out the symbolic sword; to him is vouchsafed again the Graal-sign of plenty. Guinevere returns from her alienation—or, as Isis, has again for mate the restored male form from the scattered Horus-seeds; the shining knights are again in the ring of harmony symbolized by the round table, by the round Graal-cup, by Gascoyne too perhaps.

Thus, very briefly, the main theme with its confusions; but clearly enough its plenteous material can dramatize into celebrations linked most directly with the agricultural round. In this form myth clashes with no religion, merely deepens and heightens the sense of mystery in nature. It should not be difficult to link parts of this to appropriate observances, once the essentially seasonal nature of Arthur has been recognized so that the whole myth is felt as living symbol, not distant romance.

Other themes from the subjoined outline of native deities also lend themselves to dramatic or pageantal treatment; the strangely imagination-haunting forms of Celi the piping god of the secret vegetation-fire, and Nyhelennia, the young northern Demeter with her apples, swans and stars, or Brigid the home-crafts patron.

Each generation is a new start, and in this only is the world's hope. Each generation, also, recapitulates; and though too much may be made of the fact, by too detailed a looking for particular stages of pre-history (for the child is a modern adapting to society as it is, as well as a much-modified savage)—yet the totemism and tribalism in youth are there, as the Baden-Powell movement and its allied and derived movements testify. What they have, notably, failed to do is to link the satisfaction of the myth-needs of the group with the texture of society as a whole. Towards what, in fact, do youth movements move?

The objective of a regenerated countryside is definite enough for any youth group to build towards. A regenerated countryside must be essentially regional; and regionalism in turn has an important, perhaps the decisive, word to say in the world's future shaping. As Philip Mairec recently wrote (*New English Weekly*, 2 May 1946): "Only by affirming what is most real in regional, local and communal life will mankind be able to meet the challenge of the planetary, when every country will be within a few hours' reach of each other, and all engaged in one conversation. This means a new economic, as intensive as our world has become extensive, a cultural effort which no world council will initiate for us, which must be begun by, and grow in and from, one people: perhaps it will begin in England. But here or elsewhere, this is the sign for which the workers of the world are waiting, and nothing else will command their full cooperation." A large enough objective, in all conscience, for a score of youth movements. The success of the Young Farmers' Clubs shows the existence of a body of young enthusiasts for the things of the countryside which is uncatered for, probably unsuspected by, the palliating town-escapists who have largely dominated the counsels of youth movements. Youth is, ultimately, realist; and play-organization, unless it moulds towards the world of real life, loses grip on the growing mind. Even the government's desolatingly unimaginative war-time youth organisations had success because based on national need, the factor of realism. How much greater, after the countryside has been opened up for scores of thousands of evacuated city children for the first time, would be the success of something combining woodcraft with husbandry, hardihood with a reverence for life, a sense maybe of eventual ownership with a sense of the mystery and poetry of the seasons?

Myth should be at the root of such a sense, of such an impetus. Any competent youth leader or educational worker, given a few hints, can devise a score of ways whereby in different shapes the drama of the year can be brought home in play-acting. Myth should vary and, develop. Initiation ceremonies in particular may be magnificently symbolical.

The Native Deities

These particular social aspects of myth are not necessarily, however, the poet's direct business; drama and initiation ceremonies may be poetic, but poetry is not usually dramatic. More directly mythical and more immediately exciting to the writer who feels the impulse to personify natural factors is the consideration of the native gods of the British Isles. Largely though not entirely Celtic, they form a cosmogony which can be set forth as distinctively as the Scandinavian or Greek, though perhaps not so definitely. England faces east and west with two great rivers, and over both aspects presides a god. Lud of Ludgate and the Thames is the Irish Nuada ('noo'aha'), of the White Light and thc Silver Hand, as in Wales he is Llud Lavereint; Nodens of the Severn-side Brythonic-Roman altar, is the Welsh Nud, who again is Nuada. So that King Lud and King Nod are double aspects of the same Zeus in a Neptune aspect, represented as a young man with rays coming from him, in a four-steeded chariot, accompanied by winds and Tritons who are waves; a god of great waters and the powers of the heavens. So too the sun-gods face east and west; Stonehenge, orientated to the rising sun, belongs probably to Lugh ('loo') lam-fáda, "of the long hand," the son of Remoteness (Cian); the Irish heavenly race, the Sons of Dana, may be his hosts of light; he is the god-founder of the great games at the Lammas festa, the Irish Olympiad, and owns the swift horses. In Wales he is Lleu, "light", or Llew Law Gyffes, "lion of the sure hand," has a horse of yellow-white footsteps and weds "flower-aspect," Blodywedd. Dunkery Beacon, orientated to the west, is obviously dedicated to the god of the setting sun, traditionally Bel, another aspect perhaps of Lugh, who is also a midsummer god who fights diseases and helps craftsmen.

Westward the Irish Sea opens to the Atlantic, and the sea becomes a great and angry enemy, as well as a means of communication: Lir or Leir ("sea") is a dour and ancient figure, his horse is Enbarr, the wind-foam; in Wales as Llyr he is parent of Branwen and Creuddylad or Cordelia, a gracious spring goddess of sea-waves and flowers; she alone is able to soften her father's grimness. But men develop and recover from the first panic at the Atlantic's rollers, and the old god is parent to a young and magnificent sea-god of merchandise upon sea-ways, Manannan of Man, a wind-god with a magic horse, sword and cloak; like Zeus his home is on an island—Man is the Crete of the British Isles. With the sea come infinity, speculation and yearnings towards the western sunsets, and Manannan has the sunset-land Tir-fa-tónn beneath the waves, a water elysium. The hills and funerary mounds however are the general abodes of the dead; thither go the heroes, and there are now the race from heaven, those children of Dana, Tuatha de Dánann, who arrived in Eire upon Bealtaine shrouded in mist; and the Dagda ('daw'ga') their leader comes to rule the land of the Sidhe ('shee'), dwellers in mounds; his is the fertility-cult with. a cauldron of plenty. (Arawn with his wind-dogs is the rather horrific corresponding hades—ruler of Wales.) The Dagda seems to correspond to the dark Welsh mother and earth goddess Don, "darkness," who is mother of the gods; and she in Ireland is Danu or Donu, Dagda's daughter and the Dánann mother. As Ana ("riches" or "prosperity") hers is the round earth and its symbol the mystic round cake, eaten semi—sacramentally; and the great sense of aboriginal motherhood goes on into the Christian St. Anne and the mothering-cake of mid-Lent. England's Dagda seems to be the Concealed One, Celi or Coeli, the mysterious piper on the hills and the secret good fire, perhaps the earliest deity traceable in England, who becomes King Coel and Cole and Coilus of Colchester, where coal was mined early in sub-history, whence may come the Culdees, the mysterious way-guardians.

As Manannan expands Lir, so Aenghus Ōg expands the dark Dagda his father; he is a growth god of the Boyne, is surrounded by birds like St. Patrick, and plays a love-harp. He becomes a swan to woo a swan maiden. He is also weather as it affects fertility, for he defeats the Fomorians of bad weather and sleeps in a glass dome which is the sunlit heaven. And Nyhelennia, Niwalen or Helen surely in the same way expands her father King Coel; she is the gracious young goddess of the votive tablets found by the English Channel with baskets of apples and children and a greyhound, a goddess of wind and fertility, of ways and uplands—there is a sea-connection, and links with leafy ways and armies; she girdled London with a wall. In Wales Elen is mistress of a heavenly host of stars or swans, and seems with her sisters of Arfon to form a dawn-group; she again connects with roads—tracks are often there called "elens"; "elen" also means an elder-tree, however. Don expands into a lovely daughter, Arianrhod, "Silver-Wheel," or the constellation of Corona, who is allied to a travel-god of the Milky Way, Gwydion, he who leads the daemonic revels upon Glastonbury Tor, the English Venusburg.

Fertility gives rise to a lovely myth of birth and the spirit in Ceridwen, a Welsh Ceres, who undergoes in pursuit of Gwion mystic transformations possibly corresponding to ritual ceremonials for the aspiring initiate; for Gwion has transgressed, tasting of the sacred Cauldron of Inspiration. At last as a black hen she swallows him as a wheat-grain, and he is reborn as the mystic poet Taliesin, found in the weir, which is the darkness and the waters of birth: he who has ever been and ever will be upon earth, the mystic inspiration; the incarnation of poetry— probably a pre-Celtic concept.

Magic is the chief element in the Welsh equivalent of Aenghus Og, Myrddin ("multitude") or Merlin, who may be the white light of the moon and that very brilliant and milky effect that the sun does often produce in the sky in northern climes. He confines the dragons of bad weather under Snowdon. He too has a glass house; his mate is probably the dawn, the Lady of the Lake; Caermarthen is his Caer or castle. Magical heads seem to be the belief behind Bran the giant son of Llyr.

The weather is a permanent conflict in the British cosmos, and weather contests are partly regular and seasonal, party day-to-day struggles, hand-to-hand chancy fights as it were. The Irish Children of Danu fight the Firbolg or Fomorians; the Welsh Don's son the weather-god

Amaethon eternally fights Arawn's wind-dogs; Gwythyr fights Gwyn ap Nud for Creiddylad (Cordelia), and Diarmaid fights Finn over Grainne who is Eire. After each contest the woman is shared out, Persephone-like, between the warriors, winter and summer dividing the world. Cuchulainn is the sun and the idealized Celtic warrior who transforms amazingly and fights many foes of whom the greatest seems to be Lugaidh ('looy'), probably here the monster darkness who after Cuchulainn's death is slain in revenge for him by Conell Cernach, his reincarnation.

Fire and civilization seem almost one thought in the British climate, and the fire-goddess Brigid is powerful as patron of crafts, the home patron; she, too, has another of these cauldrons which, although primarily the Irish peasant's great cooking-pot, may very well also represent an early basin-like substitute for the laborious stone circle as a means of telling the seasons, hence their control for the securing of crops, the "cauldron" itself therefore the source of plenty. The St. Brigid nuns continued the heathen perpetual fire of fertility. Kai in Wales, the English Sir Kay, is a culture-hero, the fire drill, the Celtic Prometheus. Celi, again, is perhaps the purely English figure. It must always be emphasized, however, that all these Celtic myths also belong to England, which knew most if not all of them before they retreated westward, and has many links with them still.

Fire is also war, and Celi, at any rate in his later form of Camulus, was a war-god of Essex; so was the Dagda as Irish leader, and hence his daughter Brigid, who is Brigantia or Belisma the great and warlike goddess of southern Yorkshire and Strathclyde, patron of the Brigantes. Nûdd and Gwynn were Welsh warleaders. The snake-haired and bearded god perhaps called Sul who glares at us horrifyingly at Bath, thinly disguised as a Gorgon (although gorgons were always female), may also be presumed to be a Celtic war-god.

Very Celtic is the power of oratory, and a most typical god is Oghma, giver of the Ogham script to Ireland, who may be assumed to be the same as the Gaullish Ogmios-figure recorded by a Greek traveller as drawing along captives by a rope proceeding from his mouth. Peculiar to Gaul and Britain, too, are three figures given a Latin veneer as the Deae Matres, unknown to classical mythology, who are matronae, matris and the Three Witches (lamiae trēs) of Benwell, Cumberland. They are the Three White Ladies of numerous woods; they haunt the springs; they descend upon the rivers and fuse into single river incarnations—Clota of the Clyde, Sabrina of the Severn, Abnoba of the Avons, Divona of the Dee; here and there detaching and identifying with a local goddess—an Arianrhod or Berecynthia. Not only Leir and Cordelia move directly into English concepts. Nod and Lud are not unknown to the English nursery, Sir Kay remains fiery in the later Arthurian recension, King Cole piping in the Chiltern Hills does not seem strange; Brigid, Briget, or Bride remains a crafts patron in the London institute. Helen or Helena or Nelly appears strongly evocative with her Foundling Hospital connections; St. Anne, Hebrew mother of the Immaculate Virgin, is enriched by identification with the great earth-mother. The very English-sounding Puck is Pucca Trwyn of Wales. Thus do imaginings and traditions fuse and the centuries blend in the myth world.

To sum up these aspects: myth is ancient, it is also new. Symbol and myth of a sort mankind will have; if starved of them in tradition or religion, their perverted forms spring up in diabolism or Nazism or elsehow. Seasonal myth needs reviving, reshaping in living ways; without it a cult of the soil may indeed happen, but will lack warmth and imagination. This kind of thought is natural in children, who summarize in themselves the history of the race; and for them symbol and myth can surely become means to an appreciation of man's power of cooperation with the seasons, and could give warmth and direction to a youth movement directed to the land. Seasonal celebrations for the countryside generally can be based on themes from native myths.

It is indeed possible that, through rituals based on myth, man's actual awareness may increase. A renewal may occur in that Dionysiac consciousness which was to Nietzsche the matrix of culture, smothered since Socrates in abstract knowledge of the Apollonian culture-type. To plan consciously for this, however, is to defeat the very meaning of mythical experience, which is a spontaneous participation or nothing. Indeed if any of the movements sketched cannot come about without a certain spontaneity it may be better that they should not happen for a while. For the fact must be faced that the contemplation of superhuman, as distinct from legendary shapes, projected by but abstracted from human thought, is not possible at every period of civilization. Shapes such as the dancing of the maruts for Indra, their swords imaging the vernal light, whilst Indra the fire-god un-looses the rivers, would have meant little to the typical eighteenth century mind; and all nature-powers, male or female, were identified in the middle ages with the powers of darkness, male devilry or female witchcraft.

Personification, however, is not the whole of myth. Whenever symbolism is used poetry becomes semi-mythical; for the symbol is the less human form of myth and links inevitably with it. Now symbolism is being increasingly recognized as a mode of thought lacking in this century but vital for the balance of the human mind. The more intelligent modern reaction to symbolism as a mold of thought finds clear expression in Richard Hope.[2] The modernist, he says, tries to clarify the part by abstracting it from the whole. But the meaning of every abstract concept "resides in the Whole from which it has been abstracted; and the more abstract and exact it becomes, the less meaning does it possess." It follows therefore that a concept in order to have meaning must "retain its connection with Infinity...retains a marginal inaccuracy which...gives it meaning...It retains a modicum of symbolic universality...The skilful thinker balances out the marginal inaccuracies of his concepts, works by his sense of the wholeness of the situation." Mr. Hope finds in thought generally to-day such an overplus of the abstract that it amounts to a "situation of universal meaninglessness." He concludes that "our language will be meaningless until we give back to our abstract concepts the symbolical, magical wholeness from which we have endeavoured to wash them clean." The poet, therefore, by inducing symbolic thought is doing a work of considerable significance for civilization.

It remains true that personified myth is probably the original matrix of imagination, and to it in one shape or another we are bound to return, again and again. Myth can be traced as a quite constant matrix in the past. For Nietzsche, the Greek tragic sense was born from religious myth by music. A parallel development may be worked out for Tudor drama, parented between the cathedral-step morality plays and an intoxication with song and eloquent speech.

The Archetype as Cosmic Myth

Myth has so far been given here its main historic sense of the

[2] Two articles in the New English Weekly, 22 Nov. and 6 Dec. 1945, under title of "The Meaning of Atomics".

incarnation of seasonal and diurnal, earthly and heavenly forces. But an immense illumination of the inner significance of myth has now occurred through the work of C. G. Jung. "Themes of a mythological nature...these motives and symbols Jung names archetypes...archetypes form centres and fields of force...of the continuity and order...of the unconscious," states the summary of Jung's work approved of by himself as a "concise presentation"—Jolan Jacobi, *The Psychology of C. G. Jung.*

Another definition given is: "psychological processes transformed into pictures." The images of the archetypes "are the same in all cultures. We find them repeated in all mythologies, fairy tales, religious traditions and mysteries." The night-sea-voyage and the sea-monster are the sun's night-travelling beneath the earth; forms such as the World-Tree, the Sphinx, the eternal child, humanized animals, stand for "certain figures and contents of the collective unconscious." Applying this scheme to literature, Maud Bodkin, in *Archetypal Patterns in Poetry,* accounts satisfactorily for many type-shapes in major poems of the past with reference to her subjective experience of them. They include the sunlit heavenly mountain, the cavern or watery deep of hell beneath or within it, the night journey which here becomes that of rebirth or visionary initiation symbolized by the Graal, the golden bough of life-renewal and perhaps also vision, the blessed and blossoming guarded paridisal garden, the clear yet milky river of life sequences such as the heavenly circuits intimating divine life (Plato, the *Phaedo*) and paradise-hades: figures embodying doomed and transient youth, and idealized fatality: Faust-figures, ambitious for knowledge or power, defiant of checks, contrasting with a shadow-self of evil as Faust with Mephistopheles or Othello with Iago; or in other aspects in conflict with a passionate fatal temptress: woman's ideal projection of man, such as the bold sea-captain: woman-figures such as the mother-goddess of fertility, the inviolable ideal (Eurydice), and the embodiment of visible beauty. To the psychotherapist the poet's imagination seems the same as a dream; "fantasies and visions furnish", says Jacobi, "material equivalent to that of dream for psychological interpretation." Nietzsche is collated with a deeper thought: "In sleep and dream we work through the whole task of former humanity." Jung himself says that the archetype is "an eternal presence, and it is simply a question whether consciousness perceives it or not"; archetypes are "organs of the soul." The archetype is preexistent and immanent, already there in the dark: "the form...is perhaps comparable to the axial system of a crystal which predetermines as it were the crystalline formation...without itself possessing a material existence... an invariable core of meaning." "They (the archetypes) are only formally determined," says Jacobi, "not in regard to their contents." As distinct from Plato's ideal concept of the archetype, Jung's "has inherent in its bipolar structure the dark side as well as the light."

Finally Jacobi sums up the Jungian objectives in terms that scarcely need transposition to apply to the precise purpose of the present book: "The sum of the archetypes signifies for Jung the sum of all the potentialities of the human psyche...To open this store to one's own psyche, to wake it to new life and to integrate it with consciousness, means therefore nothing less than to take the individual out of his isolation and to incorporate him in the eternal cosmic process...It becomes a teaching and a way...To release the archetype's projections, to raise its contents into consciousness becomes a task and a duty." Here therefore is the scientific justification for the poet's certainty that his dream-forms are in a peculiar sense true and his own task a valid one. "What the imagination seizes as beauty must be truth," wrote Keats; and what the imagination seizes is in fact nine times out of ten the archetype. "Archetypal images and experiences…still work to-day in the psyche," says Jacobi. "Only where faith and dogma have hardened into empty forms… in our highly civilized, technicalized, rational-minded western world have they lost their magical force and left man helpless and alone."

With James Joyce's *Ulysses* and *Finnegan's Wake* we have a large-scale demonstration of the mythopoeic faculty in the modern mind, so that Earwicker's whole life-scheme is seen deriving from instinctual bases. "Earwicker," says Edmund Wilson of *Finnegan's Wake*, in *The Wound and the Bow*, "resolved into his elemental components, includes the whole of humanity. The river…comes to represent the feminine principle itself… this stream of life which, always renewed, never pausing, flows through the world built by man. The daughter is identified with a cloud…the Anna Livia Plurabelle chapter describes a lively woman's coming-of-age; in the end, the mature river, broader and slower now, will move towards her father, the sea. The corresponding masculine principle is symbolized by the Hill of Howth…he is a fortress, he is Dublin, he is all the cities of the world." "There are also a stone and an elm on opposite sides of the Liffey which represent the death-principle and the life-principle (Ygdrasil)." "*Finnegan's Wake* advances with astounding strides the attempt to find the universally human in ordinary specialized experience which was implied in the earlier book by the Odysseyan parallel." "Joyce's purpose. . . to bring out in Earwicker's consciousness the processes of universal history…all implicit in every human being." Again, "the whole of human history and myth from the impulses, conscious and dormant...of a single human being..." The core of these gigantic studies in mental process is in fact the archetypal process, a clothing of experience with associational fantasy shapes chosen by the dream—self as material functional to the dream's purpose.

Between James Joyce and Jung it begins to appear that this myth process is much more than merely a main cultural shape of the past. It seems that it is the very pattern upon which the moving mind of man is built. If so, then it seems obvious that the extent to which a work of art makes vivid some part of this common human pattern in us all must be the extent to which it will appeal to our instinctive emotional levels. Myth becomes the central factor in the question of communication as between writer and reader in the literary process; qualified of course by all the other factors, expression, intellectual content, defence-formation by readers and so on. It may indeed prove to be a prerequisite for the transmission of other arts; this is suggested for graphic art by the discovery of the pattern of' the Golden Flower. Myth becomes a common individuation, a common ground emergent into the individual's unconscious and thence into, his consciousness from the mass-dreams of the race. Myth appears as the essential shape of the cosmos of man, both externally in the turning year and interiorly as the process whereby he assimilates the particular events of his life into his own pattern.

Some New Valuations of Myth

On the whole writers have been slow to grasp the immense implications of this discovery, though its power has been demonstrated politically in the myth-enslavement of a great people and religion has always known how to use the emotive force of participation in feelings of death and resurrection. Only rarely do writers seem to understand that, as used by poets, symbols, the typical speech-figures of myth, feel towards a language universal in the sense of being itself the root from which other systems have grown: the language after which Rilke, most inward and aware of poets, aspires: "One often finds oneself at variance with the external behaviour of a language and intent on its innermost life, or on an innermost language, without terminations if possible—a language of word-kernels...grasped in the speech seed...How often one longs to speak a few degrees more deeply! ...one gets only a minimal layer further down" (letter to Frau Wunderly-Volkart, 1920). Prose and poetry do so many things in various hands besides aiming at the deepest effect upon a maximum public that many lesser tasks have overlaid the perception of a greater. However, minds concerned with poetry have been moving in the symbolical-mythical direction, and new writers when challenged discover in themselves reasons for the myths that are found in their writings. Each of these reflections or rationalizations educed in correspondence with the writer is suggestive and illuminating as regards the use each poet makes of myth 'in his or her own work. Adam Drinan emphasizes the need for new myth and inclines to deprecate the elder myth; his own work concentrates upon the local and racial aspects. "We must make our own myth. For whom?...Don't you think the myth must come from the people, not from the artist? I can't see it coming in Mayfair or Wimbledon. I can see it coming from Suilven: and perhaps from Bow...we can't do it ourselves. There can be no synthetic myth... After the masses make the story, the poet can sing it. For now we can only sing the masses making it, a very different thing." "Myth from the people can only succeed revolution. Mayakovsky made no myth. But Lenin was the myth. We shall have a Lenin, though he may not be one man. Meanwhile, I study and sharpen my tools, praying I may not be born too soon. T he Sutherland evictions. There's a myth for you…I find in the U.S.S.R. a place for poetry as nowhere else in the world. Myths made in the heat of action, known to the whole people such as hasn't been in our countries for centuries. The ancient myth is the outcome of the ancient form of society. The myth subsists in the subconscious after that form has changed. To restore that myth unaltered is just what Fascism does in the conscious art-form." For that reason—because any reconstructed myth, he felt, moved towards undesirable political ends—Drinan does not associate himself with the work of the present group, although his work runs obviously parallel with its sympathies in its localism, in the breadth and intensity of its Gaelic historic and regional detail, as well as in the type-shapes he uses. One might suggest that not all Marxists view poetry in the same way, and that in fact the communal element is of the essence of myth. George Thomson in *Marxism and Poetry* (1945) says: "Our poetry has been individualized to such a degree that it has lost touch with its source of life. It has withered at the root... The bourgeois forms have become 'classical', our younger poets have discarded them. But they do not know where to turn for new forms...They must seek inspiration from the people." Whereas Thomson has little constructive to suggest to fulfill this programme, the cosmic shape concept provides what he needs. How can the poet seek from the people except by way of the unconscious layers that still run in common between the most individualized and the least sophisticated within one culture, by the "vision expressed in symbols," as Thomson himself describes Shakespeare's poetry?

A more limiting reaction to the myth-idea is that of Frank Kendon, the lyrical poet. "Myths...are as near to the truth (and are believed) as the people themselves can come, 'and they *express*, not control, the direction of movement and the springs of action...Myths to be effective sources of power must not yet be seen as myths. Once you have said 'let's pretend' you have killed all the vital power...The fact that myth has vanished and nothing has replaced it shows that man does not need it any longer. No doubt there are myths rife today, too; but you and I cannot choose them, I think, because we can't see them (any more than a fish can see water). Perhaps Science is the new myth. Perhaps Relativity is, or Jeans' astronomy, or the all-embracing microbe, or the more-than-all-embracing vitamin...It is fundamental to myth that it can and will be superseded by a nearer approach to naked truth as generation succeeds generation. Personified nations...American optimism, English hidden idealism—these seem to me to be something like the true myths of the moment. And money is the great myth too..."

Drinan and Kendon may be taken as typical of minds poetic and sympathetic, but non-mythopoeic. Obviously if one accepted Kendon's view that current myth cannot be known there would be an end of this discussion. There is an element of truth in it; one may reiterate that if a myth movement cannot happen naturally, it had better not happen at all. The question lies in the nature of the artist. The separation implied between the creative faculty working fully only in whole-hearted belief, and the inhibiting effect of consciousness, is over-sharp. At his best the artist surely is the person who can examine clearly his motives and groundwork yet is not thereby hampered in productivity; and the average writer or artist is usually at least half-conscious of his objectives and methods—it is a rare artist who has no intellectual account whatever to give of his work (though it may commonly, and even usually, be a wrong one). Similarly the mythical poet: deliberate invention and arrangement of complex frameworks did not prevent the mythopoeic flow in either Dante or Milton. Virgil wrote quite consciously of myths slightly over-ripe in his own day; there was already, however, a nearer approach to objective truth in Lucretius.

Very different is the account of myth given by those practising it. Morwenna Donnelly, whose exquisite "Beauty for Ashes" is obviously using myth in a way different from any of those so far considered, points out that in Gaelic writings the various elements in man's nature were given mythical form, "symbolism which conveyed the distinctions of the whole individuality." In her own poem the "symbolic people" are, besides the boy Peregrine and his mother Bella, Cucogry his soul, Lughaidh his spirit, Aedh Ruadh O Domhnaill or Red Hugh O'Donnell representing his ancestors, and his guardian saint Cairneach of Cluain-Laodh. "In myth the Irish were projecting objectively an idea of life, as well as their experience of it...The people who created the myth of Ireland infused into it a tremendous imaginative grandeur; they created a super-stature of being in Cúchulainn." This draws in a most valuable comparison, from the practice of the great stream of Irish tradition, with the view suggested above as emergent from Jung and Joyce, that all myth is inherent in the subconscious of every man. This Irish personification of the instruments comprising the orchestra which is man seems to be an, approach to the same truth front the opposite direction, as it were, such allegory being the reverse of the hyper-realistic approach represented in literature by Joyce's magna opera and in mental medicine by the approach of Jung. It is probably significant that it is the Dubliner Joyce using Irish life and consciousness for his material who thus arrives at confirming the validity of an ancient Irish poetic convention.

Morwenna Donnelly has a hope that myth may revivify whole nations; she quotes O'Grady to the effect that the legendary and mythical history of a nation is that nation's dream of what it would like to be, "and in that sense" (she says) "I think one could have a forward-feeling myth—a nation re-creating itself in its imagination. Perhaps, even if we cannot lay again the foundations of our civilization, we can revitalize it in this way." She points a very useful warning about method to those essaying the mythical path in her reply to a question about W. B. Yeats' use of myth: "I think myth is unsatisfactory when it is used recollectively, with a kind of racial nostalgia for the forms of a past culture, or with the sole emphasis on its aesthetic content. Unless one can reinterpret the meaning behind myth, it merely becomes a historical curiosity—an outworn vehicle of expression."

In James Kirkup we have a writer who moves naturally in mythopoeic fashion. He has no need to study or contrive myth, the superhuman shapes of his imagination are myth; "how much more real," he says of their effect on himself, "than the figures of actual life!" He has gone in this beyond the Surrealists. For Surrealists, products of a generation influenced by Freud, typically produce associational fantasies delving into the unconscious and deriving thence their strange and on the whole unpleasant effects by parallels with the unconscious of others. Freudian influence supplied them with a clinical approach to the primitivism of the unconscious; and in abandoning the intellectual-moral censor surrealism really went sub-human, not primitive.

Surrealism was defined in André Breton's 1924 manifesto as: "Pure psychic automatism by which it is intended to express, verbally, in writing, or by other means, the real process of thought. Thought's dictation, in the absence of all control exercised by the reason and outside all aesthetic or moral preoccupations. Surrealism rests in the belief...in the omnipotence of the dream and in the disinterested play of thought... In the course of many attempts I have made towards an analysis of what, under false pretences, is called genius, I have found nothing that could in the end be attributed to any other process than this." At that period Breton was, he himself says, "preoccupied with Freud." The denial of reason is underlined by him, writing in 1936: "a prevailing view that I look upon to-day as being extremely mistaken, the view that thought is supreme over matter. Surrealist thought rests to-day in dialectical materialism and insists on the supremacy of matter over mind." It will be noted that all this ignored the equally Freudian conception of the superego constructed during life based on parental images and acting as a check on the. instincts. However, Surrealists often practise better than they theorize, and Picasso and Dali, amongst visual artists, frequently integrate in an archetypal and therefore mythical way, as Kirkup recognizes. Neither the Freudian nor the Surrealist supplied, be it noted, any social function for the writer; he functions for them merely as a projector of his individual processes.

However, psychotherapy has meanwhile moved on; the Jungian movement has further distinguished between the personal unconscious and the universal or racial unconsciousnesses, from the racial level of which emerge the above-defined archetypes, which behave as though informed with purpose. Kirkup's forms represent some parallel in poetry to the archetypes, for they have a compelling dream-force that integrates as well as moves the emotion, and indeed goes some way in the purgation of the emotions by pity and fear: a function which their best friends would hardly claim for the Surrealist writers. Speaking of the element common to his own poetry and to mine which we decided to call "cosmic shapes," Kirkup says: "The concept of a larger-than-human shape is one that I find excites me and makes me want to describe and capture it in its own universal atmosphere. It happens to affect me in such a way that I feel urged to write about it and when I do write about it, my writing generally seems to be in the form of poetry. The greatest shapes have their being in the unconscious and are perhaps images retained from one's tininess as a child surrounded by seemingly enormous figures. It is significant, I think, that my poems about cosmic figures are primarily concerned with human or near-human shapes. The superhuman form or archetype has a sheer height and a physical largeness which generally seem to compel a large poem, but often human beings—generally those of 'simple' nature—possess cosmic stature, and are embodied in poems which are comparatively smaller—like Wild Wilbur and The Idiot.

"The types found in ballad poetry—Tam Lin, Loving Andrew, The Outlaw Murray, Hynd Etin, along with the more general 'demon lover,' 'mother,' 'son,' and 'lady' types—seem to be the nearest approach to what I mean, and certain figures of tragedy like Lear, Faustus, Oedipus, and' mythical figures like Jason, Medea, Narcissus, Proserpine, Orpheus, Zeus, Neptune and Prometheus, are all, in my sense, cosmic shapes. This seems to link my conception of the superhuman type—the Sailor (in whom all sailors, including Ulysses, Columbus, Palinurus, and even Noah, are one), the Gardener, who is vegetation, the Lover, the Prince, the Shepherd, the Father, the Fool, the Sleeper (cf. 'The Sleeping Beauty'—a fertility or regeneration type)—with a fundamental sense of tragedy and doom, such as is found in the ballad and the early German Sturm und Drang drama especially, the inherent sense of disaster in existence. The larger and more 'universal' the type, the greater become his tragic potentialities. There is always a feeling of the ultimate darkness, of the inevitability of the life-process and its eventual tragic resolution.

"This sense of tragedy is to my mind most deeply felt and most movingly expressed in the music of Sibelius, in the best of Elgar (e.g. the 2nd Symphony); in the poetry of T. S. Eliot, Whitman, Baudelaire, Milton, Dante, and the German Romantics; in the psychology of Jung; in the paintings and drawings of Blake, Samuel Palmer, Rouault, in Picasso's giantesses and agonized anatomies; and in the concepts of the fool, the angel, the shepherd and the poet in the art of Cecil Collins. Legend and fairy-tale and folk-tale all have a part in it—and the 'magic' or the enchanted quality that is the greatness of the best (generally French) Surrealist work.

"These tremendous shapes are charged with an essential consciousness of universal reality, and with an intensely emotional cosmic restlessness, longing, scheming, a perpetual aspiration towards self—realization and perfection, which is never satisfied, but which can never be disregarded or denied.

"These shapes and the worlds they inhabit, though based on our present existence and all our conscious and unconscious life, are more real to me than the human beings and the events in the world around me."

It will be noticed that Kirkup's list of cosmic shapes very largely coincides with Maud Bodkin's and Jacobi's accounts of archetypes, neither of which he had seen before writing the above.

* * * *

In *Cosmic Legend*—so named since Arthur, the central figure used, though a myth, has recently been rehabilitated by T. D. Reed as an historical figure and therefore is rather legendary than purely mythical—the cycles of the past are experienced is seasonal drama which is also allegorical of man's life: and in this any streamlined or new technique is obviously out of place. To some extent the movements in this might be held to reflect the states of consciousness surrounding the successive figures of the Jungian account of psychoanalysis, although the paradisal opening does not; that is, the Dolorous Stroke is an emblem of the Shadow or Adversary; the Graal an emblem of the vision of an Anima; Arthur as a wise risen lord is the Wise Old Man, and the completed ring a Mandala. None of these possible identifications was in my mind while the poem was in gestation, so that it is a wholly unknowing deployment of them.

Towards the old-new mythical and symbolic impulse in poetry therefore converge various pointers indicative of its inspirational value for the present and future. Any movement in writing, and indeed in any art, necessarily has a relationship to the knowledge of its own day, and no less has this one to the later findings of therapeutic psychology.

So strongly has the conviction that myth is not merely valid over large areas of the poetic field generally, but that it is the appropriate poetic gospel for this generation in particular shaped itself in the minds of several of us that the need to express it as a truth not peculiar for ourselves but for general acceptance impelled the statement that follows, expressing, however inadequately and tentatively, a belief that we feel has only to be put forward to find some response from those who have seen through the barren intellectualism of the 1920's and the political dogmatisms of the 1930's as they showed themselves in modish poetry—useful though these movements were in sharpening the tools of an art and enlarging its scope: from those who are looking for some general direction in the present chaotic trends, amongst which one has been traced by Herbert Read under the title "Neo-Romanticism" and another, referred to above, launched by Henry Treece and J. F. Hendry as "The Apocalypse": this in the latest version being said by Hendry to "describe the liberation of feelings that are breaking down the old social order".

That the growth of myth, symbol and legend-feeling runs closely with the new organic feeling for the land is evident, if only in the common factor of emotive primitivism. Some of us are more conscious of this than others; but in all who are sensitive this current of contemporary mythical tendencies is flowing in one shape or another. Our decade at last begins to take on its distinctive pattern, and criticism is set its appropriate problem—to determine the purpose and proper scope of myth, symbol, legend, fantasy and their kindred.

Cosmic Legend

I

Twelve are the starbeams running light about the zenith-pole by night,
twelve the armoured months revolving weave the sword-dance bright:
brother-band of Maruts, youthful nobles, with the god of fire
shining constantly upon the earth with him their one desire
seven rivers bound with ice-chains to unleash and bid the spring.
Indra of the fire and sunrise
for the death of Vrita, cold
dragon coiling manifold,
is dancing with his arms and eyes
speaking very silently
under earth and in the skies.

Here like ascending domes haled from the earth's foundations
crebrant with twittering leaves the great trees come
dim-patterned mushrooms now in a larger than human meadow
misted and wreathed in a most fertile gloom.
The snowdrop and the violet lurk in the year's beginning yet,
the dews are cold the young grass wet, the moon updraws the sap
beneath the tree-bark from the roots' web-fingers and long tap.
Coos the ringdove with incipient domesticity,.
fishes dart in water manifold in progeny.
The May-king leads the celandine smiling over field and hill,
Adonis the white hunter tips his arrows for the kill.
On mountain-side the moon Selene loves Endymion's sleep,
monthly in her waxing waning dotes upon his fleece-touched cheek.
Adonis will not Aphrodite, Endytnion cares but for his sheep:
yet goddesses of love and death still the young men seek.
Dark the young strength of Arthur's name, pale as the fatal horse his fame
who Gascoyne took with iron hook (swimming serpent of the night),
fisher of the northern mere and islands scarfed with light.

The cup is filled the cup has power
the waters of new vision flow,

the crops upstart, and into flower
the later grasses glow.
The deep mist drowns the northern land
and channels of the yellow south
floodwater fills; the lance upstands
and pierces the balloons of drought.
Within the storehouse fill the shelves,
The people in the copper throne
intensely burnished, see themselves:
the people and the king are one.

Legend of the earth's beginning, of the unaccomplished state
innocent of crime and virtue, Isis and her Horus-mate
son and husband, master tale whereon the race-myths variate.

II

I would not throughout creation see the shadow that deep-grows
past the sunlight down the moonlight in the lichened rocks and shadows.
Now Isis, Magna Mater, Cybel, flies incumbent upon night
as a veil blown billowing outward from a window filled with light.
Stiffly gulls in circles flying crying round the unlit tower
through the omnipresence of a moonlit shade and shower:
these her familiars as in a mist thick-charged and visible
she sits aloof and wave-drifted, dark, concentred, very still.
Cloudy wreaths creep round and vanish, spectral crowns arise and fail,
anchorless as lantern-lighted mountain swaying in a gale.
Earth-born children of the ages posture their memorial gloom,
heave upon the mouldering spaces marbles to the urn-decked tomb:
silk-heeled squires and swathed penmen gleam enormous white as doom—
solemn light across the pavement from the windows arching high
alternates with silent dusty darkness, stiff and dry.
his yet to reconcile with the dust of Horus-son
man and spirit; but the toilers of the world not yet had known
earth and heaven to bridge, or clutch with massive hand un¬skilled
when the Mother threw her girdle. As magicians Babel build

levering forces, turned to evil; with divine pre-aim unfilled
their measureless grey strength miswilled.
Pharaohs, communes, demes and nations weltering perished from some
rule
by godhead written and for earth designed
to quench from evil fiery desolate man.
The cruelty that worms the heart of love
feeds upon jealous sad despair; great pain
mingles with every sweetness fleshly grown.

The Cup is dry, the land is blowing with the dust of Horns slain.
The fated Mother hooded cut his stalk of life; she weeps again
lament for Thammuz and Adonis. Death-in-life Osiris reigns
on shadowed earth.

Excalibur is fixed within the magic stone.

Guinevere and her twelve maidens singing weep and weeping moan
in the chapel perilous beside the entranced neophyte;
the cup has floated far away from the questing knight.
See the temples of brown Egypt fill with eyes within, and cool
grows the intent of souls. Habit and air and fire
fall from the spirit.

Isis floated then
in darkened garments, lined with crescent moons, without desire.
Lakes with silver seeded, darkened under trees inverted green
bore her on the cosmic voyage for the Horus-dust divided.
when the god betrayed was cut and scattered many-sided
among all men; and she the heavy searcher. for the fragment-truth

hid on earth in many temples—quest through lands of age and youth:
Arthur at the close of day by the death-queens rowed away,
Adonis by the boar at bay pierced, lies gory-thighed,
Adonis-Attis gardens planting shallowly, the girls inchanting
weep to the sacred numen-tree in whose laden hollow
the form of carven Attis they may show.

O enwoven in the darkness: so to a faithless century,
ghostly mother, also coming: in the night a breded tree
is domed enormous to the sky with leaves that whisper and branches
whine
brushing up among the stars, touching at the zenith's bars,
until they fall sometimes in fire through an arc entranced and fade
burnt for the glamour of earthly tales:
soft mansion of innumerable veils
that shield around from penetrable shade
ancient Isis: so within the night of drought and death
amid harsh breaths a softer breath is met.
Weaves a loom of eerie dream,
woven forms that mime and cry
and empassioned sleepers seem
bound in weird reality
when the fluttering shape is sent
charged with meaning's inner gleam
and swathed in moving lineament.

Then are the windows' pale blank overhang
of shifting shades on many a. muted way
of that dun empire, glittering from a ray
through frond-lit trees as throbbing hum
touches the sleeping ear. So come
white morning and still pools of truth
showing still image in that vigil, youth.

Isis searches night by night in heaven and earth and stars (they say)
fragments of the ever-living Horus; and from day to day
what is found she joins, but never whole again has she
the child and mate she bore arid slew in the land beside the sea.
That is the sorrow eternal, the sorrow of Isis unfree.

And even as your partial forms, O Isis—and even as she—
neither in light nor dark, come terribly
the hours of knowledge clear and dim
that build upon the loom for him,

the watcher, his flax-hearted thought
then with an image closely caught;
and when the intense hour is done
in memory is clearly laid
thought shapely as the informing shade
that lives when life and death are one.

Flows the blood of Mithra's bull, the waters under the moonpull
fall and draw out from the pool, the grain floats far away:
the Graal is vanished from the chapel where the knight lies gray.
I would not throughout creation see this shadow that deep-grows
even in sunlight and in snows:
cursed is this mad and musical mephitic air—
speak then I no more, there is horror in my hair.

NADIR

The bed of darkness whereinto light bends
where thought begins and toward which it tends:
here round and found the silent stones are rolled
wherewith the caster makes the vital mold:
there constantly the changing clays are poured;
then taken, hard and changeless, to be stored
with all the records of the dead that lie
time past, in barren dull rigidity.

Yet is no past, no future, and no fate
but being, jetting from the increate.
The breath whereon the universe is poised
exhales, indraws, undreaded and unnoised.
So does the large-expanded ocean breathe
in mists that on dim silent headlands wreathe.
By forms from this unseeing mold we live;
time here goes meaningless as some old sieve
no longer straining the grey death-dust through.
Simultaneity is the sole view
of the eternal eye that never shone

because it is that which it looks upon.
The eye in matter veiled can only see
the wild destruction danced by Shiva, he
whose traceries are spread before man's face;
not so the gathering in depths of space,
the exhaltation germinal and vast
of Brahma's breath sustaining first and last.

III

Prose:
I have made my ceremonies; the crisis
comes. None can reproduce, no water flow,
until the sword is from its sheath pulled.
Only I, the medicine-man Gawain, instructing
at midnight Galahad, the pure one of
spring—I alone can save you, faithless
with the fallen leaf. I prove to you,
O my dead people, once again that
I alone am your strength.

In the first ray beating touching on the centre altar-stone
to the eye prepared at vigil-end, the vessel of the sun,
cup and heart, to Galahad.

Life runs along the central vein;
on the broadened ray the yellow seeds are floating in a rain:
so the neophytes entranced can move their hands and feet
as from the stone the sword leaps out, as the pulses beat
strongly in the waiting people—rising of the slain,
movement-ripple as the crowd
with smile and speech move each to each.
Now from a deep blue cloud
the oarless barge of sleep
carries again twelve figures from its deep,
surround that fisher king who lives again
his simple folk to greet.

IV

Horus in Isis can fulfil, man and woman have their will
each of each; the night is still, the secret forces rise.
Glory in the darkness: Isis has the power that prisoned lies
in the search and in the shadow warm, creative, slow and wise
in the night beneath the moon, when the male forces wane
and the woman, white, pervasive, moves in restless joy and pain,
tremulous and flowerlike, with shining knowledge wan.
The face that dances silently through the star-powdered sky
with a yellow mirror, lips that flicker movelessly,
is the vessel of her strength unfolded riding by.
All the silver mazes drawn by Aphrodite orbed at sea
lead but into one deep cavern soft and warm and free
where the man at last at rest his peace extends; the cave is she.

On the sun-filled plain and mountain comes the power to man;
all Adonis flame-ringed chases with a hunter's cry
down the golden frets and clanging corridors of sky.
Engine-muscled implemental on the earth, the man in pain
sweating cuts and cutting binds, threshes heavy grain.
On the weary plain go wending the yoke-cattle dusty grey
beneath the hammers of eternal heat and showering sparks all day
from the sun's colossal forge white-blinding from of old.
Behind the trees at forest-edge in black and crooked fantasy
wave and ripple rich on ripple hangs the sheeted corn in gold.

As Rā in angry pleasure runs along the western rim
man the hardwon sheaf is carrying with wasted limb:
nightly then the garnered taking. she transmuting not in vain
shapes conception; Isis blows through her unknowing brain,
every motion hers is filled with thoughtless wisdom, she who is
the urgent lifecup and the circle.
Horus mangled lies
in a thousand pieces, cut by his ambition (so
mankind is lost in its inventions' curious vain show).
Horus, Isis—rhythm of the aeons in the earth and air;

the careworn and divided one—the brooding and the bare.
Man that taketh woman...Horus to the ancient Isis there.

On sanded waste a youth with a maiden oxen-eyed
slowly wandered hand in hand on feet that searched no path, but wide
went, with only footpalms knowing how they walked, for so
enwrapped they were that eye and mind did large and single grow.
Isis hovering sought and muttered in their touches soft and slow.

Crebrant is the land; the throne restored and shining; seasons swing
again beneath twelve signs, the noble youths that dance about the
spring
dance to the completed ring.
Persephone sometime is captive, Mithra now shall mediate
knowing life and death; the people comforted endure to wait:
for thee circle is fulfilled, life and death have been explored
and deepened summer ripens Attis-Arthur, the wise risen lord.

Prose of the Myth Fusion Employed

First Movement:

In the sky and from sky to earth dance the star-beams, a flashing sword-dance by twelve glorious youths of equal age (Maruts, Korētes, Salii, Knights). They are fertility daimons dancing eternally for the freeing of the waters, seven rivers imprisoned by Vritra; the feat is performed by Indra (the god of fire, lightning and volcano) for the coming of the May King, the spirit of Adonis loved by Aphrodite, of Endymion loved by the fertility-moon Selene, of all vegetation. Fishes and doves are symbols of fertility; Arthur the fisher-king catches Gascoyne the world-fish of reproduction (Sesha, the world-serpent). As Attis he is loved by the mother-goddess, as king he is loved by Guinevere. The Graal dwells in the land, by the waters of plenty.

Second Movement:

The god-king is smitten with the Dolorous Stroke, Adonis is wounded in the thigh, Attis is emasculated by the mother-goddess, Horus is cut up by his enemies, Arthur's kingdom is desolated, fertility is gone, the Graal vanishes, Osiris the underworld undersoil death-in-life god reigns. Excalibur is immovablc in the stone.

The eternal mother-lover who is essentially the moon, Isis-Aphrodite, Magna Mater, Cybele, Anahita, laments for the scattered Horus, for Thammuz, for Attis-Adonis; Selene watches over Endymion, Guinevere weeps with her maidens. All nature is waste.

Arthur is rowed away over the death-waters; Horus (who is also the scattered seed) is dispersed throughout the land. In his death must die also the initiate in the chapel perilous. The grain is floated away. The sacred Bull bleeds under the knife of Mithra.

It is the indrawing of creation's breath, the darkness of Brahma, the triumph of Shiva.

Third Movement:

Appears the hero, the returning year, the medicine man, Gawain-Galahad, the herb-healer. His is the vigil of the initiate, and with him watch all the initiation-test novices. The dead knight-king is in the chapel perilous; by him the Graal-aspirant awaits the vision. If he fail, if the novices fail, they too die. The proof of the success of the initiation is in the resurrection of the god-king, the new birth of the year, the new flame of spring. Galahad initiated by Gawain alone can draw the symbolic sword from the stone, free the reproductive powers from the chill of death; he rides out with the unconquered lance and to him comes the vision of the Graal, the Cup, the female emblem; and where the Cup is, there is plenty and moisture.

Fourth Movement:

Isis collects into a whole her scattered child Horus, Arthur arises from sleep, comes again from the west; the initiation is completed. He is the same yet different; he identifies in his renewed youth with the hero, he is Attis, he is Adonis, loved again by the mother-wife-goddess. He is now the six-months' sojourner on earth, the season of growth and fruition; but Perse phone must later spend six months in captivity with Dis of the underwor1d. The Lord is risen, the seasons revolve again. He is now the mediator, knowing both life and death; he is agent, as Mithra, of the resurrection of all men. The circle is completed.

The four parts of the completed cycle may therefore be summed in the phrases: Spring paean—the trance of death—the efficacious magic—resurrection and fulfilment.

A Note on Variant Elements

A word is due to the scholar of mythology.

I am aware that not all the mythical figures quite fit into this generalized myth; the death of the hero remains (probably advantageously) mysterious—whether he is motivelessly sacrificed by the mother-goddess or cut up by enemies: herein therefore it his been left inconsistent. Similarly, the confusion between Gawain and Galahad—or whether Galahad is Gawain, or a risen Arthur; and the confusion between the short seasonal cycle (spring death and late summer life) and the longer yearly cycle (autumn death and spring life); both are unresolved.

More detailed divergences I here merely note, again without attempting to synthesize opposing conceptions. In brief, Attis-Adonis-Thammuz is, essentially a youth loved by a goddess; only after tragic death does he become divine. There was for his Phrygian followers, a mystic feast in which women also partook. The Attis initiate theoretically died with his hero and rose with him; presumably a western version of well-known Indian mystical initiation methods.

Mithra, however, is from the first a mediator between god and man; he is also the sun (his is a Persian cult) and agent of the resurrection of all men, the sacrificer of the divine bull in whose blood his followers were washed. The ritual was an all-male one, a favourite with soldiers. The Mithra initiate did not die—the bull's death was all-sufficing; but he rose direct to the new life, up seven ladders into heaven.

Bibliography

Carr-Gomm, Philip, *Journeys of the Soul: The Life and Legacy of a Druid Chief* (Oak Tree Press, 2010).

-----, *What Do Druids Believe?* (Granta Books, 2006).

Davies, Edward, *The Mythology and Rites of the British Druids* (J. Booth, 1809).

Godwin, J.G., ed., *The Poetical Works of Robert Stephen Hawker* (C. Kegan Paul, 1879).

Greer, John Michael, *The Druidry Handbook* (Weiser, 2006).

Haycock, David Boyd, William Stukeley: *Science, Religion, and Archaeology in Eighteenth-century England* (Boydell Press, 2002).

Hutton, Ronald, *The Druids* (Continuum, 2007).

Jacobs, Margaret, *The Radical Enlightenment* (George Allen and Unwin, 1981).

James, David, *The Patriarchal Religion of Britain, or a complete manual of ancient British Druidism* (Whittaker and Co., 1836).

Jenkins, Geraint H., *Fact, Fantasy, and Fiction: The Historical Vision of Iolo Morganwg* (Canolfan Uwchefrydiau Cymreig a Cheltiadd Prifysgol Cymru, 1997).

-----, ed., *A Rattleskull Genius: The Many Faces of Iolo Morganwg* (University of Wales Press, 2005).

Morgan, Owen, *The Light in Britannia* (Daniel Owen and Co., 1890).

-----, *The Winged Son of Avebury* (Daniel Owen and Co., 1921).

Mortimer, Neil, ed., *Stukeley Illustrated* (Green Magic, 2003).

Nichols, Ross, *The Book of Druidry* (Aquarian, 1990).

-----, *Prophet, Priest and King: The Poetry of Philip Ross Nichols*, ed. Jay Ramsay (Oak Tree Press, 2001).

Paine, Thomas, *The Writings of Thomas Paine*, ed. Moncure Daniel Conway (G.P. Putnam's Sons, 1908).

Piggott, Stuart, *The Druids* (Thames & Hudson, 1975)

-----, *William Stukeley* (Thames & Hudson, 1985).

Raoult, Michel, *Les Druides: Sociétés Initiatiques Celtiques Contemporaines* (Editions du Rocher, 1983).

Reade, W. Winwood, *The Veil of Isis, or Mysteries of the Druids* (C.J. Skeet, 1861).

Spence, Lewis, *The History and Origins of Druidism* (Rider and Co., 1947)
-----, *The Magic Arts in Celtic Britain* (Rider and Co., 1945)
-----, *The Mysteries of Britain* (repr. Newcastle Publishing, 1993).
Steiner, Rudolf, The Druids (Rudolf Steiner Press, 2001)
-----, *Man in the Past, Present, and the Future* (Rudolf Steiner Press, 1966).
-----, *How to Know Higher Worlds* (Anthroposophic Press, 1994).
Stukeley, William, *Stonehenge: A Temple Restor'd to the British Druids* (repr. Garland, 1982).
-----, *Abury, a Temple of the British Druids* (repr. Garland, 1982).
Thompson, James, *The Castle of Indolence and Other Poems* (University of Kansas Press, 1961).
Weston, Jessie, *From Ritual to Romance* (repr. Peter Smith, 1993).
Williams ab Ithel, J., ed., *The Barddas of Iolo Morganwg* (Weiser, 2003)

Starseed Publications
2204 E Grand Ave.
Everett, WA 98201
www.lorian.org